OECD Studies on Water

Financing a Water Secure Future

OECD

BETTER POLICIES FOR BETTER LIVES

Please cite this publication as:
OECD (2022), *Financing a Water Secure Future*, OECD Studies on Water, OECD Publishing, Paris, https://doi.org/10.1787/a2ecb261-en.

ISBN 978-92-64-35158-5 (print)
ISBN 978-92-64-78290-7 (pdf)

OECD Studies on Water
ISSN 2224-5073 (print)
ISSN 2224-5081 (online)

Photo credits: Cover image © Nuria Kreuser/Shutterstock.com.

Corrigenda to publications may be found on line at: www.oecd.org/about/publishing/corrigenda.htm.

Preface

The importance of water security to broader economic development and resilience is increasingly internationally recognised, as reflected by the annual G20 Dialogue on Water as well as the preparations for the 2023 UN Conference on Water; the first of its in kind in nearly 50 years. Investments that contribute to water security span a range of essential infrastructure systems to deliver clean drinking water, reliable sanitation and to manage water resources and water risks. They deliver substantial benefits across multiple policy agendas, notably food and energy security, urban development, public health and education. The COVID-19 pandemic has also starkly demonstrated the importance of ensuring access to safe water, sanitation and hygiene as a critical element of reducing the transmission of infectious diseases.

The economic case for investments in water security is robust and with climate change and other drivers exacerbating pressure on water systems, the value of investments in resilience is further heightened. Economic losses related to water insecurity are estimated to include USD 260 billion per year from inadequate water supply and sanitation, USD 120 billion per year from urban property flood damages, and USD 94 billion per year of water insecurity to irrigators. At the same time, the global costs of achieving SDG 6 on water and sanitation exceed USD 1 trillion per year, or 1.21% of global GDP. Yet, financing flows have long remained well below identified levels of need. The world is not on track to meet the SDG 6 and lack of financing is well-recognised as a major impediment.

The analysis presented in this report confirms that addressing the financing challenge requires more than calls for increased funding. It requires accelerated and concerted action on multiple fronts to: (1) make the best use of existing assets and finance, (2) strengthen the enabling environment for investment, (3) pursue strategic investment planning to ensure resilient investments in the context of uncertain future climatic conditions, and (4) mobilise additional sources finance from various public and private sources. Policy makers and financiers can seize new opportunities that arise from growing interest in sustainable finance, such as the development of taxonomies for sustainable activities, green and blue bonds, as well as increased policy impetus and investor appetite to align finance with environmental ambitions.

These findings draw on analytical work and discussions at the Roundtable on Financing Water; the only dedicated forum on financing water at the international level. Since its establishment in 2017, the Roundtable has engaged several hundred policy makers and practitioners to mobilise the full range of sources of finance to contribute to a water secure future. The release of this report provides a strong foundation for new initiatives such as the OECD Global Observatory on Financing Water Supply, Sanitation and Water Security, which will provide a dedicated knowledge hub to share good practices and support peer-to-peer learning.

We hope you will find this report inspiring. We encourage you and all stakeholders to join us to advance this agenda to scale up financing for water security and sustainable growth.

Mathias Cormann

Secretary-General, OECD

Foreword

This report distils key messages from the Roundtable on Financing Water, a joint initiative of the OECD, the Government of the Netherlands, the World Water Council and the World Bank, and related analytical work on financing water. The report benefitted from the engagement of several hundred participants in Roundtable meetings organised over the past five years, including global, regional (the Americas, Asia, Europe) and thematic meetings (on agricultural water and on climate action). Through partnerships with member countries (Israel, the Netherlands and the United States), key regional players (Inter-American Development Bank, Asian Development Bank, European Investment Bank) and other key organisations (the United Nations Food and Agriculture Organization), the Roundtable's meetings have allowed for a deeper exploration of the contextual factors that influence financing approaches in different regions and investment types. This provides the basis for an up-to-date summary of the key challenges and opportunities in the water financing landscape and sets out a vision for future OECD work on financing for water security and the Roundtable.

Kathleen Dominique led the work to develop this publication and has managed the Roundtable since 2017. The author team included: Kathleen Dominique, Helen Laubenstein, Stephanie Lyons and Harry Smythe. Xavier Leflaive, Simon Buckle and Walid Oueslati provided guidance. Data provided by the CDP survey of corporates disclosing water risks informed the analysis in Chapter 2. The report benefitted from valuable comments from Marta Arbinolo, Wiebke Bartz-Zuccala, Simon Buckle, Jane Ellis, Guillaume Gruère, Raphaël Jachnik, Xavier Leflaive, Mireille Martini, Michael Mullan and Mikaela Rambali of the OECD Secretariat, as well as from Mariem Khemiri, Project Officer, World Water Council. Sama Al Taher Cucci and Beth Del Bourgo provided excellent support on communications and Ines Reale provided invaluable administrative assistance.

The work was overseen by the OECD Working Party on Biodiversity, Water and Ecosystems and benefitted from valuable inputs and comments from delegates.

The OECD is grateful to the Government of the Netherlands, the World Water Council and the World Bank for their excellent co-operation in the context of the Roundtable on Financing Water, without which this report would not have been possible.

This document was approved by the Environment Policy Committee by written procedure on 29 October 2021 and prepared for publication by the OECD Secretariat.

Table of contents

Tables

Figures

Boxes

Glossary

- **Bankability** refers to the financial sustainability of projects to be financed on market terms, and considers *inter alia* creditworthiness, performance, resilience, sustainability and growth prospects.
- **Costing**: refers to the assessment of the expected costs of an operation, covering both the capital cost (as one-off investment or as an annual repayment schedule) and/or the recurrent operational expenditures, as the case may be, as well as financing costs.
- **Financing**: financing provided with the expectation of a financial return, in the form of interest or dividends.
- **Funding**: refers expenditure derived from the collection of fees, tariffs, subsidies and other income.
- **Conditional guarantees**: are guarantees of loan repayment recognizing certain unknown conditions or circumstances.
- **Pooled financing**: refers to the aggregation of individual project loans by the legal entity which raises the money for the individual project loans.
- **Project financing**: generally, this refers to the financing of a standalone project, which has revenue directly associated with it.
- **Renewable freshwater resources**: Total freshwater resources that are offered by the average annual natural inflow and runoff that feed each hydrosystem (catchment area or aquifer).
- **Reserves**: are money or other legal commitments set aside to be used to cure defaults in obligations of the borrower.
- **Revolving funds**: are pools which when the repayment of individual project loans is made, those repaid funds are made available for new project loans.
- **Sanitation**: delivery of sanitation services (toilets, latrines, etc.), wastewater collection and treatment. The notion covers both on-site (or off-grid) and centrally piped services.
- **Water abstraction (or withdrawal)**: is water physically withdrawn from the environment. Part of that water may return to the environment. Typically, a number of industries abstract water for cooling purposes – then return the water to the environment in a suitable condition for use by other purposes. However, a significant part of the water abstracted from the environment is consumed.
- **Water consumption**: water use that reduces either the quantity or quality of water that is returned to the environment. Consumed water is not necessarily abstracted from the environment (it can be generated from other sources, e.g. recycled water). A variety of water uses do not consume water (e.g. shipping, swimming, the environment). These uses should however be taken into account in water resource management (e.g. through environmental flow and quality requirements for environmental purposes).
- **Water losses, leakage, non-revenue water**: The first two are synonymous and refer to physical losses, while the latter also includes water that is supplied but not paid for.
- **Water security:** achieving and maintaining acceptable levels for four inter-related water risks: too little water (scarcity and droughts), too much water (floods), too polluted water (lack of suitable quality water for a particular purpose), and degradation of freshwater ecosystems. These risks can also increase the risk of (and be affected by) inadequate access to safe water supply and sanitation.

List of acronyms

ACRE	Agriculture and Climate Risk Enterprise
ADB	Asian Development Bank
AFD	Agence Française de Développement
APEC	Asia-Pacific Economic Cooperation
ASEAN	Association of Southeast Asian Nations
BAU	Business as usual
CAPEX	Capital expenditure
CBA	Cost benefit analysis
CFM	Climate Fund Managers
CreW	Caribbean Regional Fund of Wastewater Management
DBP	Development Bank of the Philippines
DFCD	Dutch Fund for Climate and Development
DFI	Development Finance Institutions
EAFRD	European Agricultural Fund for Rural Development
EC	European Commission
EFSI	European Fund for Strategic Investment
EIB	European Investment Bank
EIP	Ecosystem Investment Partners
EPA	Environmental Protection Agency
ESG	Environment, Social and Governance
EU	European Union
FAMM	Metropolitan Water Fund of Monterrey
FAO	Food and Agriculture Organisation
FMO	Dutch Entrepreneurial Development Bank
GCF	The Green Climate Fund
GDP	Gross Domestic Product
GLAAS	Global Analysis and Assessment of Sanitation and Drinking-Water
GUARDIAN	Gramalaya Urban and Rural Development Initiatives and Network

IADB	Inter-American Development Bank
IBNet	International Benchmarking Network for Water and Sanitation Utilities
IDA	International Development Association
IDH	The Sustainable Trade Initiative
IFC	International Finance Corporation
ILI	Infrastructure Leakage Index
JICA	Japan International Cooperation Agency
LGUGC	Local Government Unit Guarantee Cooperation
MCC	Millennium Challenge Corporation
MDB	Multilateral Development Bank
MPWI	Multipurpose water infrastructure
NbS	Nature-based solutions
NGO	Non-governmental organisation
NRW	Non-revenue water
O&M	Operation and Maintenance
ODA	Official Development Assistance
OPEX	Operation expenditure
PPP	Public-private partnerships
PSE	Producer support estimates
PSOD	Private Sector Operations Department
PWRF	Philippine Water Revolving Fund
PWS	Payment for watershed services
RRG	Renewable Resources Group
SAB	Sustainable Awareness Bonds
SDGs	Sustainable Development Goals
SPV	Special purpose vehicle
SRF	State Revolving Fund
TCFD	Task Force on Climate-related Financial Disclosures
UN	United Nations
UNFCCC	UN Framework Convention on Climate Change
USAID	US Agency for International Development
WMO	World Meteorological Organisation
WSS	Water supply and sanitation services
WTO	World Trade Organisation
WWF	World Wildlife Fund

Executive Summary

Water-related investments deliver substantial benefits for water security and sustainable development. "Water-related investments" refer to a broad range of investments that contribute to water security through the delivery of water and sanitation services, the management of water resources and water-related risks ("too much", "too little" and "too polluted"). Beyond the water sector, water-related investments connect multiple other sectors and policy agendas, including agriculture, energy, urban development, public health and education. Due to their cross-cutting and underpinning nature, such investments are central to achieving the Sustainable Developments Goals (SDGs), global climate and biodiversity goals and can contribute to a green and resilient recovery from the COVID-19 crisis.

At the same time, the economic and social consequences of the COVID-19 crisis have intensified financial pressure on water and sanitation service providers at the very time when such services are more vital as ever for public health. This pressure may limit or delay future water-related investments due to constraints on public and household budgets. There is an increasing recognition of the importance of water resilience for economic resilience in light of the accelerating number and intensity of catastrophic floods as experienced recently in Germany, Belgium, the People's Republic of China, India as well as historic drought in the Western United States. This underscores the need to understand the potentially cascading water-related risks and interdependencies across the economy, including but not limited to the material financial risk for investor portfolios.

While investment in water security makes economic sense, this does not always translate into investment at scale. The widespread under-valuing of water resources and of the benefits associated with water investments by both public and private actors constrains financing opportunities. The Roundtable on Financing Water[1] and related analytical work has, since 2017, contributed to a better understanding of the distinctive bottlenecks that hinder the mobilisation of the full range of sources of finance to contribute to a water secure future. These bottlenecks include weak enabling environments, insufficiently robust strategic planning and prioritisation, a lack of attractive risk-return profiles for specific projects, and the local, small-scale nature of many investments. Water-related investments typically lack distinct revenue streams and assets that can be used as collateral given that such investments are usually part of a larger system for the delivery of water-related services and management of resources, lacking specific ring-fenced revenue (Baker, 2022[1]).The Roundtable has also identified a range of tailored financing approaches for water-related investments and policies to enable their uptake.

An enduring financing gap, with scope for better allocation of existing resources

The world is not on track to meet the SDG 6 on water and sanitation largely due to insufficient levels of water-related investment. This is underscored by estimates of investment needs for SDG 6 at global level, as well as regional level analysis (in Europe and Asia-Pacific) (OECD, 2020[2]; ADB, 2020[3]). Estimated global costs of achieving SDG 6 exceed USD 1 trillion per year, or 1.21% of global gross product (Strong et al., 2020[4]). To achieve universal and equitable access to safe and affordable drinking water for all by

2030, the present value of the additional investment needed is around USD 1.7 trillion, which is about three times the current investment levels (Hutton and Varughese, 2016[5]).

Climate change is increasing pressure on water systems and heightens the value of investments in resilience. Many of the impacts of climate change manifest through changes in the hydrological cycle, such as increased frequency of floods (coastal, riverine and storm-driven) and droughts, increased variability and intensity of rainfall, reduced snowpack feeding headwaters of major rivers and wildfires, among others. Climate change also affects demand for water (for irrigation, or for cooling heat island effects in cities, for instance). Decisions regarding water infrastructure typically rely on engineering, modelling and planning that bases projections of future needs on historical patterns of water availability and use. However, these assumptions are an increasingly unreliable guide to future conditions. As old assumptions about a (relatively) stable climate are replaced by dynamic climatic uncertainty, new approaches to policy frameworks, institutional arrangements and investment planning are needed (OECD, 2021[6]).

Water-related investment has historically been financed by public budgets, including international transfers, with contributions from service and resource users via tariffs, abstraction charges, and other economic instruments. The historic reliance on public budgets and concessional finance can undermine incentives for accountability and performance in the sector and crowd out private sources of finance. According to OECD data, commercial finance mobilised by development finance for water and sanitation in ODA eligible countries remains very limited accounting for just over 1% of total commercial finance mobilised by blended finance (OECD, 2019[7]).

Water-related investments constitute a minor share of total investments by private investors in infrastructure as of 2020 (an estimated USD 17 billion out of just over USD 1 trillion) (OECD, 2020[8]) and, hence, do not seem to benefit much from the rapidly growing market for sustainable investment focused on Environmental, Social and Governance aspects (ESG). Moreover evidence suggests that existing funding may be poorly targeted, failing to reach the projects that can deliver the greatest benefits and reach the communities most in need (Andres et al., 2019[9]; Leflaive and Hjort, 2020[10]). In most instances, public and development finance are not used as a catalytic force to crowd in additional capital (OECD, 2019[7]).

Finally, funding and financing flows for water-related investments are far outweighed by funding flows to other sectors, such as agriculture, energy and urban development, which can increase pressures on water resources and exacerbate exposure and vulnerability to water-related risks. Indeed, investments in these sectors and activities often fail to adequately account for their implications for the water sector and water policy objectives, including the SDGs. This underscores the need for greater alignment of financing flows with water security, climate and broader policy objectives.

Concerted policy action is needed to finance a water secure future

The importance of concerted policy action from governments to provide the conditions the effective use and mobilisation of finance cannot be overstated. The Roundtable and related work since 2017 has highlighted the multiple opportunities to scale up funding and financing by improving the risk-return profile of water-related investments and through tailored financing vehicles (such as funds) and instruments (such as use of proceeds bonds). Appropriate financing approaches for water-related investments need to address the specificities of the water sector, such as the need for long tenors, small ticket sizes, limited creditworthiness and the lack of clearly-defined revenue streams. This requires adapting proven financing approaches as well as innovation to address current and emerging challenges.

Ensuring that existing financing flows deliver expected benefits and scaling up financing for water-related investments is unlikely to materialise in the absence of concerted policy action at multiple levels (national, sub-national) and on multiple fronts:

- Addressing the financing challenge is not merely about getting more funding to fill a financing gap. It is critical to **make best use of existing assets and finance**, including timely asset management, capital expenditure planning, and targeted allocation of public subsidies, seizing opportunities to reap economies of scale and improve performance.
- **Strengthening the enabling environment** for investment. This includes ensuring robust policies, regulations and institutional arrangements related to the delivery of water and sanitation services, ensuring water resources allocation and adequate quality. The enabling environment also includes the policy framework for investment, which influences the availability of diverse sources of capital and deployment of adequate financing mechanisms. A recently-developed scorecard of indicators to support blended finance for water-related investments can inform policy dialogues aimed at strengthening the enabling environment (Money, forthcoming[11]). Moreover, governments can develop financing approaches (e.g. revolving funds) that provide consistent levels of funding certainty overtime. This can provide a strong signal to the water infrastructure project developers that planning and project development efforts will be rewarded with funding (Gebhardt, Zeigler and Mourant, 2022[12]).
- Optimising future investment needs through **strategic investment planning**, including more systematic consideration of long-term trends, notably climate change and options to design more robust and flexible investments in the context of uncertainty. Governments can signal their intention and financial capacity to tender water projects over a multi-year time span. Project-level analyses need to be supplemented by the design, review and assessment of investment pathways. New analytical methods are being developed to support and inform the transition from a focus on resilient projects to the resilience of the system as a whole at the relevant spatial scale (Brown et al., 2020[13]).
- **Mobilising additional[2] sources of funding and finance** by strengthening the risk-return profile of investments, lowering the cost of capital and seizing opportunities to deploy a range of financing vehicles and approaches. Governments can foster the development of commercial finance and capital markets able to lend at an affordable cost and appropriate long term maturity to water-related projects. Intermediaries have distinctive roles to play to facilitate activities along the investment value chain with the aim to bridge the gap between the demand for and supply of finance. Recent analysis of the landscape of intermediaries takes stock of the wide range of functions they perform and identifies gaps, misalignments and areas for improvement (Lardoux de Pazzis and Muret, 2021[14]).

Looking forward, the OECD's programme of work on financing water aims to raise the level of ambition, broaden engagement and contribute to key international processes and initiatives, including the United Nations Global Acceleration Framework for SDG 6. Key activities in the OECD programme of work will focus on three pillars, interconnected with the Roundtable on Financing Water. These include:

- Launching the OECD Global Observatory on Financing Water Supply, Sanitation and Water Security to collect and share good practices on financing water-related investments.
- Developing Diagnostic Tools to assess the strengths and weaknesses of countries' enabling environments for investment, including an OECD Framework for Financing Water to guide country-level action.
- Develop analytical work to support aligning financing with a water secure future. This will include a conceptual framework and tools to inform strategic investment planning and deepen the understanding of the materiality of water-related risks for the financial sector.
- Together with governments, financiers and international partners, the OECD will continue to work towards building a more water secure future.

References

ADB (2020), *Financing water security for sustainable growth in the Asia-Pacific region*, Asian Development Bank. [3]

Andres, L. et al. (2019), *Doing More with Less Smarter Subsidies for Water Supply and Sanitation*, The World Bank Group, http://www.worldbank.org/gwsp. [9]

Baker, M. (2022), "Critical disconnects between donors and domestic realities", in *Investing in Water and Growth*. [1]

Brown, C. et al. (2020), "Resilience by design: A deep uncertainty approach for water systems in a changing world", *Water Security*, Vol. 9, p. 100051, http://dx.doi.org/10.1016/J.WASEC.2019.100051. [13]

Gebhardt, J., R. Zeigler and A. Mourant (2022), "Water Infrastructure Financing: The Experience of the U.S.", in *Investing in Water and Growth*. [12]

Hutton, G. and M. Varughese (2016), *The Costs of Meeting the 2030 Sustainable Development Goal Targets on Drinking Water, Sanitation, and Hygiene*, http://www.worldbank.org/water. [5]

Lardoux de Pazzis, A. and A. Muret (2021), "The role of intermediaries to facilitate financing for water-related investment". [14]

Leflaive, X. and M. Hjort (2020), "Addressing the social consequences of tariffs for water supply and sanitation", *OECD Environment Working Papers*, No. 166, OECD Publishing, Paris, https://dx.doi.org/10.1787/afede7d6-en. [10]

Money, A. (forthcoming), "Country-level indicators to support blended finance for water related investments", *OECD Environment Working Paper*. [11]

OECD (2021), *Losses and Damages from Climate Change*. [6]

OECD (2020), *Financing Water Supply, Sanitation and Flood Protection: Challenges in EU Member States and Policy Options*, OECD Studies on Water, OECD Publishing, Paris, https://dx.doi.org/10.1787/6893cdac-en. [2]

OECD (2020), *Green Infrastructure in the Decade for Delivery: Assessing Institutional Investment*, Green Finance and Investment, OECD Publishing, Paris, https://dx.doi.org/10.1787/f51f9256-en. [8]

OECD (2019), *Making Blended Finance Work for Water and Sanitation: Unlocking Commercial Finance for SDG 6*, OECD Studies on Water, OECD Publishing, Paris, https://dx.doi.org/10.1787/5efc8950-en. [7]

Strong, C. et al. (2020), *Achieving Abundance: Understanding the Cost of a Sustainable Water Future*, https://www.wri.org/research/achieving-abundance-understanding-cost-sustainable-water-future (accessed on 7 February 2022). [4]

Notes

[1] Further information on the Roundtable on Financing Water is available here.

[2] In this context, "additional" refers to sources of funding and financing that otherwise would be have been mobilised in the absence of specific interventions.

1 Introduction

This chapter sets the context and provides background for the following chapters of the report. It summarises the activities of the Roundtable on Financing Water since its establishment in 2017 and the related analytical work on financing water-related investment.

Finance has long been recognised as a central driver towards the achievement of universal access to water supply and sanitation, the sustainable management of water resources and the management of water-related risks (floods, droughts and pollution) (Winpenny, 2015[1]; OECD, 2018[2]; OECD, 2019[3]). Since its establishment by the OECD and partners in 2017, the Roundtable on Financing Water[1] has provided a unique forum for action-oriented engagement between the water and the finance communities to promote the strengthening of enabling policies and the acceleration of investment that contributes to water security and sustainable development. An initiative of the OECD, the Government of the Netherlands, the World Water Council and the World Bank, the Roundtable draws upon political leadership and technical expertise, with discussions substantiated by robust analytical work. The substantive work undertaken has helped to characterise the scale of the financing challenge and explore options to address it through improved enabling environments and tailored financing approaches.

The scope of the Roundtable is global and focusses on water-related investments broadly defined. These include the diverse range of investments that contribute to water security through the delivery of water and sanitation services, the management of water resources and water-related risks ("too much", "too little" and "too polluted"). This can include a range of infrastructure types (including conventional "grey", and nature-based solutions, or a combination thereof) as well as large, centralised infrastructures and small-scale, decentralised systems. Water-related investments may also include investments designed for other purposes, which contribute to water management (e.g. green roofs or permeable surfaces that limit rainwater runoff). Beyond investments in the water sector, water-related investments connect multiple sectors and policy agendas, including agriculture, energy, urban development, public health and education, among others.

Since 2017, Roundtable meetings have engaged several hundred participants representing governments and regulators in developed, emerging and developing economies, as well as private financiers (e.g. institutional investors, commercial banks, asset managers, and impact investors), development financing institutions, bi-lateral donors, international organisations, academia and civil society organisations. A wide range of experience and good practices have been shared. Yet, ultimately, many of the fundamental challenges remain.

Through partnerships with member countries (Israel, the Netherlands and the United States), key regional players (Inter-American Development Bank, Asian Development Bank, European Investment Bank) and other key actors (the United Nations Food and Agriculture Organization), the Roundtable's meetings have allowed for a deeper exploration of the contextual factors that influence financing approaches in different regions and themes. The list of Roundtable meetings to date follow, with links to meeting summaries provided:

- First meeting of the Roundtable on Financing Water, Global meeting, April 2017, Paris (OECD, 2017[4]);
- Second meeting of the Roundtable on Financing Water, Global meeting, co-convened with the Government of Israel, September 2017, Tel Aviv (OECD, 2017[5]);
- Third meeting of the Roundtable on Financing Water, Global meeting, November 2018, Paris (OECD, 2018[6]);
- Fourth meeting of the Roundtable on Financing Water, Regional meeting focused on the Americas, co-convened with the U.S. Government and the Inter-American Development Bank, June 2019, Washington, D.C. (OECD, 2019[7]);
- Fifth meeting of the Roundtable on Financing Water, Regional meeting focused on Asia, co-convened with the Asian Development Bank, November 2019, Manila (OECD, 2019[8]);
- Sixth meeting of the Roundtable on Financing Water, Regional meeting focused on Europe, co-convened with the European Investment Bank, December 2020 (virtual) (OECD, 2021[9]);

- Seventh meeting of the Roundtable on Financing Water, Thematic meeting on Financing Agricultural Water, co-convened with the U.N. FAO, January 2021 (virtual) (OECD, 2021[10]).
- Eighth meeting of the Roundtable on Financing Water, Thematic meeting on Climate Action, co-convened with the U.S. Department of State and the U.S. Environmental Protection Agency, September 2021 (virtual) (OECD, 2021[11])

Working in partnership is a key feature of the Roundtable, in recognition that a focus on water security alone will not be sufficient to manifest the action required to finance a water secure future. This requires going beyond policymakers responsible for water to engage with policymakers from sectors impacting water security (agriculture, energy, urban planning, among others), and the range of financiers (institutional investors, commercial banks, asset managers, impact investors, development financing institutions and bi-lateral donors), corporates, NGOs and experts who can help to drive action. The Roundtable strives to build on and collaborate with key international initiatives, such as the Dutch Valuing Water Initiative, the Water Data Initiative of the Australian Water Partnership and the UN-Water Global Acceleration Framework for SDG 6.

This report distils the key messages and lessons learned from the Roundtable discussions and related analytical work. It provides an up-to-date summary of the key challenges and opportunities in the water financing landscape and sets out a vision for future OECD work on financing water and for the Roundtable. The report represents an important milestone in the development of the OECD programme of work with key new initiatives being developed (see further details on forthcoming initiatives in Chapter 5).

References

OECD (2021), *6th meeting of the Roundtable on Financing Water, Regional meeting Europe, 7-8 December. Summary and discussion highlights*, https://www.oecd.org/water/6th-Roundtable-on-Financing-Water-in-Europe-Summary-and-Highlights.pdf (accessed on 28 June 2021). [9]

OECD (2021), *7th meeting of the Roundtable on Financing Water, Thematic meeting on Agricultural water, 27-28 January. Summary and discussion highlights*, https://www.oecd.org/water/Summary-Roundtable-Financing-Agricultural-Water.pdf (accessed on 28 June 2021). [10]

OECD (2021), *8th meeting of the Roundtable on Financing Water, Thematic meeting on Climate Action, 23-24 September. Summary and discussion highlights*, https://www.oecd.org/water/Summary-and-Highlights-Roundtable-on-Climate-Action-23-24-September-2021.pdf (accessed on 7 February 2022). [11]

OECD (2019), *4th meeting of the Roundtable on Financing Water, Regional Meeting Americas, 26-27 June, Washington DC. Discussion Highlights*, http://www.oecd.org/water/Summary-RTmeeting-26and27June.pdf (accessed on 2 June 2020). [7]

OECD (2019), *5th meeting of the Roundtable on Financing Water, Regional meeting Asia, 26-27 November, Manila. Summary and Discussion Highlights*, http://www.oecd.org/water/Summary_The_Fifth_Roundtable_%20on_%20Financing_%20Water_in%20Asia.pdf (accessed on 2 June 2020). [8]

OECD (2019), *Making Blended Finance Work for Water and Sanitation: Unlocking Commercial Finance for SDG 6*, OECD Studies on Water, OECD Publishing, Paris, https://dx.doi.org/10.1787/5efc8950-en. [3]

OECD (2018), *3rd meeting of the Roundtable on Financing Water, Global meeting, 12 November, Paris. Summary and Discussion Highlights*, http://www.oecd.org/water/roundtable-financing-water-2018-summary-and-highlights.pdf (accessed on 2 June 2020). [6]

OECD (2018), "Financing Water, Investing in sustainable growth, Policy Perspectives", *OECD Environmental Policy Paper No. 11*, https://www.oecd.org/water/Policy-Paper-Financing-Water-Investing-in-Sustainable-Growth.pdf. [2]

OECD (2017), *2nd meeting of the Roundtable on Financing Water, Global meeting, 13 September, Tel Aviv. Summary and Discussion Highlights*, http://www.oecd.org/env/resources/Roundtable%20on%20Financing%20Water%20second%20meeting%20--%20Tel%20Aviv%20Sept%2013%20--%20summary%20final.pdf (accessed on 2 June 2020). [5]

OECD (2017), *Roundtable on Financing Water, Inaugural meeting 12-13 April 2017, Paris. Discussion Highlights and Roadmap for Future Work*, http://dx.doi.org/10.1787/19970900. [4]

Winpenny, J. (2015), *Water : Fit to Finance? Catalyzing national growth through investment in water security.* [1]

Notes

[1] Further information on the Roundtable on Financing Water is available here.

2 The Challenge of Financing Water-related Investments

This chapter provides insights into the challenges related to financing water-related investments and why concerted policy action is required to overcome them. It helps characterise the order of magnitude of the challenge by highlighting estimates of investment needs and financing capacities for select regions (Europe and Asia-Pacific). It also presents data related to investment in agricultural water and trends in development finance for water. Finally, the chapter documents how water risks could translate into material financial risks, including by generating financial impacts on corporates.

2.1. Scope and definitions

The scope of this report is the range of investments that contribute to water security through the delivery of water and sanitation services, the management of water resources and water-related risks ("too much", "too little" and "too polluted"). Investments in water security comprise a very heterogeneous range of activities. For example, investing in a wastewater treatment plant is very different from financing a nature-based solution to protect a city from flood risks. Similarly, financing the construction and start-up of a new desalination plant raises different challenges and opportunities than financing the refurbishment of one already in operation.

Investments in water security can include a range of infrastructure types (including conventional "grey", and nature-based solutions, or a combination thereof) as well as large, centralized infrastructures and small-scale, decentralized systems. This broad category may also include investments designed for other purposes, which contribute to water management (e.g. green roofs or permeable surfaces that limit rainwater runoff). At the same time, the range of financiers is also very diverse: with different mandates, investment objectives, risk appetites and liquidity needs. Additional classifiers for water investments include scale (from watershed to household); function (water supply, wastewater management, flood protection, etc.); and operating environment (ownership, governance and regulation) (Money, 2017[1]).

Beyond investments in the water sector, water-related investments connect multiple sectors and policy agendas, including agriculture, energy, urban development and public health, among others. Box 2.1 provides a view of the range of water-related investments and description of sub-sectors. The Glossary provides definitions of key terms.

Box 2.1. Water-related investments: Description of sub-sectors

- **Water resources management**: Conservation and rehabilitation of inland surface waters (rivers, lakes etc.), ground water and coastal waters; prevention of water contamination.
- **Bulk water supply**: The production of water to be distributed to various end-users, including drinking water supply. Bulk water supply may be produced from the abstraction of surface or groundwater or through non-conventional sources, such as desalination or wastewater reuse.
- **Storage and conveyance**: The infrastructure required to store and transport bulk water supply to various end-users. This includes reservoirs, pipelines, channels and other forms of water supply distribution.
- **Water supply services**: The production and distribution of high quality water at standards required for consumption as drinking.
- **Sanitation services**: Sanitation services consist of the provision of facilities and services for the safe disposal of human urine and faeces.
- **Wastewater collection and treatment**: refers to the safe collection and treatment of sewage and wastewater. The treatment can be executed on several different levels: preliminary, primary, secondary and tertiary. May include waste to energy activities.
- **Irrigation**: The production, distribution and application of water to land in support of agricultural production.
- **Flood protection (riverine, coastal)**: Interventions intended to manage the risk of flooding caused by coastal and river flooding. Flood is defined as the overflowing of the normal confines of a stream or other body of water, or the accumulation of water over areas that are not normally submerged.
- **Urban drainage**: Interventions to manage runoff from storm water.

- **Multipurpose infrastructure**: encompasses all constructed water systems, including dams, dykes, reservoirs, hydropower and associated irrigation canals and water supply networks, which may be used for more than one purpose for economic, social and environmental activities

Source: (Dominique and Bartz-Zuccala, 2018[2])

2.2. Why financing water security is a policy issue

2.2.1. Water-related investments deliver substantial benefits for water security and sustainable development

The global benefits from strategic investment in water security could exceed hundreds of billions of dollars annually. A partial estimate of the scale of global economic losses related to water insecurity include: USD 260 billion per year from inadequate water supply and sanitation, USD 120 billion per year from urban property flood damages, and USD 94 billion per year of water insecurity to existing irrigators (Sadoff, et al., 2015[3]). As of 2020, 2 billion people around the world do not have access to safely managed drinking water, while 3.6 billion people lack safely managed sanitation services and 2.3 billion lack basic hand washing facilities (UN-Water, 2021[4]).

The impacts of water-related risks can propagate through multiple channels, such as through impacts on human health from increased disease and morbidity due to poor drinking water quality and lack of access to safely managed sanitation; disruptions in industrial operations or supply chains due to water-related disasters; impacts on agricultural production and commodity markets due to water scarcity and droughts. These impacts could translate into a material financial risk for sovereigns and local governments, corporates, insurers and financiers. These risks can materialise at multiple scales, from the household to corporate level, to industry and sector scale to systemic risk. For example, a recent study by the Dutch Central Bank estimated that the financial sector in the Netherlands has a combined exposure of EUR 83 billion to facilities located in extremely water-stressed regions in its equity portfolios (amounting to approximately 17% of all equity holdings). Pension funds account for 94% of this exposure, given their relatively large equity holdings (De Nederlandsche Bank (DNB), 2019[5]). Looking only at specific sectors for which water is considered "vitally important" (such as agriculture, mining and energy production) the exposure to businesses operating in extremely water-scarce regions remains significant, at EUR 37 billion (De Nederlandsche Bank (DNB), 2019[5]).

2.2.2. A strong economic case for water-related investments does not translate into financing flows commensurate with needs

Pervasive under-valuing of the resource and benefits associated with investment by both public and private actors constrains water financing opportunities. Water-related investments generate a mix of public and private benefits in terms of valued goods and services as well as reduced water-related risks. For example, public benefits of water supply, sanitation and wastewater treatment include improved public health and ecosystem functioning. Private benefits of water resource use may include good health, better incomes and livelihoods, improved education outcomes, along with financial returns on industrial or agricultural production that rely on water use. Many of the benefits from water-related investments cannot be easily monetised, undermining potential revenue flows (OECD, 2017[6]).

Due to the nature of local service delivery and resource management, water-related investments are often relatively small-scale and fragmented. Water and sanitation services are, by definition, locally sourced and provided. At the same time, the sector requires strong public regulation due to the public good dimension of a number of benefits delivered by such services as well as due to its monopolistic market structure

(OECD, 2019[7]). For the management of water resources, well-designed allocation regimes are essential to avoid over exploitation (OECD, 2015[8]). Appropriate financing approaches for water-related investments would account for and help address the specificities of water-related investments, such as the need for long tenors, small ticket sizes, limited creditworthiness and the lack of clearly defined revenue streams. Financing terms should be commensurate with the useful life of the project. Long tenor financing of long-lived projects is also attractive because it spreads cost recovery over time, which is more equitable for rate payers, where applicable (Baker, 2022[9]). At the same time, different types of financiers will have different risk-return appetites, which can be suitable along distinct phases of the project cycle (development, construction and operation) (Gietema, 2022[10]).

While investment in water security makes economic sense, this does not always translate into investment at scale. "Water-related investments" refer to a broad range of distinct investments in a very heterogeneous landscape. "Water infrastructure" is a broad term that encompasses a wide range of activities – from the river basin or catchment scale to the household tap, traversing projects as diverse as water supply and sanitation, flood protection, irrigation and reservoirs (Money, 2017[11]). Water projects with such disparate scales and purposes entail different levels of capital intensity and repayment periods, distinct credit, commercial and legal risks, and varied economic, financial and social returns (Money, 2017[11]). These investments reflect distinct risk-return profiles and project attributes, which influence the suitability of various financing approaches (Money, 2017[11]; OECD, 2019[12]).

As water-related investments vary widely across sub-sectors and according to a country's policy and institutional settings, it is important to note that the options for securing financing from public or private (concessional or commercial) sources present different opportunities, advantages and disadvantages. For example, short-term investments (e.g. to reduce non-revenue water, or expand water supply and sanitation (WSS) service coverage) may be more appealing and better suited to commercial financiers, while larger, longer-term investments (e.g. water network extensions with long repayment periods) may be better suited to concessional finance or blended finance involving institutional investors (World Bank, 2017[13]). This reflects the diverse typology of both projects, the diverse nature of the benefits delivered and potential investors across the water sector (OECD, 2019[12]).

Similarly, financiers vary widely in their extent of knowledge of the water sector, performance objectives, tolerance of risk, income objectives and time horizon (Money, 2017[11]; OECD, 2019[12]). For most types of financiers, interest is primarily driven by the attractiveness of the risk-return profile, which depends on i) a stable revenue stream and ii) how the range of risks and returns related to water security investments are shared between public and private actors (OECD, 2018[14]). Due to the sector's inherent complexity and distinct characteristics, investors might perceive water-related investments as more risky and generally less attractive than other sectors (Streeter, 2017[15]; OECD, 2010[16]). Features of water-related investments that pose challenges for financing are summarised below.

Lack of clearly defined revenue streams and weak enabling environment for investment

The management of water resources and delivery of water and sanitation services provide a mix of public and private benefits, with many benefits (e.g. improved public heath, improved ecosystem functioning) not easily quantified and monetised (OECD, 2016[17]). This makes it difficult to translate benefits of investments that contribute to water security into revenue flows, particularly for avoided costs or cross-sectoral benefits. (OECD, 2018[14]) A weak or poorly designed enabling environment that fails to clearly define and provide a framework for the appropriate valuing and pricing of water resources and services can limit the scope of governments and service providers to access critical sources of revenue and finance.

Water investments are typically different from infrastructure projects for which common project financing techniques are used. In infrastructure financing, such projects have direct revenues that can be ring-fenced, such as landing fees at airports and tolls on highways. In these cases, the project's revenue is usually the credit for the financing. Only rarely does a water "project" have a distinct revenue associated with it, such as a desalination project which involves a high-tech desalination plant that typically falls outside routine technical competence of a water utility or where the water is used by a specific user which pays directly for the water produced (Baker, 2022[9]).

Water and sanitation projects are usually part of systems for the delivery of water supply and sanitation services to an area, normally an administrative division like a village, a town or a city. As such, they must be recognised as part of the whole water system, and be financed in the context of the whole system. That is, they are not financed on the revenue generated solely by the project itself because there is none, but by the revenue of the whole system. That revenue might be from tariffs, from general taxes or from transfers from national governments to local governments or to water utilities. Further, the way the scope of an investment is defined or designed drives financing options. This is consequential for financing collateral projects. For example, the delineation of an urban area by a legal definition or regulation influences the definition of nearby rural areas. A more expansive definition of an urban area might permit adjacent areas to be incorporated into a development financing program (Baker, 2022[9]).

In the case of water supply and sanitation services, utilities often do not succeed in collecting enough revenue through tariffs to cover operational and capital expenditure (Alaerts, 2019[18]). According to the UN-Water Global Analysis and Assessment of Sanitation and Drinking Water (GLAAS) report, over half of countries surveyed stated that water tariffs are at a level which allows the recovery of only 80% of operating costs (O&M), to say nothing of capital costs (UN-Water, 2019[19]). A lack of creditworthiness constrains their ability to obtain finance and they are often perceived as high-risk borrowers (OECD, 2019[7]); notable exceptions suggest this does not need to be the case. Raising water tariffs to achieve cost-recovery can face constraints in terms of affordability and political feasibility (Leflaive and Hjort, 2019[20]). Issues such as underdeveloped financial sectors, ineffective or absent regulation, operational inefficiency or low rates of cost recovery in water services provision can all undermine the sector's potential to secure finance (Pories, Fonseca and Delmon, 2019[21]).

Flood protection, as another example, is usually spatially distributed and not associated with a specific revenue stream. Costs are typically borne through taxes. Governmental revenue flows can pose additional risks for investors, especially in politically or economically less stable countries, or where water budgets are not ring-fenced (Alaerts, 2019[18]). Due to the benefits in terms of risk reduction, investments to manage water-related risks, such as floods or drought, could provide an opportunity to mobilise the insurance sector.

Mismatch between the needs and characteristics of the supply and demand side of finance

Water infrastructure is typically capital intensive, long-lived with high sunk costs. This calls for a high initial investment followed by a long pay-back period (of about 20 to 30 years) (OECD, 2018[14]; Cardascia, 2019[22]). . However, commercial banks principally finance projects with short-term horizons, seeking quick returns (Cardascia, 2019[22]). Long tenor finance on affordable terms is often unavailable. Borrowers may lack marketable collateral. Risks and associated expected financial returns shift over time according to the phase of the project cycle. They are lowered when a project is maturing and/or due to appropriate blending with public support instruments. Different types of financiers and financial instruments in one phase can replace or add to instruments deployed in earlier phases (Gietema, 2022[10]).

Further, water projects, often developed at the local level, tend to be small compared to the size of deals sought by financial providers (whether commercial investors or development finance providers). Investors prefer transactions in the range of USD 20 to 1000 million and thus avoid small and context specific investment classes (Alaerts, 2019[18]; OECD, 2018[14]). The limited size of projects and modest financing needs raise the transaction costs due to the lack of scale.

Finally, inconsistency of water-related policies across sectors impedes efficient cross-sector planning and capturing potential synergies. Infrastructure interventions usually fall under different administrative authorities and ministries (environment, health, agriculture, urban planning, etc.), raising challenges for policy coherence and requiring different approaches for cost-recovery and financing. Often, relevant stakeholders operate in single-disciplinary silos, resulting in overlapping roles and inefficiencies and undermining additional sources of funding (Alaerts, 2019[18]; Cardascia, 2019[22]). Existing financing mechanisms are usually unable to support the design and implementation of cross-cutting interventions.

The emergence of taxonomies seek to provide more clarity to the market about what is considered "sustainable" by providing definitions of investment opportunities that contribute to low carbon, climate resilience or environmentally beneficial investments. Taxonomies may also screen out investments in relation to a given environmental goal that impact negatively on one or more other such goals. Such tools can potentially direct significant volumes of finance towards projects screened against pre-defined and agreed upon criteria. While these taxonomies may be a powerful tool to channel public and private funds towards sustainable activities, the extent to which the taxonomy may support environmental objectives will depend on how the technical criteria and thresholds are defined (OECD, 2021[23]).

The protection of water resources is an explicit objective of the EU taxonomy, which could raise awareness of investment opportunities in the water sector. 'Do No Significant Harm' criteria could help to better protect water resources, for example via reduced pressure on the water resource through changes in agricultural practices. Other water-related investments, which may not be considered as "sustainable activities" under the taxonomy's criteria, e.g. supporting access to water supply to previously underserved communities, could lose visibility and attractiveness for investors seeking sustainable finance opportunities, depending on how these activities are categorised (OECD, 2021[23]).

Lack of data and limited sector knowledge

The risk-return profile, and thus the attractiveness of an investment, depends crucially on financiers' ability to assess investment and operation risks. However, there is a lack of appropriate analytical tools and data to assess complex water-related investments and to track records (OECD, 2018[14]). Regulatory requirements for water risks disclosure and reporting by financial institutions are broadly lacking (Cardascia, 2019[22]). A lack of credit ratings and limited information about the creditworthiness and performance of borrowers deters financiers.

Overall, lenders have limited experience with the water sector and the related risks. Financial products often do not match the characteristics of the sector. At the same time, project developers often have limited capacity to prepare bankable proposals. Water infrastructure projects often suffer from poor preparation of project pre-feasibility and design, weak pipeline identification structuring and implementation (Cardascia, 2019[22]). There is hence a mismatch in knowledge and capacity between stakeholder groups (Alaerts, 2019[18]). Since investments in water security are often context specific, it is challenging to scale up financing models or to replicate lessons-learnt from previous projects; this adds transaction costs that can deter financiers' interest (OECD, 2020[24]). Table 2.1. provides a summary of risks related to water-related investments.

Table 2.1. Summary of risks related to water-related investments

Type of risk	Specifications and examples
Macroeconomic and business risks	**Transfer risk:** due to mismatch between revenue and debt servicing currency **Operating and construction risk** including: • weak performance of utilities • risks related to a variety of technologies and innovative approaches (e.g. nature-based solutions [NbS]) **Credit risk**: inability of counterparty to honour contractual arrangements **Termination risk:** risk of early termination of long-term contracts **Market risk:** demand for service
Regulatory and political risks	**Regulatory risk** including: • change in tariffs • economic regulation may be weak or absent • regulation on private participation in infrastructure **Political risk:** • in the case of government procurement contracts • due to potential for political interference in the tariff setting process
Technical risks	**Performance risks:** • due to lack of experience and data for innovative approaches (e.g. NbS) • due to obsolesce of utilised technologies given the long-term nature of contracts and multitude of technologies applied. • in the case of WSS investments: performance risks can also arise due to aging infrastructure and leakage
Commercial risks	Risks affecting the revenues from a particular project (affordability, willingness to charge, willingness to pay)
Environmental/ social risk	**Environmental risk:** • variability of water resources availability due to climate change can reduce performance of water infrastructure, for example hydropower production • increasing water scarcity can lead to increase of cost of bulk water supply; • potential negative environmental impacts of large multi-purpose water infrastructure **Social risks** including: • resettlement of households that will be flooded down stream of dams • affordability constrains related to tariff increases

Source: Authors, based on (OECD, 2019[7])

Increasing pressures and growing uncertainty due to climate change

Many of the impacts of climate change manifest through disruptions to the hydrological cycle, such as increased frequency of floods (coastal, riverine and storm-driven) and droughts, increased variability and intensity of rainfall, and reduced snowpack feeding headwaters of major rivers, among others (Masson-Delmotte et al., 2018[25]; Bates et al., 2008[26]). Observed warming has been linked to changing precipitation patterns, intensity and extremes, and to changes in runoff to rivers, lakes and wetlands, in addition to melting of ice and reduced snow cover (Bates et al., 2008[26]). Over varying timescales, these changes in the global hydrological cycle impact water resource availability and quality (Huntington, 2006[27]). Climate change also affects demand for water (for irrigation, or for cooling heat island effects in cities, for instance).

Decisions regarding water infrastructure typically rely on engineering, modelling and planning that base projections of future needs on historical patterns of water availability and use. For example, infrastructure design, planning and operating procedures are often based on the assumption that future climatic and hydrological conditions will be broadly similar to those of the past (Haasnoot et al., 2019[28]; OECD, 2013[29]). However, these assumptions are an increasingly unreliable guide to future conditions. Approaches for decision making under uncertainty are increasingly relevant to ensure robustness and flexibility to uncertain future conditions (OECD, 2021[30]).

As old assumptions about a stable climate are replaced by dynamic and changing climatic uncertainty, new approaches to policy frameworks, institutional arrangements and investment planning are needed. Climate change is one of a range of uncertainties, which also include demographic, economic and urban settlement trends, among others. This requires recognizing that water infrastructure built today will effectively lock in our choices for decades or centuries while the global climate continues to change, and that regulatory frameworks and water allocation regimes, if not flexible, will make water management rigid when it needs to be adaptive and agile (Smith et al., 2019[31]). Emerging and systemic threats, including the impacts of climate change, intensify the challenge of financing water-related investments and underscore the value of flexible and robust approaches to financing long-lived capital intensive infrastructure (Box 2.2).

Box 2.2. Systemic threats intensify the financing challenge

Emerging and systemic threats intensify the challenge of financing water-related investments. Incorporating resilience into water-related investments is needed to ensure that system-wide enhancements are made to help absorb and rebound from residual risks (for which further risk reduction is prohibitively expensive) as well as events that may be difficult to predict. These may include pandemics, social change, political disruption, landslides, cyber-attacks, climate and weather-related challenges such as droughts, storms, floods, wildfires, etc. Combined with optimal investment in risk reduction measures, resilience can minimise the costs of recovery in the event that threats materialise.

Climate change poses a systemic threat to the reliable provision of water services, the management of water resources and water-related risks, which will vary across regions in terms of the nature and magnitude of impacts (Linkov et al., 2019[32]). Temporal and spatial climate patterns are changing and, in some cases, projections are highly uncertain, rendering historical trends an inadequate basis for decision-making. Water-intensive assets that have operational lifetimes of many decades, even centuries, need to take a forward-looking approach to investment that address the novel challenges associated with a shifting water cycle (Matthews, 2019[33]). Project developers are only beginning to explore how to use new metrics, such as the value of resilience in the context of disruption, climate transformation, and high levels of uncertainty about the pace, direction, and types of impacts we can expect (Haasnoot et al., 2019[34]).

Experience to date with water-related investments suggests that many investors are forward-looking, strongly recognise the value of policy coherence in supporting investment conditions, and are actively interested in investment opportunities that fulfil objectives across multiple policy domains (OECD, 2018[35]).

Over recent years there has been a growing effort to situate water-related priorities and investments within a broader resilience paradigm, to promote a "new way of thinking about risk so that we can make wise financial decisions" (Linkov et al., 2019[32]). A resilience-led way of thinking would entail a shift in water sector financing norms for vulnerable countries and populations, and could help to trigger financial and technological innovation for the water systems of the future (Linkov et al., 2019[32]).

Source: (Linkov et al., 2019[32]), (Matthews, 2019[33]), (Haasnoot et al., 2019[34]), (OECD, 2018[35]).

2.3. Exacerbated challenges related to the COVID-19 crisis and opportunities related to the recovery

The COVID-19 pandemic has starkly demonstrated the importance of access to safe drinking water, sanitation and hygiene for human health. At the same time, the related economic and social consequences of the crisis have intensified financial pressure on water and sanitation service providers. During the first wave of the COVID-19 outbreak, water demand decreased significantly in multiple contexts. While domestic water use increased slightly, industrial and commercial water consumption dropped by 27% on average during the first months of the COVID-19 outbreak in 2020 (GWI, 2020[36]). In some areas industrial and commercial water consumption dropped by significantly higher percentages of up to 75%, e.g. in Kampala, Uganda (Danilenko, 2020[37]). While utilities in North America, Europe, Japan and Australia are likely to be more financially resilient than those in other regions, the financial impacts of the pandemic have impacted utilities in both OECD and non-OECD countries (GWI, 2020[36]). In addition to impacts on WSS service providers, the crisis contributed to numerous impacts on irrigation services due to fiscal constraints, interruptions of supply chains and lack of availability of labour (Waalewijn et al., 2020[38])

Revenue falls for utilities were also caused by suspended action against non-payers or tariff discounts in response to the COVID-19 crisis. Over 75% of the reviewed utilities of a global survey[1] waived measures against non-payers during the first months of the first wave of the pandemic (GWI, 2020[36]). As a consequence, in Sub-Saharan Africa, for example, utilities collected only 35% of their billing during the first months of the COVID-19 crises, compared to 69% before the pandemic (Gasson, 2020[39]). In Osaka in Japan, the Municipal Waterworks Bureau waived the fixed charges for water and wastewater for July to September 2020, resulting in a reduction of the combined tariff by 60.4%. The COVID-19 outbreak was also a reason for the 15.3% tariff decrease in Adelaide in Australia in 2020 (GWI, 2020[40]). Overall, falling collection rates from residential customers and reduced billings from industrial water users created significant financing challenges for water utilities.

The pandemic also postponed or stopped planned or on-going water infrastructure projects due to travel restrictions and supply chain disruptions. As one example, the procurement process of an advanced water purification plant in Los Angeles was held up as a result of the pandemic (GWI, 2021[41]). In the Philippines, the water investment program for Manila was suspended in 2020 due to COVID-19 (GWI, 2021[42]). Globally, the number of finished water infrastructure projects dropped in 2020. Not only project implementation but also project preparation slowed down in that year, with utilities focusing on operational priorities rather than capital ones (Scotney, 2021[43]).

In 2021, water tariffs rose again by an average of 3.7% year-on-year (GWI, 2021[44]). This helped ease the financial situation of water utilities. Overall, the impacts of the pandemic on water utilities' finances differ globally, depending on their resilience to financial shocks and changes in water demand.

While the water sector was hit by the pandemic, it also benefitted from immediate relief measures launched by governments and development banks and it continues to benefit from recovery packages in the future. For example, EBRD put together the Vital Infrastructure Support Programme, which provides bridging loans for municipalities that deal with liquidity shortages due to lockdowns. The largest recipient is Morocco's national water utility with EUR 50 million (GWI, 2021[45]). In Europe, the European Commission aims at allocating 30% of their EUR 1.85 trillion recovery budget[2] to sustainable investments, which can potentially contain water-related investments (European Council, 2020[46]). Over the next decade this would amount to over EUR 503 billion, as laid out in the EU Green Deal, which will mobilise at least EUR 1 trillion of sustainable investments (European Commission, 2020[47]). Further, the French recovery program *France Relance* includes the pillar 'Ecological development' which suggests several water-related infrastructure investments (see Box 2.3).

From a macro-economic view point, public budgets have been negatively affected by the pandemic. Government deficits and debt increased sharply in many emerging-market economies in 2020 (OECD,

2021[48]) and by 2023, public debt ratios are likely to exceed 2019 levels by 14 percentage points in the median OECD economy (OECD, 2021[49]). These developments could reduce governments' capacity to provide funding for water-related investments and could postpone necessary infrastructure projects in the water sector.

Box 2.3. COVID-19 recovery packages and their role for water-related investments

The EU's recovery instrument *Next Generation EU*

In July 2020, the European Council agreed to the EUR 750 billion recovery instrument *Next Generation EU*, aiming at boosting private investment, supporting ailing companies and accelerating the green and digital transitions.

The following selected elements could potentially provide funding for the water-related investment projects:

- The Recovery and Resilience Facility of EUR 560 billion provides loans and grants to EU member states and defines that the according plans need to "significantly contribute to addressing the green and the digital transitions" and the supported measures should "avoid adverse impacts in climate and the environment" (European Commission, 2020[50]).
- EUR 15.3 billion have been made available to upgrade the programme InvestEU, containing the new Strategic Investment Facility, which, with the upgrade, aims to generate up to EUR 150 billion of investments for the green and digital transitions.
- In the past, the European Fund for Strategic Investment has supported water-related projects, for example through a EUR 330 million loan for a flood defence project in the Netherlands or a EUR 200 million loan for a water and waste water infrastructure project in Italy (EIB, 2019[51]; EIB, 2018[52]). A top up could allow similar water-related investments in the future.
- The European Agricultural Fund for Rural Development (EAFRD) has been reinforced with EUR 15 billion to support structural changes necessary in line with the European Green Deal.

  One of the aims of the EAFRD is the support of agri-environmental farming practices, which can include measures to improve water quality or water resource management.
- The cohesion policy programmes will be topped up by EUR 55 billion between now and 2022.

  One of the Cohesion Policy's objectives is to support regions to preserve their natural environment and to finance water and waste-water infrastructure. 13% of its funds between 2014 and 2020 were dedicated to the environment and resource efficiency and 6% to climate change adaptation and risk prevention (European Commission, 2020[53]). The financial reinforcement of the programme could support water-related projects in the future.

Source: (European Commission, 2020[54])

The French Recovery Package *France Relance*

In 2020, the French Government launched the recovery plan *France Relance* in response to the COVID-19 crisis. The recovery package aims at creating jobs and relaunching the French economy to 2019 growth levels by 2022, focussing on the three pillars: 'ecological development', 'competitiveness' and 'cohesion'. Under the pillar 'ecological development', endowed with a budget of EUR 30 billion, several categories and proposed investments include water-related investments. These include:

- EUR 300 million to support the revival of biodiversity and the prevention of risks, notably to adapt to the effects of climate change and to strengthen resilience. This includes financing projects to manage and restore coastal, maritime and aquatic ecosystems and dam reinforcement to improve the safety of people and goods downstream and the capacity for use by or for the public of these structures.

- EUR 250 million in metropolitan France to strengthen investments in the modernization of drinking water and sanitation networks as well as treatment plants, with a focus on the treatment of sludge in rural areas. This aims to improve the resilience of the drinking water supply to the risk of drought and to mitigate water contamination through more effective treatment in wastewater treatment plants.
- EUR 50 million will be allocated specifically to accelerate the implementation of the "Overseas Water Plan" for overseas territories.

Source: (French Government, 2020[55])

2.4. Orders of magnitude of water-related financing needs and capacities

2.4.1. *Investment needs are massive and the gap is persistent*

Beyond this backdrop of systemic change and growing pressures, sound investment planning for financing water-related investments is impeded by a robust projections on investment needs and the state of existing assets. Projections on financing needs are diverse and can vary by several orders of magnitude. Estimates for investment needs vary widely due to data limitations and different methodological approaches. Estimated global costs of achieving SDG 6 exceed USD 1 trillion per year, or 1.21% of global gross product (Strong et al., 2020[56]). To achieve universal and equitable access to safe and affordable drinking water for all by 2030, the present value of the additional investment needed is around USD 1.7 trillion (Hutton and Varughese, 2016[57]), which is about three times the current investment levels. Looking at food production and agriculture, at least USD 300 billion are estimated to be required annually to meet the SDGs related to food security (UNCTAD and Convergence, 2020[58]).

2.4.2. *Regional perspective – Europe*

In Europe, a regional perspective is particularly relevant because EU member states share a common level of ambition. They enjoy financial and technical support from the European Commission. The EU water *acquis* and similar policies contribute to (comparatively) robust monitoring and data collection, which support cross-country comparison and peer learning.

Investment needs

Current annual average expenditures on water supply and sanitation are estimated at a total of EUR 100 billion across EU member states, with large variations across countries. Eight member states spend less than EUR 100 per capita each year, while six countries allocate more than EUR 250 per capita annually on WSS services (OECD, 2020[24]).

Investments in WSS need to increase significantly in order to reach and maintain compliance with common European standards (OECD, 2020[24]). OECD analysis provides estimates for the additional investment needs, including compliance with selected water directives[3] and to achieve required efficiency improvements. Sanitation represents the lion's share of the total additional expenditures, while urban growth plays a minor role in driving additional needs in the future. On a country level, all member states with the exception of Germany will need to increase annual expenditures for water supply and sanitation by more than 25% in order to reach and maintain compliance with the selected directives. At the higher end of additional investment needs, Romania and Bulgaria need to double (or more) the current level of expenditures (OECD, 2020[24]). Figure 2.1. depicts the additional expenditures per annum required by 2030. The estimates for the additional yearly expenditures are a sum of the expenditures of a business as usual scenario (reflecting the costs of connecting new city dwellers, driven by urban dynamics with no new policies), the costs of maintaining and reaching compliance with selected directives and efficiency improvements, required under the revised Drinking Water Directive, compared to a baseline of estimated current expenditures on WSS.

Figure 2.1. Per Annum additional expenditures by 2030

Business as usual (BAU) + Compliance + Efficiency vs. baseline

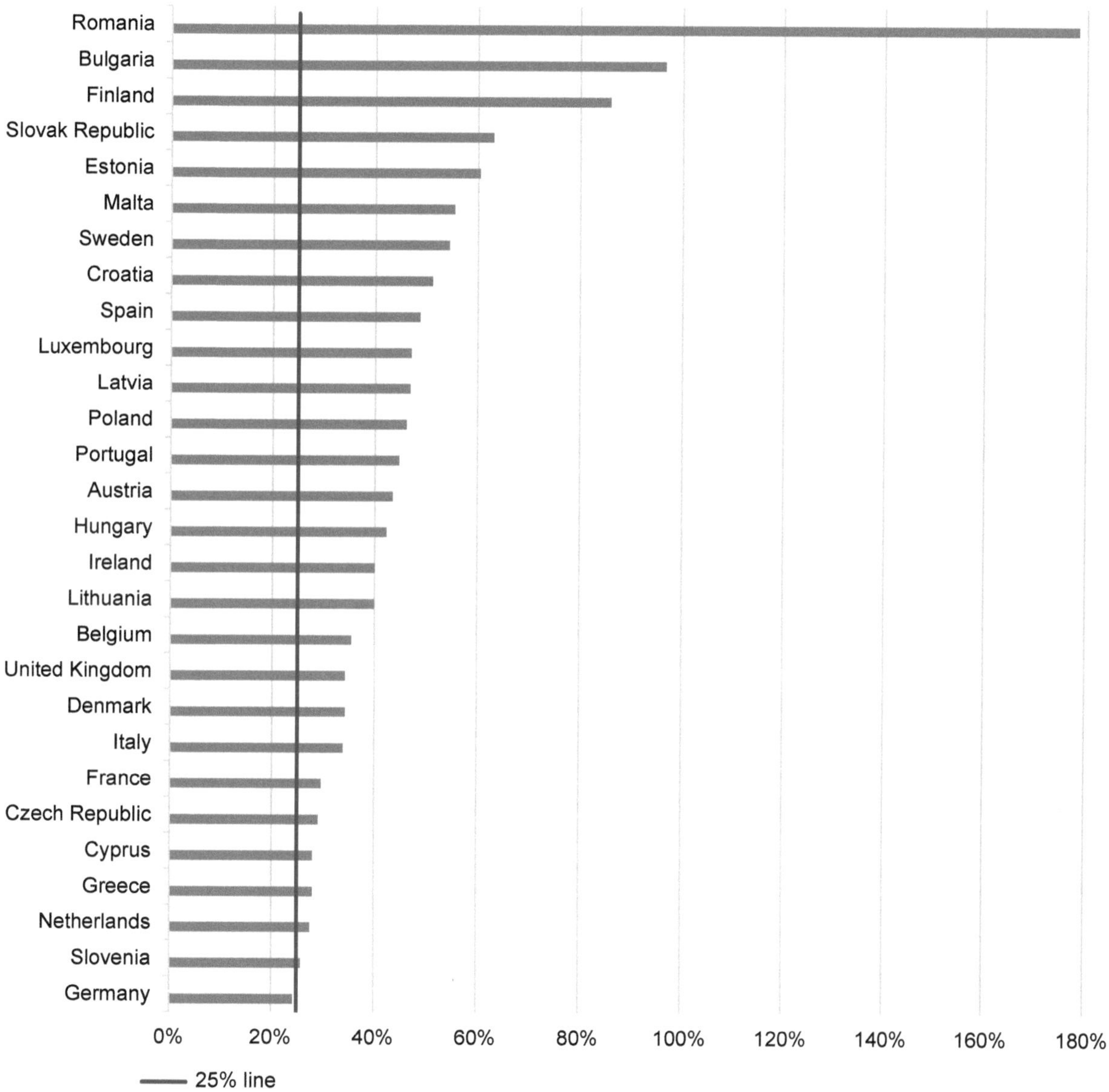

Source: (OECD, 2020[24])

Note: BAU (business as usual) scenario (same level of effort with no new policies, driven by urban population growth) and estimated costs to reach efficiency and compliance with DWD and UWWTD compared to the costs of the baseline scenario (member states' current expenditure level on WSS and flood protection).

Sources of funding

EU members vary in terms of the combination of sources of finance used for water supply and sanitation. Figure 2.2. visualises the shares of public spending and revenues from water tariffs as sources of finance for water supply and sanitation services. Close to 100% share of public spending implies the absence of water pricing, while a high percentage of revenue from water tariffs, on the other extreme, means that the majority of capital and operational expenditures are financed by the consumer. In the EU-13[4], public budgets cover 43% of the funding for WSS services and 29% in the EU-15.

Figure 2.2. Sources of finance for water supply and sanitation services for the EU-28

(2011-2015 annual average)

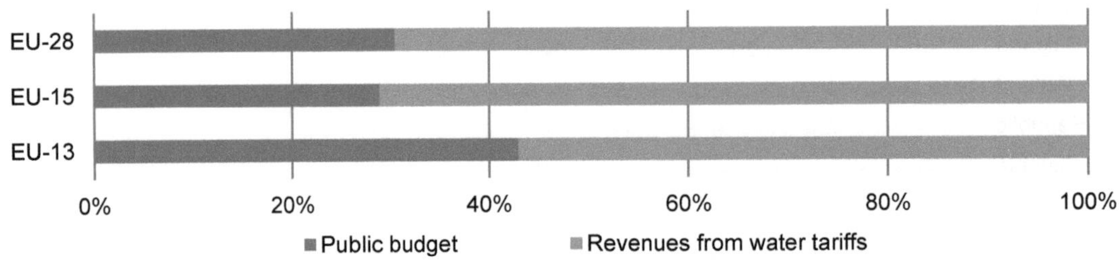

Source: (OECD, 2020[24]), based on EUROSTAT (General government expenditure by function, Final consumption expenditure on environmental protection services by institutional sector, Final consumption expenditure of households by consumption purpose, Mean consumption expenditure by detailed COICOP level).

In some countries, public budgets for WSS heavily rely on EU funding (notably the EU-13), some states rely essentially on water tariffs (Denmark, England and Wales), while others cover the costs through taxation (Ireland), which here is presented as part of public budget. The three main sources of funding and their potential use in the future are summarised below:

- ***EU transfers*** play an important role in the EU-13 countries, covering up to 17% of estimated total expenditures for WSS and in some countries, the lion's share of public funding (e.g. in Estonia). However, EU support through cohesion funds is projected to decrease in the future, further widening the financing gap and intensifying the need to mobilise alternative sources of finance.
- Water ***tariffs*** contribute to cost recovery and provide a source of revenue for water providers. Increasing tariffs is a potential option for a number of member states. The OECD analysis (2020[24]) found that in 24 EU member states, more than 95% of the population could pay more for water services without facing affordability constraints[5] on 2011-2015 average. Figure 2.3 gives an overview of the share of households' expenditure on water supply and sanitation in their overall disposable income per country. Some countries, however, face significant affordability constraints, especially when looking at the lowest quintile. Social tariffs or income support measures could be useful tools to address these issues. A caveat arising from data analysis for Figure 2.3 is that the statistics might fail to fully capture the complexity of affordability issues. Typically, poorest and most vulnerable households may not pay for public water supply and sanitation, because they are deprived from access to any service. This is typically the case for migrants, homeless, or remote and rural communities. A second caveat is that estimates presented in the figure remain dependent on current level of household expenditures, which in turn very much depends on the extent to which water is actually priced. Hence, affordability issues will be underestimated or may even go unnoticed in countries with a combination of low overall expenditure levels and low to no pricing. On the other hand, countries with reasonably low affordability concerns despite relatively high water prices are in principle in a better position.

- The ability to raise ***public spending*** depends on current tax income and public debt levels and varies significantly among member states. Countries with a high ratio of debt to GDP, such as Greece, Italy and Portugal, have limited room to increase public budgets for water-related investments. More disaggregated analysis is required to specify financing capacity of local authorities, which cover over 50% of public investment in the EU member states.

These findings might need to be reconsidered in light of the COVID-19 crisis, which has negatively affected both public and household budgets (as discussed above). Countries would benefit from a systematic assessment of the state of existing WSS infrastructure and needs for renewal.

Commercial finance could play a role in bridging the financing gap in European member states, including in response to declining availability of EU Funds, as it is accessible in all member countries.[6] So far, it has only marginally been used for water-related investments, representing roughly 6% of total expenditures on WSS (and only 1% in the EU-13). Especially for creditworthy and near-creditworthy borrowers, there is room to scale up commercial investments in the sector. Of course, as discussed below, commercial finance needs to be paid back, through a combination of revenues from tariffs, or (domestic or international) public funding.

Figure 2.3. Share of water supply and sanitation expenditures in households' disposable income

2015-2019 average

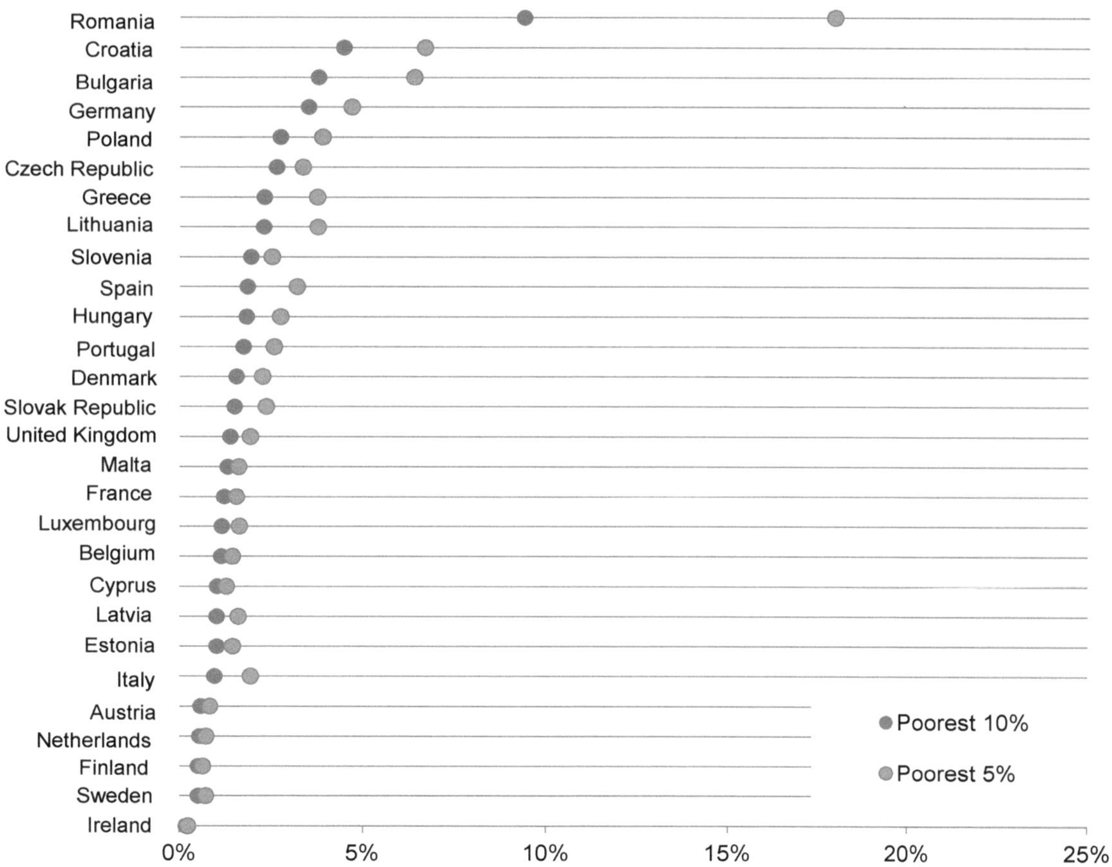

Note: Lack of household expenditure data for Sweden
Source: Authors, based on EUROSTAT (household expenditure and income data)

Estimates on current expenditures on **flood protection** are not available for most of the countries. Additional work is required to assess financing needs and capacities for water resources management to address risks of floods and droughts. Investment needs for flood protection are based on changes in the exposure of flood risks, relying on the development of indicators such as the value of assets at risk, the number of people affected and value of GDP affected. Some countries (Austria, Luxembourg and the Netherlands) face high growth factors for expenditure needs on flood protection, while others (Belgium, Czech Republic, Denmark, France, Germany, Hungary, Ireland, Poland, Romania, Slovak Republic and Sweden) are affected by moderate growth factors. Cyprus[7], Greece, Malta, Portugal and Spain benefit from low or negative growth factors, reducing the necessity to scale up investment in flood protection. (OECD, 2020[24])

2.4.3. Regional perspective - The Asia-Pacific region

In contrast to European member states, countries in the Asia Pacific region do not share a common ambition or set of regulations for water security. While the SDGs, and notably the targets under SDG 6, provide a common guideline, there is a lack of comparable data on water-related expenditure, making it challenging to estimate investment needs and financing capacities for water security at regional and national levels. Nonetheless, OECD analysis provides a broad order of magnitude of financing needs for water in the region.

Investment needs

Overall projections indicate that most countries in the Asia-Pacific region will need to allocate between 1% and 2% of GDP for ***water supply and sanitation infrastructure*** over the 2015-2030 period to achieve universal access to safely managed water supply and sanitation services for all[8]. Countries with investment needs of less than 2% of GDP, such as Timor Leste, Afghanistan, Nepal and Pakistan, can expect to face greater challenges to meet these investment needs. The largest share of the USD 198 billion total annual estimated investment needs in the Asia Pacific region fall to the People's Republic of China (hereafter 'China') (USD 60 billion/year) and India (USD 22 billion/year). At the same time large investment needs compared to GDP are concentrated in low- and middle-income countries. Several countries have water supply and sanitation investment needs of greater than USD 20 per capita per year (ADB, 2020[59]). Figure 2.4 compares countries in the region in terms of total investment needs as both a share of GDP and per capita between 2015 and 2030.

Figure 2.4. Comparative expenditure gap of water supply and sanitation infrastructure required by 2030 to achieve SDGs 6.1 and 6.2

Cost per capita (USD) and as a percentage of GDP

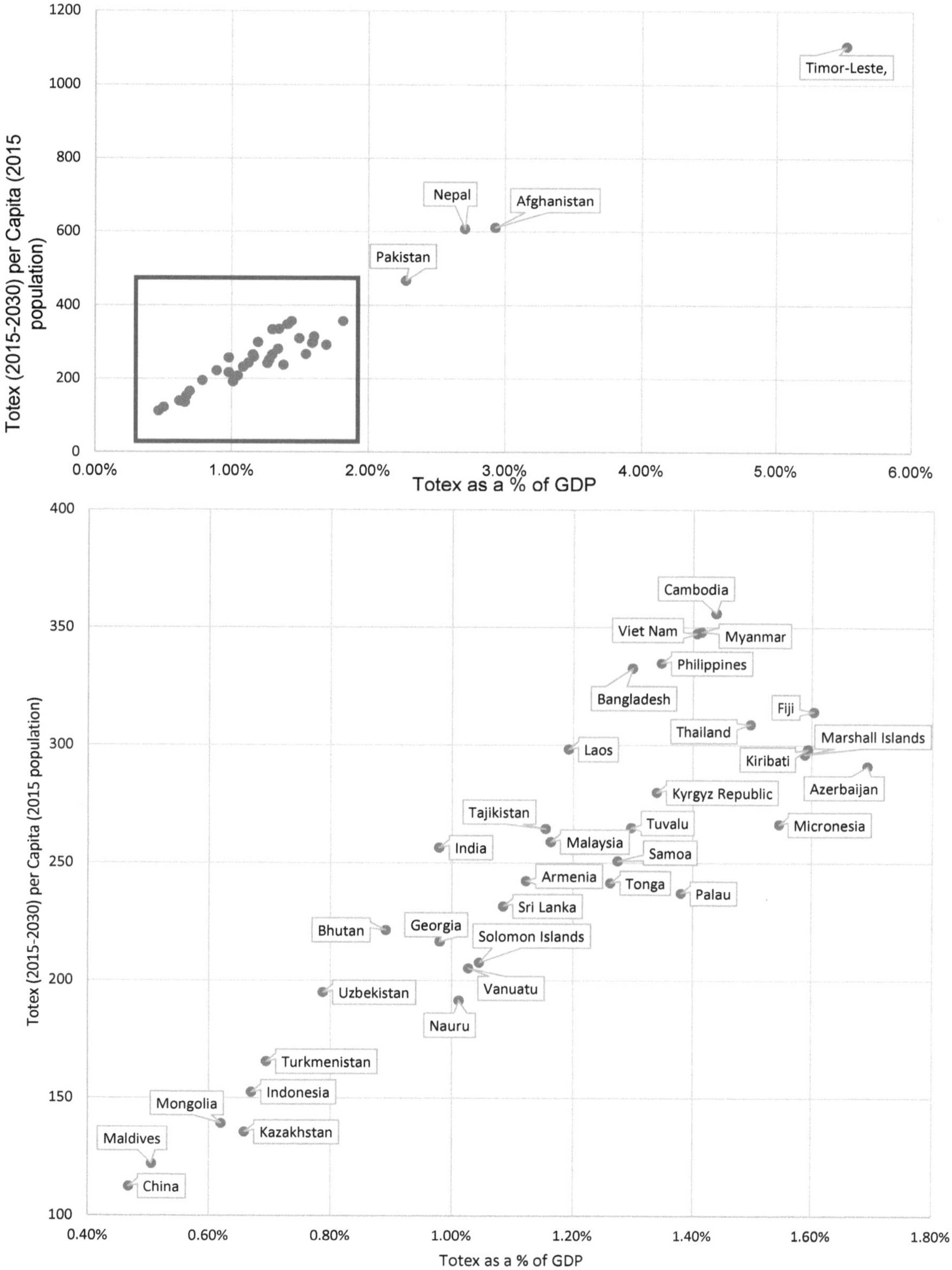

Note: No data for Australia, Singapore, New Zealand, Brunei, South Korea, Japan, Hong Kong (SAR China), Niue, Cook Islands.
Source: OECD calculations based on (Rozenberg and Fay, 2019[60])

Investment needs for flood protection are difficult to quantify and depend on both population and assets at risk of flooding. Like water supply and sanitation, the impacts on people and the magnitude of investment needs in flood protection are, for the most part, concentrated in low- and middle-income countries. Note that this is not the case for the value of assets at risk of flooding. Bangladesh, in particular, is a hotspot for flood risk in the Asia-Pacific region with over 11% of the population projected to be exposed in 2030. India is expected to experience the greatest increase in absolute numbers of people exposed to flood risks between 2010 and 2030 (over 20 million additional people). In terms of GDP affected by floods, the exposure is substantial in some countries, most notably in India (over USD 280 billion), China (USD 220 billion) and Indonesia (over USD 100 billion). In several countries, flood risks will exceed 6% of GDP in 2030. (ADB, 2020[59])

Further, ***irrigation*** needs will increase in Asia and with it investment needs. While data on current expenditure on irrigation or investment needs is not available on a country-level, regional estimates project total annual investments in irrigation to USD 6.8 billion for East Asia and Pacific and USD 5.1 billion for South Asia between 2015-2030 (Rosegrant et al., 2017[61]). Figure 2.5. presents regional estimates of annual irrigation investment needs from 2015-2030 as a percentage of GDP. The following section will give further insights into the topic of agricultural water financing.

Figure 2.5. Annual irrigation investment needs 2015-2030 in Asia-Pacific sub-regions

Percentage of GDP / year

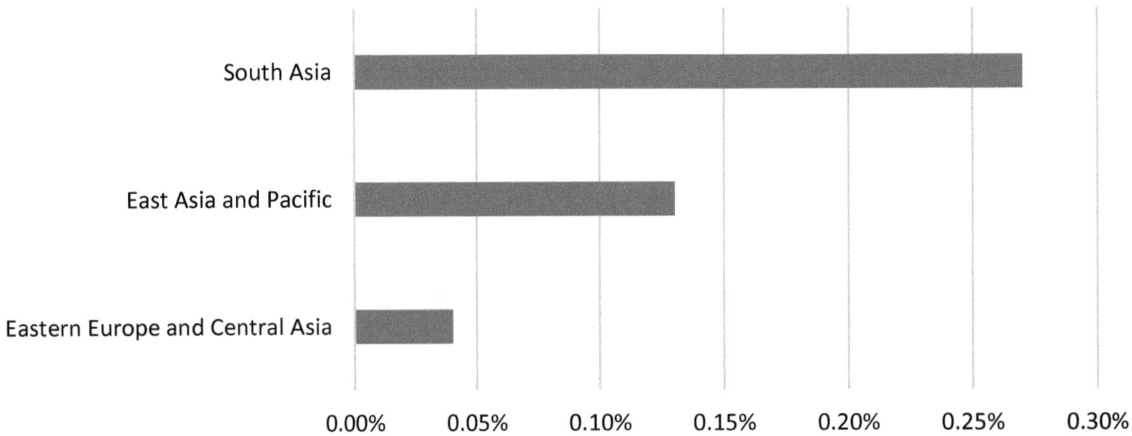

Note: EECA region includes 13 ADB countries, as well as 10 non-ADB countries.
Source: (Rozenberg and Fay, 2019[60])

Sources of funding

- ***Public budgets*** are the dominant funding source for water supply and sanitation infrastructure in countries for which data is available. Significant levels of public expenditure (more than 5% of GDP) have occurred in several countries, notably China, Bhutan, Viet Nam, India and the Maldives over selected time periods. However, the potential of taxes and surcharges to increase public funds allocated to the water sector remains generally underexplored. (ADB, 2020[59])
- ***Water tariffs*** are often relatively low and half of responding countries in the latest GLAAS survey indicated that water supply and sanitation tariffs are insufficient to recover 80% of operation and maintenance costs, let alone capital (refurbishment and replacement) costs (UN Water and WHO, 2019[62]). Many countries have limited ability to raise water prices because of affordability constraints for parts of the population. In some countries the annual tariffs in selected cities

currently represent more than 10% of the annual income of the middle quintile household. Conversely, there may also be scope to increase water supply and sanitation tariffs in a number of countries, such as Tajikistan, Armenia, Kazakhstan and others. (See Figure 2.6.) (ADB, 2020[59])

- ***Official development aid*** represents a small proportion of total expenditure on water infrastructure. In comparison to other countries, India and Indonesia received considerable amounts (on average USD 257 and 189 million per year) and data suggests that ODA may not be reaching some of the countries that most need it, such as Timor-Leste, Bangladesh, Myanmar, Afghanistan and Papua New Guinea. (ADB, 2020[59])

Although domestic ***commercial finance*** is available across Asia-Pacific countries, private investment is concentrated in only a few of Asia's lower-risk economies and few countries have gained experience in mobilising it for water-related expenditures to date. A few transactions have been supported by international donors, but these have mostly been in middle-income countries, and they have so far failed to be replicated at scale (AIIB, 2019[63]).

Figure 2.6. Microeconomic affordability: Average city water supply and sanitation tariffs as a share of annual disposable middle-quintile household income

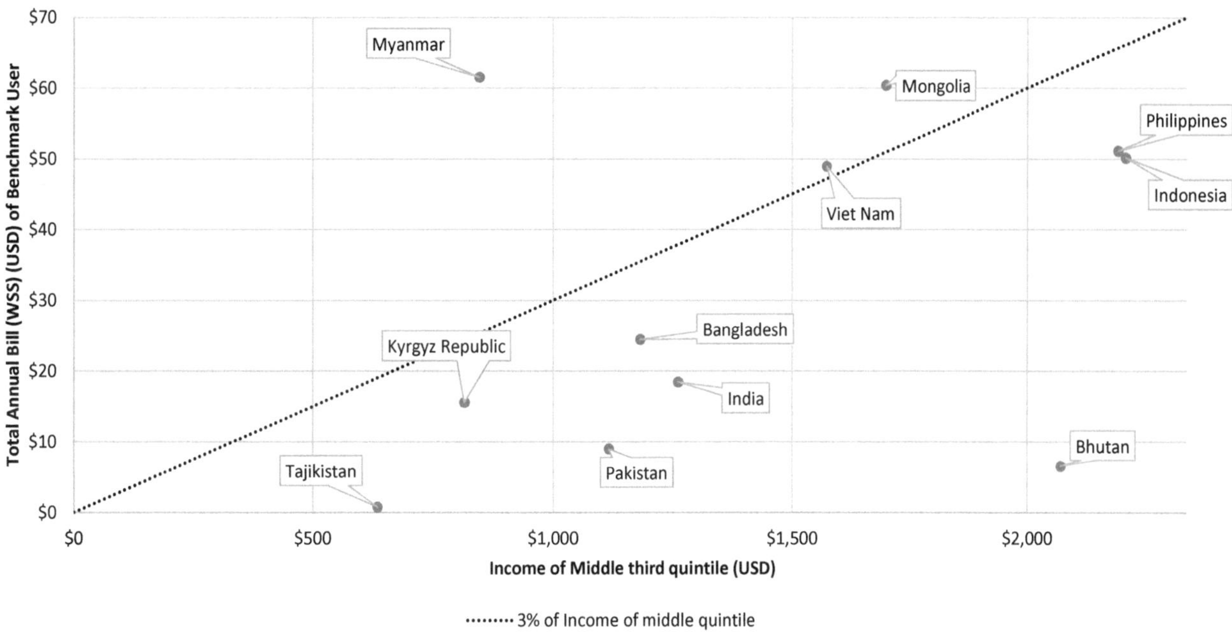

Note: Average city tariff represents year 2017, and based on available data for select cities from GWI. Annual disposable income of households is based on the middle quintile of income.
Data for tariffs from 108 cities, in 20 countries.
Source: OECD calculations based on (GWI, 2019[64]) and (World Bank, 2019[65])

Overall, tracking and projecting financing flows for water security in Asia is compounded by a significant lack of available data. Additional coordinated efforts to monitor financing flows at regional level would provide invaluable support to policy making and to the design of financial mechanism that are up to challenge and tailored to regional and country needs. Regional financial institutions have a role to play, at least to compile information on the projects and financing mechanisms they contribute to. Further coordination could also be considered through thematic regional platforms in place (the Asia Pacific Water Forum, the Asia Water Council) or regional political fora (e.g. APEC, already active on related issues such as food security).

2.4.4. Sectorial perspective – Financing Agricultural Water

Water resources are critical for agricultural production and food security. The agricultural sector is a major consumer of freshwater, accounting for 70% of the world's water withdrawals and 85% of global freshwater consumption (OECD, 2017[66]). These water needs will rise in the future and climate change will cause additional water-related pressure on the sector. Forty percent of global food production depends on irrigated agriculture, covering 20% of the world's cultivated land. The remaining 80% rely on rain fed agriculture with greater vulnerability to changing precipitation patterns (UNESCO, 2020[67]; World Bank, 2020[68]). Irrigated agriculture is at least twice as productive per unit of land as rain fed agriculture, on average, and could improve resource efficiency and intensify production (World Bank, 2020[68]).

Population growth and changing diets will lead to increased demands on agricultural productivity and efficiency. These are key drivers for freshwater scarcity. In sub-Saharan Africa and Northern and Western Africa, annual total renewable water resources per capita declined by 41% and 32% respectively between 1997 and 2017 (FAO, 2020[69]) and trends will exacerbate in the future. Climate change poses an additional layer of pressures on the sector. According to the IPCC (2021[70]), drought events are 1.7 times more likely today than on 1850-1950 average, and will further increase in frequency and intensity, particularly in Africa, South America and Europe.

The projected impact of climate change on agriculture is expected to be severe both for the sector and in terms of reduced economic growth (OECD, 2015[71]; OECD, 2014[72]). Recent events illustrate the type of impacts foreseen. For instance, the extreme drought in Europe in 2018 resulted in cereal yields declining by up to 50% for certain crops, and the heavy rainstorms in Japan in the same year led to damage for the agricultural sector valued at USD 4 billion (MAFF, 2029[73]; Gruère, Shigemitsu and Crawford, 2020[74]). In India, productivity of most crops is projected to decline by 10 to 40% by the end of the century due to higher temperatures, rainfall variability and decreasing access to freshwater for irrigation (Shrivastava, 2016[75]). Beyond increasing the intensity and frequency of extreme events, some estimates project climate change to raise global irrigation requirements by up to 20% (Hertel and Liu, 2016[76]).

The agricultural sector contributes to increased water competition with other users and sectors, particularly in some countries (OECD, 2017[66]). Due to its high consumptive water use, irrigated agriculture can have significant consequences for water resources, economic activities and ecosystem services. An estimated 41% of current irrigation water use occurs at the expense of environmental flow requirements (FAO, 2020[69]) and in some regions, intense groundwater use for irrigation have resulted in declining groundwater tables, contributing to environmental degradation and putting in question the sustainability of groundwater-irrigated food production (OECD, 2015[77]). Additionally, agriculture contributes largely to water pollution mainly through organic matter and nutrient runoffs from agricultural inputs (e.g., pesticides, herbicides or fertilisers), resulting in contamination or eutrophication (OECD, 2017[78]).

Investment needs for agricultural water

Ensuring that agriculture and food systems meet the needs of a rising population and are able to withstand, recover from and anticipate the impacts of climate change will require significant investments in agricultural systems. This will encompass investing in innovation for sustainable, productive and resilience agriculture and food systems (OECD, 2021[79]), and in particular improving the management of irrigated areas, as well as water management in rain fed cropland and pastureland areas.

There is currently no unified consistent, longitudinal or cross-sectoral database with cost or investment data on irrigation or agricultural water. The data availability for this sector is exceedingly sparse compared to other sectors and makes constructing projections on current investment levels and needs now and in the future a challenge.

Globally, about 1.2 billion people live in extremely water scarce irrigated or rain-fed areas affected by water shortages, of which 520 million live in rural areas. According to FAO (2020[69]), more than 275 million hectares of irrigated cropland would benefit from improved water management, 171 million hectares of which are under high to very high water stress and require urgent action, with regional differences. In developing countries in the sub-regions of East Asia, the Pacific and South Asia, for example, required investments to meet the projected irrigation expansion may cost an estimated average of USD 3.1 billion annually between 2015 and 2030, of which USD 1.7 billion are required to improve water-use efficiency. Soil and water management technologies have baseline investment estimates of USD 500 million per year across the three regions. Combining the acceleration of irrigation expansion[9] and improvement of both irrigation efficiency and soil and water management would require an estimated USD 6.8 billion per year in East Asia and the Pacific and USD 5.1 billion per year in South Asia. (Asian Development Bank, 2020[80]) In the Arab region, annual irrigation replacement costs of existing capital, upgrade, efficiency, and new capital investments in Arab countries in North Africa and the Maghreb are estimated to average between 0.08 - 0.16% of regional GDP. (Rozenberg and Fay, 2019[60])

Investments in water productivity need to be accompanied with investments in water allocation policies, governance and institutions to ensure that investments deliver the benefits for sustainable management of water resources (Gruère and Shigemitsu, 2021[81]; Yu et al., 2021[82]). Together with investments in innovation, infrastructure, including transportation and the provision of information and communication technologies, they are critical for improving sustainable water management and for strengthening the resilience of the sector.

Sources of funding for agricultural water

This section[10] provides estimates of funding for agricultural water, including from governments, official development assistance and other sources based on available OECD data and additional sources. These estimates are derived from an OECD analysis (Ashley and Gruère, 2021[83]) in preparation of the Roundtable on Financing Agricultural water in January 2021.

Government water-related agricultural support

Total public agriculture related support for water in 54 countries - the 28 EU member states[11] (aggregated), other OECD member countries, and 11 emerging economies[12] - increased from USD 25.9 billion in 2000 to USD 54.2 billion in 2011 and then declined to USD 41.6 billion in 2019 (see Figure 2.7.). Close to three quarter of total support was provided in non-OECD emerging countries, especially India and China (58% of total support).

Figure 2.7. Total water-related agriculture support in 54 countries

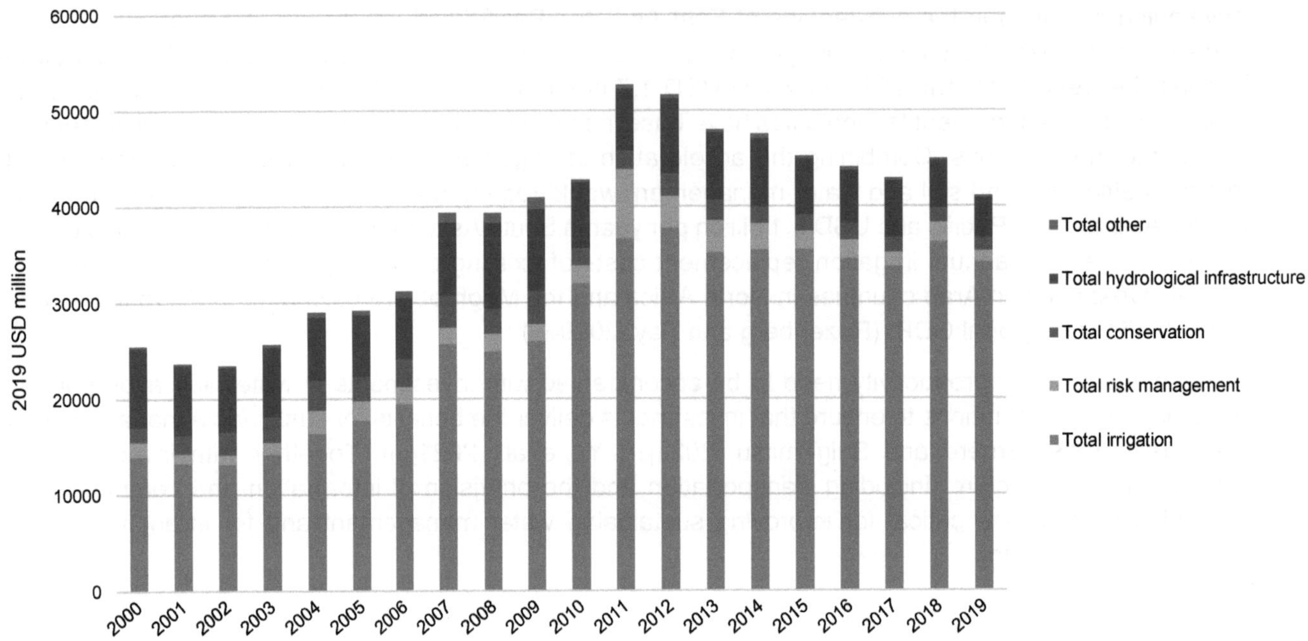

Note: Hydrological infrastructure relates to all expenses to support water use related infrastructure related to agriculture, conservation includes measure towards the conservation of water ecosystems and payment for sustainable water use, risk management includes measures to manage water risks, particularly flooding, scarcity or salinity, irrigation covers payments to encourage irrigation and development of irrigation on farm.
Source: (Ashley and Gruère, 2021[83]) based on (OECD, 2020[84]).

Seventy percent of total agricultural support for water was dedicated to irrigation (from irrigation development to support for water in irrigation), Eighteen percent of support went to agriculture-related hydrological infrastructure (comprising of all basin and sub-basin infrastructure work that may be related to agriculture water management) and the remaining part was split between conservation-related and water risk-related management expenditures. Between 2000 and 2019, governments of the covered countries spent between USD 10 and USD 20 billion per year on irrigation (USD 15.4 billion in 2019), the amounts almost entirely spent by India and China. Eight-two percent of production support for irrigation aimed at incentivising the use of water for irrigation via irrigation-related water or electricity subsidies (98% in non-OECD countries). This kind of support has the potential to encourage excessive use of water for irrigation and thus have harmful effects on surface and groundwater resources (Gruère and Le Boëdec, 2019[85]).

In terms of the activities targeted, 43% of total water-related agricultural support was related to production and 57% to enabling agricultural activities and functioning of the sector (general services). A contrasting picture emerges when looking only at OECD countries. In this case, only 24% of total support is linked to agricultural production while 86% are dedicated to enabling activities.

Similarly, irrigation investment trends differ from the 54-country-totals, when considering OECD countries only: total water-related agriculture support declined progressively from a peak in 1995 of USD 18.7 to USD 6.8 billion in 2019. Differently from the total of all covered countries, only 13% of these amounts focused on irrigation, while most of the support was dedicated to hydrological infrastructure. Domestic producer support for irrigation in OECD countries has declined from USD 2.5 billion in 1989 to close to USD 480 million in 2019. The share of support directly incentivising the use of water for irrigation declined from 88% in 1986 to 46% in 2019. Figure 2.8. and Figure 2.9. visualise these trends.

Overall, non-OECD emerging countries are spending much more on irrigation than other types of infrastructure related to agricultural water management, while the contrary is the case for OECD economies. These differences may underline varying government priorities, both related to food production and to irrigation sector specificities. However, no obvious trend of changing government support structure over time can be observed, even for rapidly growing emerging economies.

Figure 2.8. Total water-related agriculture support in OECD countries

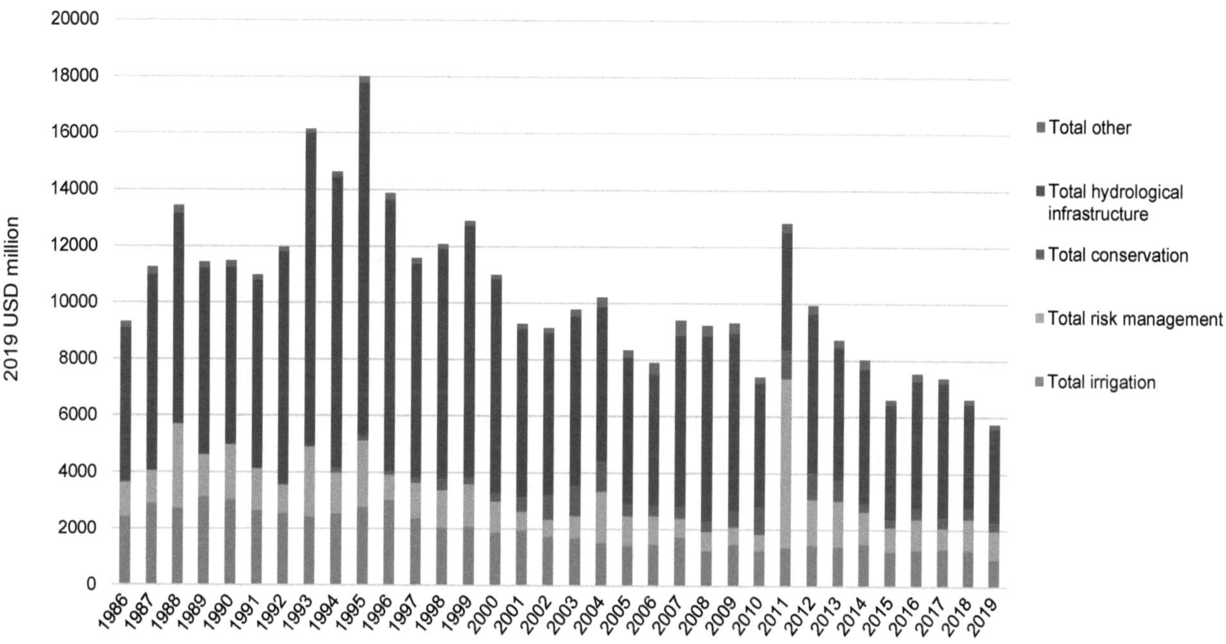

Source: (Ashley and Gruère, 2021[83]) based on (OECD, 2020[84]).

Figure 2.9. Producer support estimates (PSE) related to irrigation by OECD country

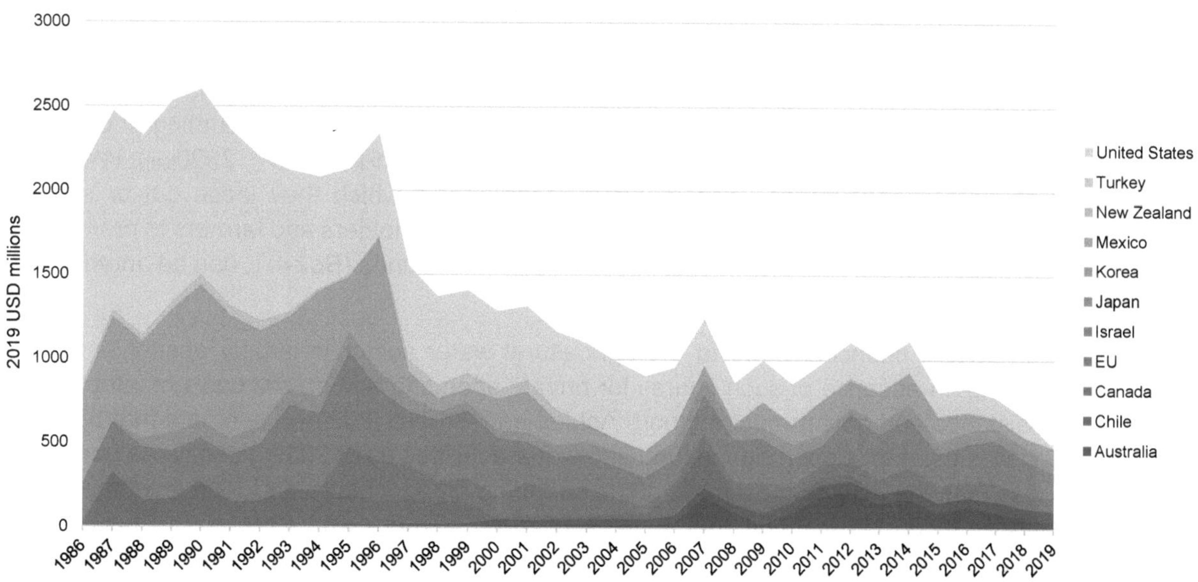

Source: (Ashley and Gruère, 2021[83]) based on (OECD, 2020[84]).

Development Assistance on agriculture and water

About USD 1 billion of official development assistance[13] (ODA) was spent annually on water-related investments in recent years, the largest share originating from multilateral agencies. Almost all of the total ODA related to agricultural water was allocated to Asian (52%) and African (44%) countries. Other official assistance[14] amounts to an average of USD 381 million annually between 2014 and 2018, of which 85% were dedicated to Asian countries. Taking these sums together, official development flows amount to roughly USD 1.5 billion annually, which remains very limited given the wide geographical scope. To give a picture of order of magnitude, this only slightly exceeds Korea's total domestic support for agricultural water, at USD 1 -1.2 billion. Looking at a sectorial context, ODA dedicated to agriculture amounted to USD 7 to 7.5 billion annually, and USD 166 to 195 billion of ODA were spent on all sectors during the same time period.

In the Arab region, as regional example, international aid flows to the agricultural water sector account for around 1% of total aid to the region, with donors committing a total of USD 2.7 billion to this sub-sector between 2008 and 2017, out of 6.9 billion committed to the entire agriculture sector. Thirty-six percent of these flows related to agricultural water went to Egypt, followed by Morocco (30%) and Sudan (14%) (FAO IWMI, 2019[86]).

Other sources of finance

Private actors have an important role to contribute to finance agricultural water investments. *Individual and groups of farmers* play a key part in financing water-related investments. They can invest in irrigation equipment and maintenance and improved land use practices with the support of credit or banking institutions. Evidence shows that in India, 80% of all types of financing sources across modernising irrigation schemes stem from farmers' own savings and that farmer-led irrigation, business-to-business and business-to-consumer alliances could be promising financing models for agricultural water in the future (World Bank Group, 2020[87]). However, farmers often face considerable barriers to access finance. Large-scale farmers require finance with long maturities, while commercial lenders prefer shorter timelines. Medium and small-scale farmers face hurdles receiving loans since their risk profile is often difficult or costly to model, thus increasing transaction costs and risks for investors. Additionally, systemic risks, such as extreme weather events related to climate change, pose a particular challenge for sector financing. Chapter 3 discusses financing models which can overcome these challenges, such as microfinance for farmers, extended tenors with blended finance, or weather index-based crop insurance.

Other investors in the sector from the private sphere are *agro-food companies* or *technology providers*, which can provide finance for irrigation-related initiatives or projects to improve climate resilience. The agro-food company Mars, for example, estimates that by rolling out wet-dry rice farming, it could avoid supply shortages and thus reach savings of between USD 60 and 180 million (CDP, 2020[88]). *Water sector companies or other stakeholders* may also invest in technologies which they lease out or set up for remunerative use by farmers. Compensation schemes between stakeholders and farmers to promote more sustainable water resource use within a landscape, such as Water Funds (Box 4.1, can be another source of finance.

Globally, data on private financing flows to the agricultural water sector is largely absent and reliable estimates are lacking. In absence of such figures for private spending and on the basis of information on development assistance and government support, Ashley and Gruère (2021[83]) estimate that a minimum of USD 43 billion was used to support agricultural and water activities as of 2019 globally. As comparison, this amount is less than the minimum estimate of the spending on agriculture and food relief measures in response to COVID-19 during the first four months of 2020 (Gruère and Brooks, 2021[89]). A better understanding of where and how to best orient financing flows for agricultural water and water services in rural areas is needed in order to support a transition towards more sustainable agricultural and food systems.

2.5. Trends in development finance for water

Overall, official development assistance (ODA) flows have increased more than 2.5 times since 2002, with ODA for water generally increasing in line with the broader trends (Figure 2.10). Over the 2002-18 period, USD 120 billion have been allocated to water-related ODA (out of a total of USD 2.4 trillion for all sectors). "Water-related" ODA includes several sub-sectors including water supply and sanitation, waste management/disposal, hydro-electric power plants, agricultural water, and water resource conservation. The share of ODA allocated to water-related sub-sectors remains relatively stable at 4-5% over 2002-18, reaching 5.15% of total ODA in 2018 (Figure 2.10). During that time the split between ODA loans and ODA grants in the water sector is relatively even at 51% for grants and 49% for loans. There is a trend to move away from grants and towards loans. In 2002, loans accounted for 44% of water sector ODA flows and in 2018, they had reached 61% of water sector ODA flows.

Among water-related ODA flows, water supply and sanitation (large systems) accounted for the largest share, capturing 21% of the total flows for water, amounting to USD 45 billion total value over the period 2002-18, followed by water supply and sanitation (basic systems) capturing a 10% of the total flows for water, amounting to USD 22 billion total value of the period (Figure 2.11). ODA for agricultural water amounts to 6% of total flows for water (USD 13 billion total value) and for hydro-electric plants amounts to 4% (USD 9 billion total value). ODA flows for waste management/ disposal and water resources conservation account for relatively small shares compared to other water-related sub-sectors. Box 2.4 provides details related to the largest ODA donor for water, Japan, and the largest ODA recipient, India.

Figure 2.10. ODA Flows by Selected Sectors, 2002-2018

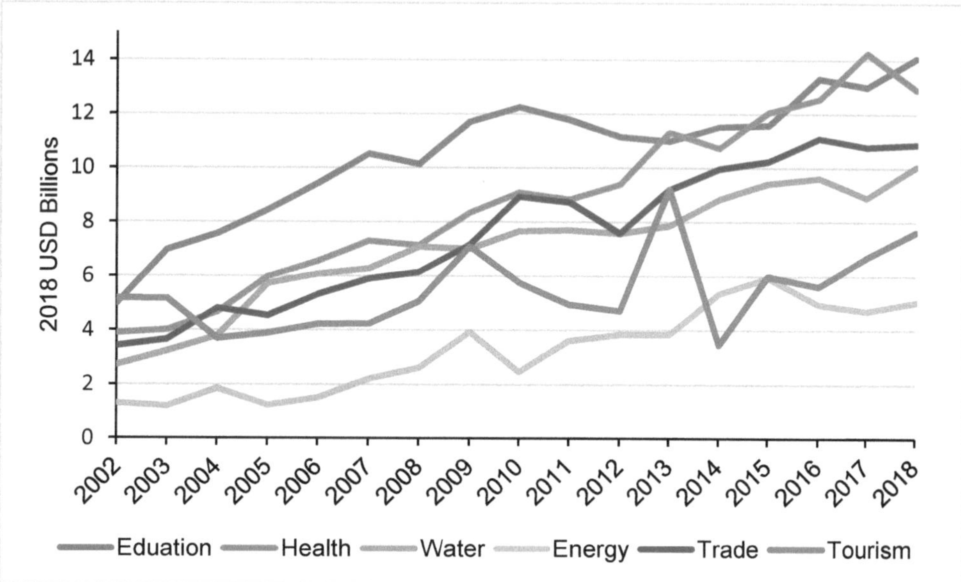

Source: Authors, based on OECD Creditor Reporting System https://stats.oecd.org/Index.aspx?DataSetCode=CRS1

Figure 2.11. ODA Flow by Water Sub-sector

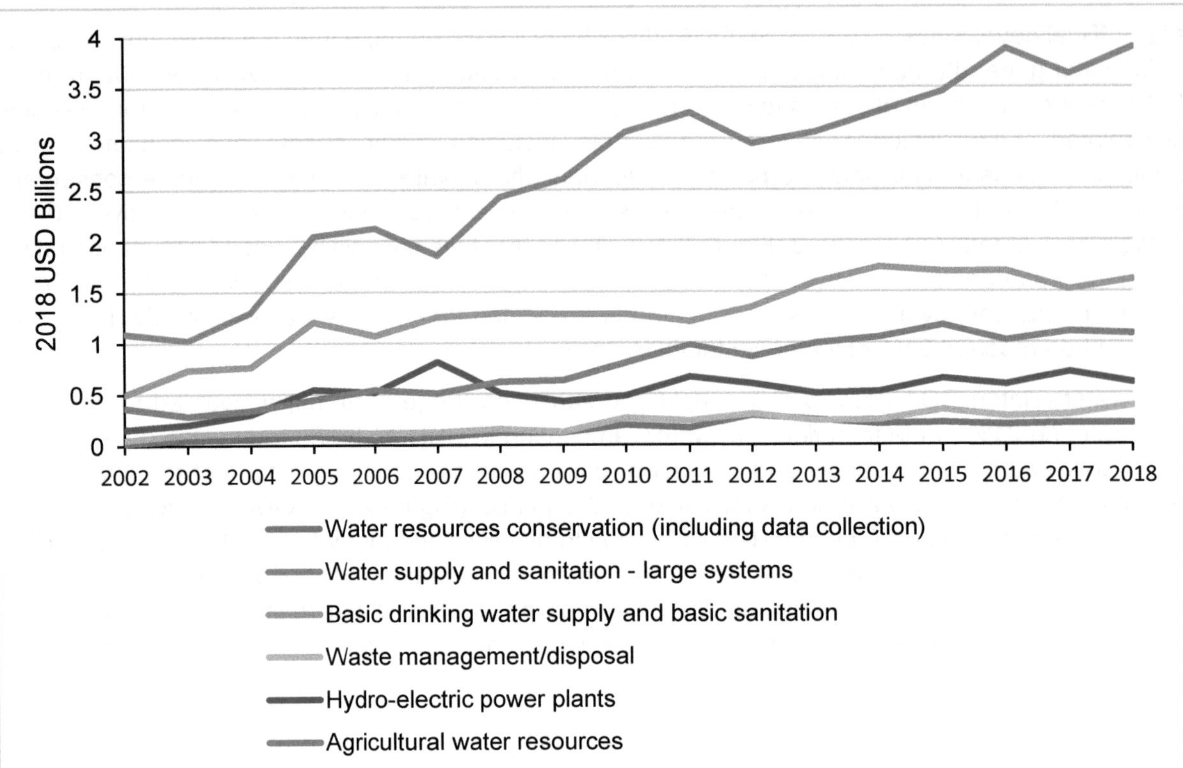

Source: Authors, based on OECD Creditor Reporting System https://stats.oecd.org/Index.aspx?DataSetCode=CRS1

Box 2.4. Largest donor and recipient for water-related ODA

Since from 2002 to 2018, Japan has been the largest ODA donor in the water sector contributing 21.5 billion in 2018 USD, 19% of all water ODA. Figure 2.12. illustrates the distribution across sub-sectors of Japan water-related ODA over the period. Water supply and sanitation accounts for the largest share of Japan's ODA for the sector, reaching nearly 65% (including both large systems and basic systems).

Figure 2.12. Distribution of Japan Donor ODA by Sector 2002-2018

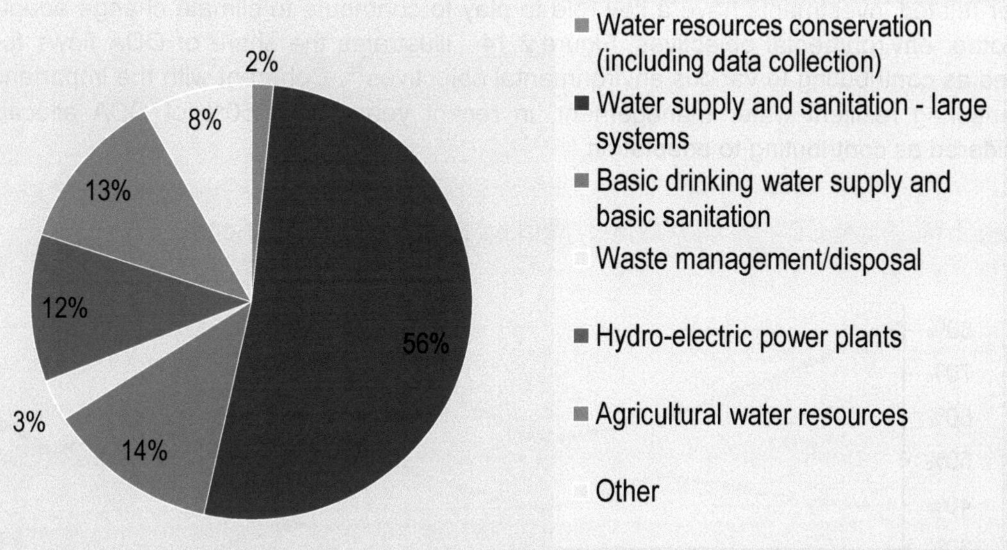

Source: Authors, based on OECD Creditor Reporting System https://stats.oecd.org/Index.aspx?DataSetCode=CRS1

In terms of recipients, India has been the largest recipient of water-related ODA, receiving approximately USD 4.6 billion over 2002-18 (USD 2018 constant prices), amounting to 6% of all water-related ODA over the period. The largest share is allocated to water supply and sanitation, nearly 70% (including large systems and basic systems). The India Government launch of a major campaign in 2014 to improve WASH services may have contributed to attracting significant levels of ODA in recent years.

Figure 2.13. Distribution of India Received ODA by Sector, 2002-2018

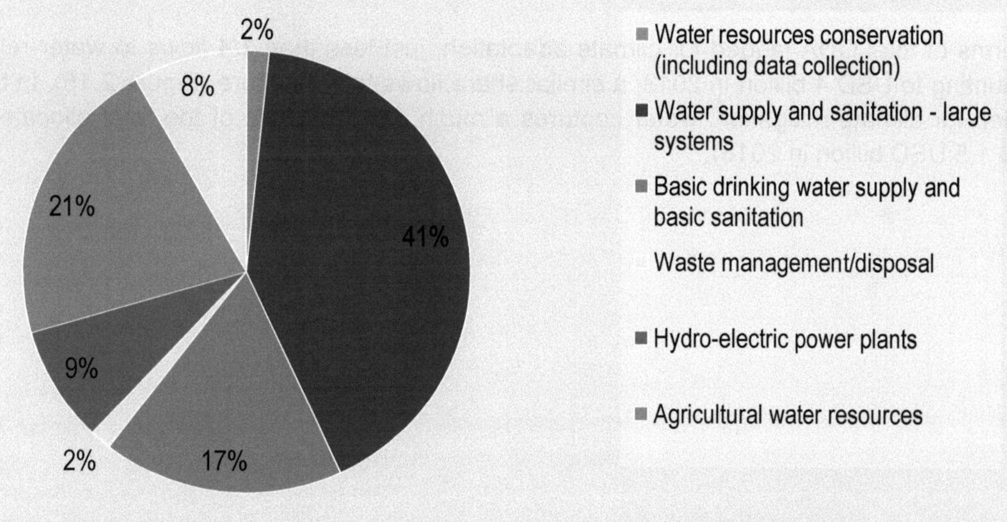

Source: Authors, based on OECD Creditor Reporting System https://stats.oecd.org/Index.aspx?DataSetCode=CRS1

2.5.1. Trends in development finance for water contributing to key environmental objectives

Water-related investments have a key role to play to contribute to climate change adaptation, mitigation and other environmental objectives. Figure 2.14. illustrates the share of ODA flows for water that are tagged as contributing to various environmental objectives[15]. Coherent with the importance of adaptation for ensuring resilient water management, in recent years, over 50% of ODA allocated for water is considered as contributing to adaptation.

Figure 2.14. Water ODA by Rio Marker, Marked Principle or Significant

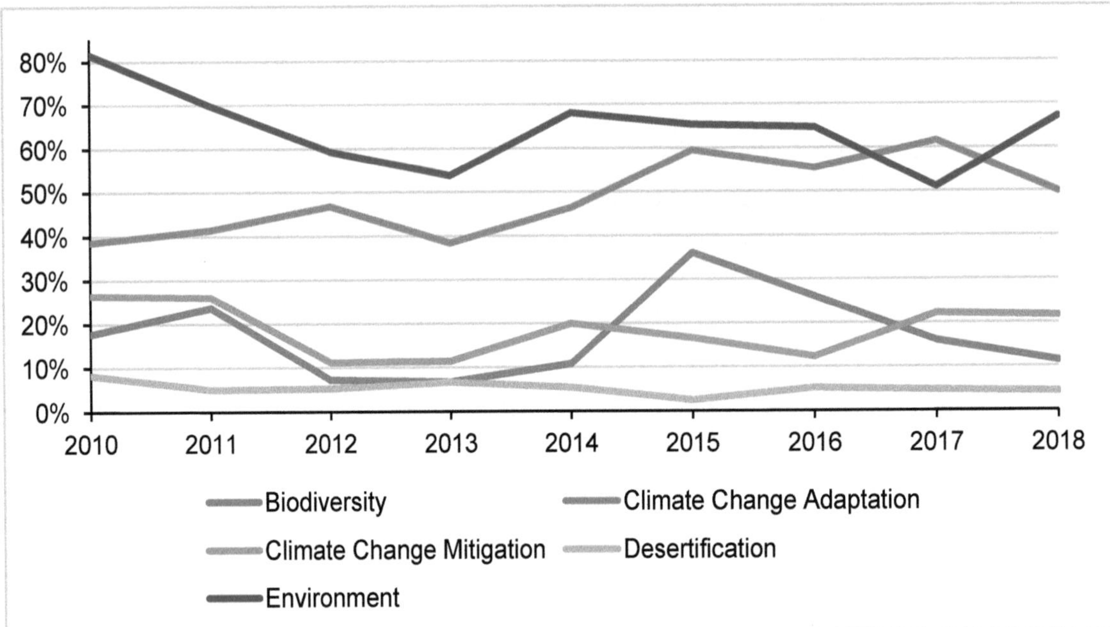

Note: Climate Change Adaptation coverage begins in 2010
Source: Authors, based on OECD Creditor Reporting System https://stats.oecd.org/Index.aspx?DataSetCode=CRS1

In terms of total ODA tagged for climate adaptation, just less than 1/4 flows to water-related subsectors amounting to USD 4 billion in 2018, a similar share flows to agriculture (Figure 2.15). In the case of ODA tagged for climate mitigation, water captures a much smaller share of the total allocated, amounting to USD 1.5 USD billion in 2018).

Figure 2.15. Screened ODA for Climate Adaptation and Mitigation, Select Sectors

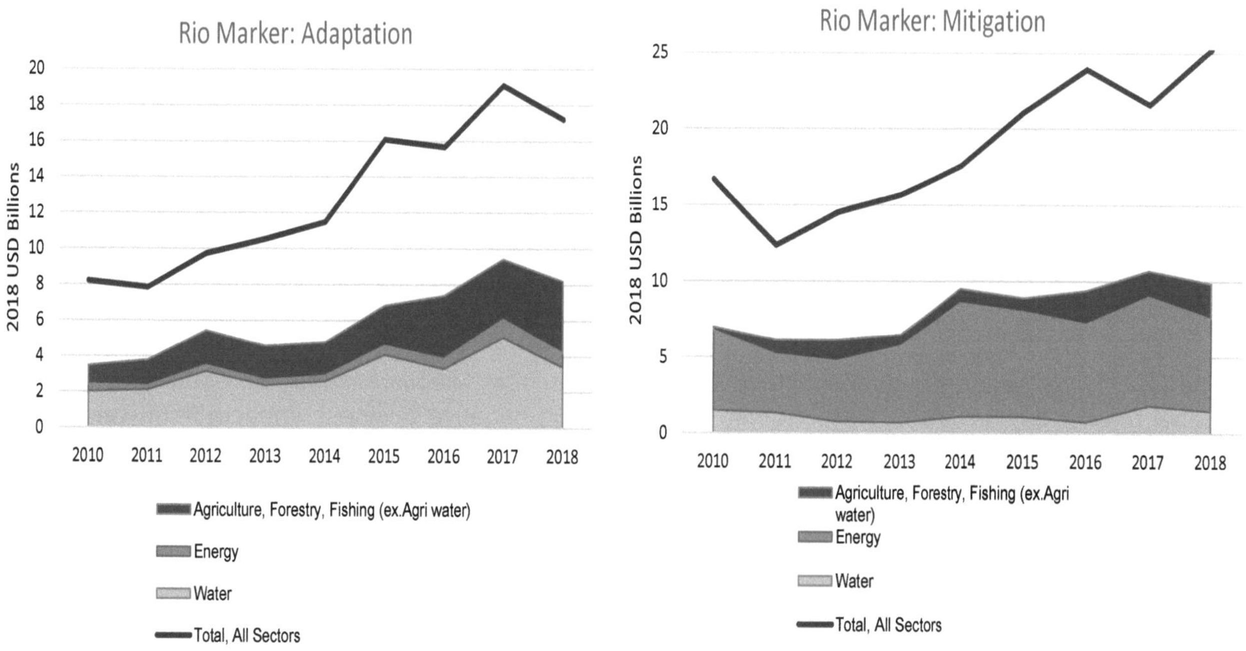

Source: Authors, based on OECD Creditor Reporting System https://stats.oecd.org/Index.aspx?DataSetCode=CRS1

Similar figures can be observed when looking at climate finance from a wider angle, including both public and private investments dedicated to climate goals. Analysis from Climate Policy Initiative (Buchner et al., 2019[90]) shows that the water sector represents only a minor share in global climate finance, compared to other sectors. In 2017-18, only about 2% (USD 13 billion) out of USD 574 billion global climate finance were dedicated to water and waste, and about 3.6% (USD 20 billion) to agriculture, forestry and natural resource management, while the renewable energy sector accounted for the biggest share of 58%. When looking at adaptation finance only, the water sector plays a more prominent role: Similarly to ODA figures, the water sector is the first recipient of climate finance dedicated to adaptation (34%, USD 10 billion), followed by the agricultural, land-use and natural resource management sector, capturing 24% of global adaptation finance flows. This highlights the important role that water-related investments play in the transition towards resilient and adaptive systems and economies.

2.6. Transcending sectors: how water risks could translate into material financial risks

The impacts of water-related risks can propagate through multiple channels, such as through impacts on human health from disease and morbidity due to poor drinking water quality and lack of access to safely managed sanitation; disruptions to industrial operations or supply chains due to water-related disasters; impacts on agricultural commodity markets due to water scarcity and droughts impacts on production. These risks can materialise at multiple scales, from the household to corporate level, to industry and sector scale to systemic risk; they potentially cut across geographical scales, from local to basin, regional and global level. They may transmit into impacts on the financial system via a variety of impact points and transmission channels (OECD, 2021[91]). Further work is required to understand and document such transmission channels, the order of magnitude of financial material impacts and how policy makers and financial institutions can address them.[16] The following section focuses on financing impacts of water-related risks for corporates. However, it is worth noting that material financial risks could impact the financial sector not just via corporates, but also via insurance, sovereign bonds, real estate funds and other channels. These issues are being explored in ongoing OECD work.

2.6.1. Financial impacts of water-related risks for corporates

Water-related risks can have significant impacts on business value, now and increasingly in the future. The financial value of water-related detrimental business impacts of over 2 900 corporates, disclosing information in the 2020 CDP survey on water security amounted to USD 16.7 billion. Companies also reported that currently identified water-related risks could potentially have impacts on business value of up to USD 336.3 billion in the future (CDP data, 2020[92]). The survey also revealed that, despite these considerable business impacts, only half of the responding companies are integrating water-related issues into their financial planning.

The CDP water security questionnaire covers corporates from various sectors, representing a quarter of global market capitalisation. Respondents report both on negative business impacts from water-related events that have occurred during the reporting period – typically the previous year - as well as potential business impacts from water-related risks that may occur in the future. The survey covers several types of water-related risks, such as physical, regulatory and technological risks as well as risks related to reputation and markets.

Looking at negative business impacts that have occurred in the last reporting period, over three quarters of the detrimental impacts reported by publically disclosing companies[17] were related to physical events, such as flooding, droughts or severe weather events (see Figure 2.16.).

Figure 2.16. Drivers of detrimental water-related business impacts reported by corporates to CDP in 2020

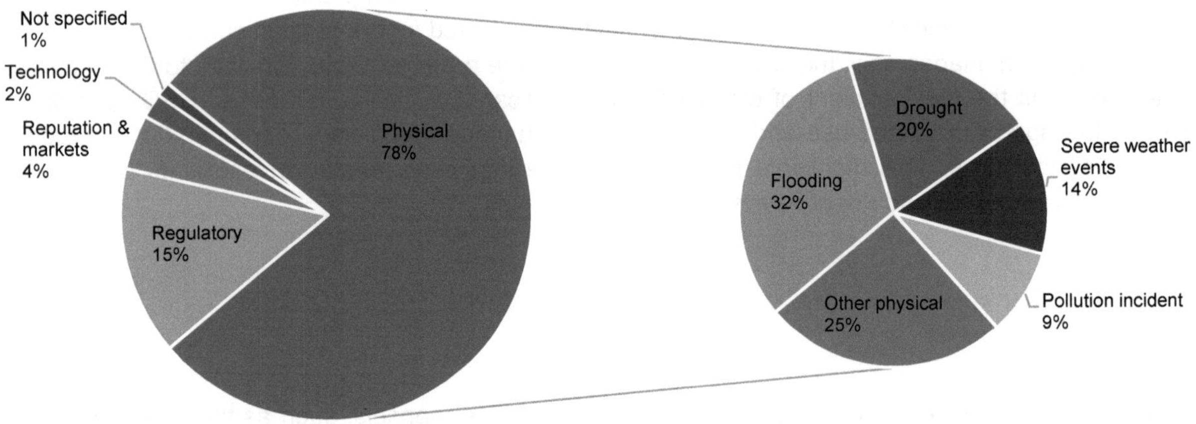

Note: Includes only publically disclosing companies. 'Other physical' events include leaching of pollutants to groundwater bodies, soil degradation, rupture of tailings dams and toxic spills and acid rock drainage and metal leaching. 'Reputation and markets' include water-related litigation, changes in consumer behaviour, community opposition and negative stakeholder feedback and increased stakeholder concern.
Source: Authors, based on (CDP data, 2020[92])

Disaggregating by sectors, USD 11.7 billion of the total USD 16.7 billion of financial value of water-related detrimental business impacts fell on the materials sector (including mining)[18], followed by the manufacturing sector with USD 1.7 billion[19] (CDP data, 2020[92]). Figure 2.17. gives an overview of the total financial value of detrimental water-related business impacts during the reporting period per sector.

Figure 2.17. Total financial value of detrimental water-related business impacts per sector

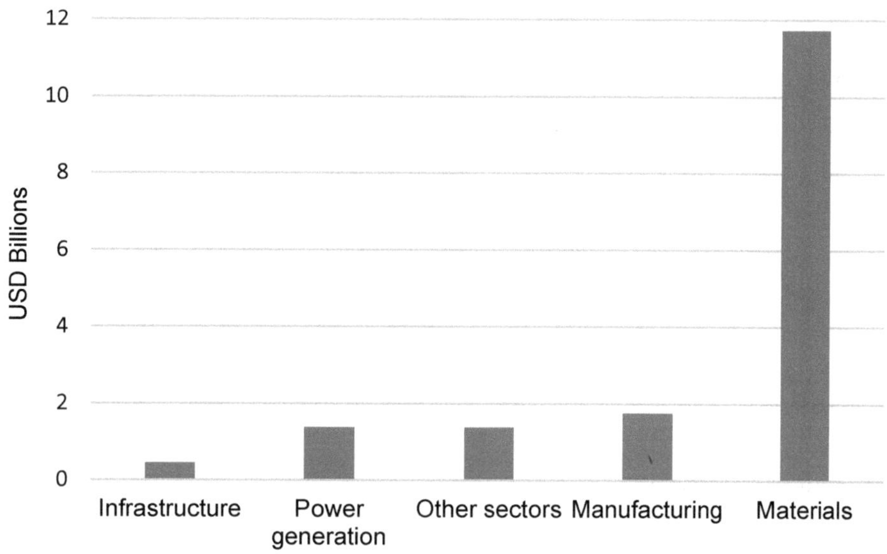

Note: Includes both publically and privately disclosing companies.
Source: Authors, based on (CDP data, 2020[92])

2.6.2. Water-related risks identified with the potential to have substantive financial or strategic business impacts

Almost half of the publically disclosing companies (44%) have identified water-related risks in their direct operations or value chains with the potential to have substantive financial or strategic business impacts now and in the future. Seventy-seven percent of the risks identified are physical risks, followed by regulatory risks (14%). Figure 2.18. gives an overview of the different types of risks and their frequency of identification. The five most frequently identified physical risks are flooding, increased water stress, drought, increased water scarcity and severe weather events. Companies report that these events could lead to reduction or disruption in production capacity, increased operating costs or supply chain disruptions. The identified regulatory risks include changes in regulations of discharge quality or volumes, higher water prices, tighter regulatory standards or mandatory water efficiency, conservation or process standards. The most frequently reported potential impacts triggered by those regulatory risks are increased operating costs for companies, reduction or disruption of production or imposed fines and penalties.

Figure 2.18. Top 8 water-related risks for corporates covered by the CDP survey

Risks identified in direct operations or within the value chain

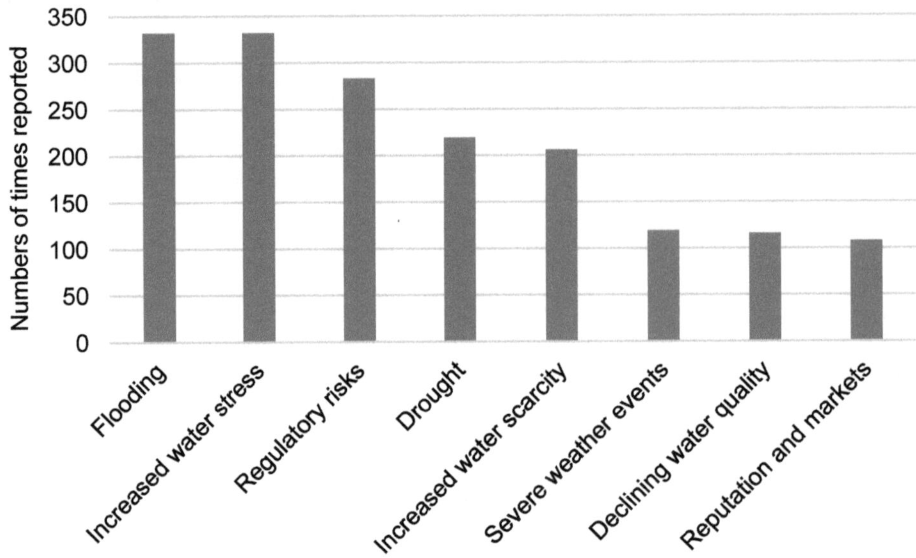

Note: Includes only publically disclosing companies
Source: Authors, based on (CDP data, 2020[92])

When looking at potential business impacts related to water, the manufacturing sector appears to be the most exposed[20], with an estimated business value at risk of up to USD 206.7 billion. Figure 2.19. gives an overview of the maximum estimated business value at risk per sector.

Figure 2.19. Maximum estimated business value at risk due to water issues per sector

USD Billions

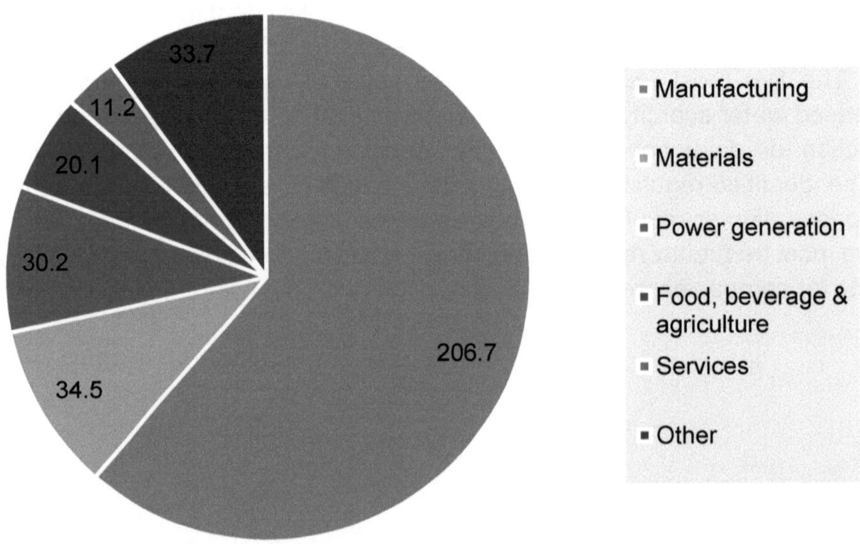

Note: Includes both publically and privately disclosing companies.
Source: Authors, based on (CDP data, 2020[92])

Further, over half of the publically responding companies from the fossil fuels, infrastructure, and power generation and materials sectors have identified water-related risks in their direct operations. Zooming into the materials sector, almost all metallic mineral mining companies have identified at least one water-related risk within their direct operations as well as over 60% of the companies from the wood and paper and metal smelting, refining and forming subsectors.

Beyond water-related risks in direct operations, roughly, one third of publically disclosing companies from the transportation service sector, hospitality and materials sectors have identified water-related risks within their value chains. Figure 2.20. visualises exposure to direct and indirect water-related risks per sector.

Figure 2.20. Exposure to water-related risks by sector

Percentage of companies per sector having identified inherent water-related risks with the potential to have substantive financial or strategic impacts on their business

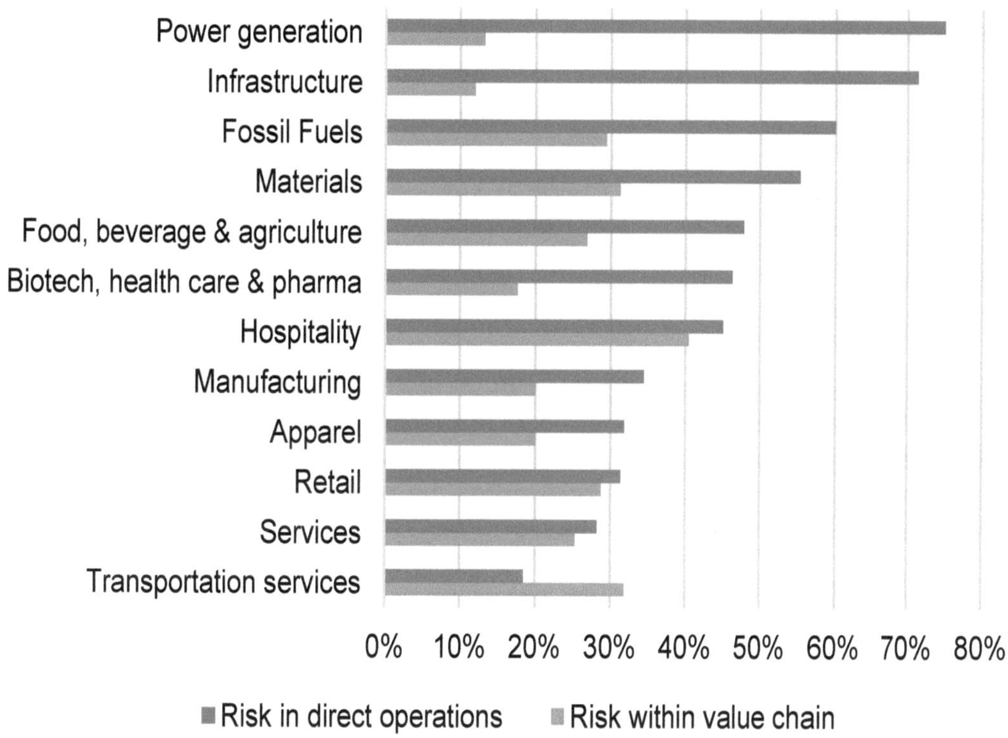

Note: Includes only publically disclosing companies.
Source: Authors, based on (CDP data, 2020[92])

China, the United States and Japan are the countries with the highest number of identified risks within companies' value chains[21]. Physical events are the major source of risk in these three countries, while in China regulatory measures also contribute notably to value chain risks (see Figure 2.21.). In the US, the largest number of risks is centred around the Mississippi River, in China around the Yangtze River, Yellow River and Pearl River.

Figure 2.21. Top 5 countries with greatest numbers of risks reported within companies' value chains

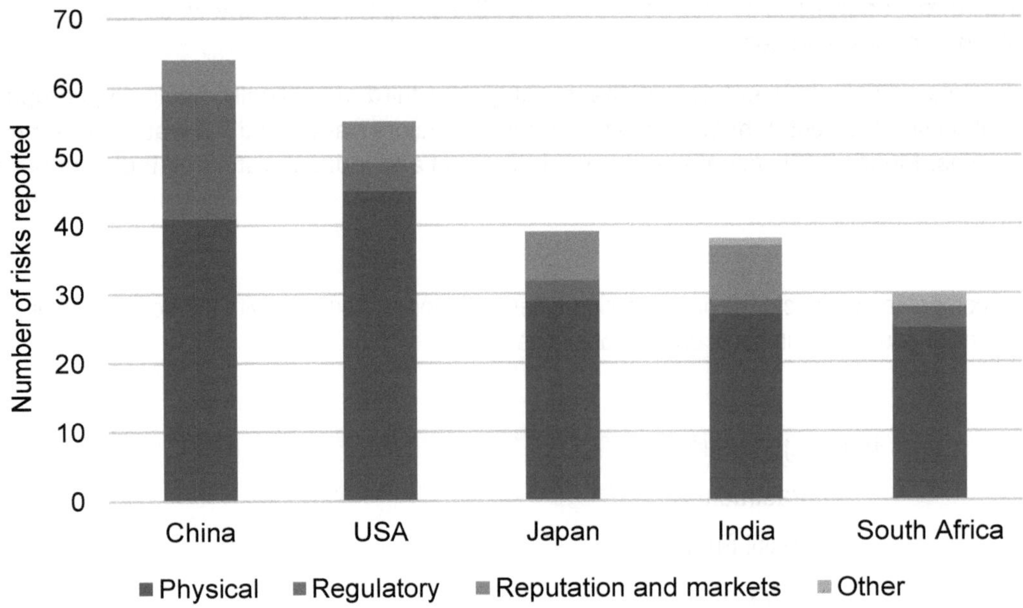

Note: Includes only publically disclosing companies. Of all publically responding companies, 10% were located in China, 18% in the USA, 17% in Japan, 3% in India and 2% in South Africa.
Source: Authors, based on (CDP data, 2020[92])

This analysis highlights how water insecurity can pose business risks and can negatively influence corporates' profits. Regular assessment and disclosure of quantifiable and consistent information on water-related risks can support businesses to better identify risks across their value chains and to integrate them into corporate decision-making. Analysis has shown that the potential financial impact of water-related risks is over five times higher than the cost of addressing these risks – mitigating water-related risks hence makes business sense (CDP, 2021[93]). Regular risk assessment and disclosure can support companies to develop forward-looking and resilient business strategies. For example, they can bolster resilience by ensuring that investment is directed towards the parts of their business exposed to the greatest risk related to water.

A company's exposure to water-related risks and how it is addressing them, therefore is vital information for investors. Without comparable and consistent data, it is difficult to impossible for investors to evaluate a company's investment performance. Corporate water-related risk disclosure can hence inform decisions on potentially material financial risks related to water and provides greater certainty for investors. Further, more disclosure and transparency could trigger action, from both corporates and investors, to support the transition to a water-secure and net-zero world.

However, today, corporate water-related risk disclosure remains limited: From about 5 500 companies asked to provide data via the CDP water security questionnaire by their investors or business customers, just above half did so (CDP, 2021[93]). In the future, regulation on water-related and nature-related risk disclosure can contribute to greater transparency about the impact on corporates of water-related risks.

References

ADB (2020), *Financing water security for sustainable growth in the Asia-Pacific region*, Asian Development Bank. [59]

AIIB (2019), *Asian Infrastructure Investment Bank Water Strategy: Water Sector Analysis, October 2019*. [63]

Alaerts, G. (2019), "Financing for Water—Water for Financing: A Global Review of Policy and Practice", *Sustainability*, Vol. 11/821, http://dx.doi.org/10.3390/su11030821. [18]

Ashley, C. and G. Gruère (2021), *Background paper for the 7th OECD/FAO Roundtable on Financing Agricultural Water, The case for action on financing agricultural water*, https://www.oecd.org/water/Background-paper-Day1-RT-on-Financing-Agricultural-Water.pdf. [83]

Asian Development Bank (2020), *Asian Water Development Outlook 2020:*, Asian Development Bank, Manila, Philippines, http://dx.doi.org/10.22617/sgp200412-2. [80]

Baker, M. (2022), "Critical disconnects between donors and domestic realities", in *Investing in Water and Growth*. [9]

Bank, E. (ed.) (2018), *Netherlands: EUR 330m EIB support under Juncker Plan for Afsluitdijk flood defence works*, https://www.eib.org/en/press/all/2018-131-eur-330m-eib-support-under-juncker-plan-for-afsluitdijk-flood-defence-works-in-the-netherlands (accessed on 7 July 2020). [52]

Bates, B. et al. (2008), *IPCC Technical Paper: Climate Change and Water*. [26]

Buchner, B. et al. (2019), *Global Landscape of Climate Finance 2019*, Climate Policy Initiative, https://www.climatepolicyinitiative.org/wp-content/uploads/2019/11/2019-Global-Landscape-of-Climate-Finance.pdf. [90]

Cardascia, S. (2019), *Session 4. Financing Water Infrastructure and Landscape Approaches in Asia and the Pacific*, OECD, https://www.oecd.org/water/Session4.Financing_Water_Infrastructure_and_Landscape_Approaches_in_Asia_and_the_Pacific%20.pdf. [22]

CDP (2021), *A wave of change The role of companies in building a water-secure world*, https://cdn.cdp.net/cdp-production/cms/reports/documents/000/005/577/original/CDP_Water_analysis_report_2020.pdf?1617987510. [93]

CDP (2020), *Cleaning up their act, CDP Global Water Report 2019*, https://cdn.cdp.net/cdp-production/cms/reports/documents/000/005/165/original/CDP_Global_Water_Report_2019.pdf?1591106445. [88]

CDP data (2020), *Analysis based on CDP water security 2020 questionnaire*. [92]

Danilenko, A. (2020), *The financial impact of the COVID-19 crisis on Sub-Saharan African drinking water utilities*, https://www.globalwaterintel.com/global-water-intelligence-magazine/21/9/opinion/the-financial-impact-of-the-covid-19-crisis-on-sub-saharan-african-drinking-water-utilities (accessed on 20 October 2020). [37]

De Nederlandsche Bank (DNB) (2019), *Values at risk? Sustainability risks and goals in the Dutch financial sector*. [5]

Dominique, K. and W. Bartz-Zuccala (2018), *Blended Finance for Water Investment*, https://www.oecd.org/water/Background-Paper-3rd-Roundtable-Financing-Water-Blended-Finance-for-water-related-investments.pdf (accessed on 27 July 2021). [2]

EIB (2019), *Abbanoa Water Investments*, https://www.eib.org/en/projects/pipelines/all/20180038 (accessed on 20 August 2020). [51]

European Commission (2020), *European Structural and Investment Fund Data*, https://cohesiondata.ec.europa.eu/overview (accessed on 20 August 2020). [53]

European Commission (2020), *Europe's moment: Repair and prepare for the next generation*, https://ec.europa.eu/commission/presscorner/detail/en/ip_20_940 (accessed on 14 February 2022). [54]

European Commission (2020), *Questions and Answers on the EU budget for recovery: Recovery and Resilience Facility*. [50]

European Commission (2020), *The European Green Deal Investment Plan and Just Transition Mechanism explained*, https://ec.europa.eu/commission/presscorner/detail/en/qanda_20_24 (accessed on 20 August 2020). [47]

European Council (2020), *Special meeting of the European Council (17, 18, 19, 20 and 21 July 2020) - Conclusion*, https://www.consilium.europa.eu/media/45109/210720-euco-final-conclusions-en.pdf (accessed on 21 October 2020). [46]

FAO (2020), *The State of Food and Agriculture, Overcoming water challenges in agriculture*, https://doi.org/10.4060/cb1447en. [69]

FAO IWMI (2019), *Towards a new generation of policies and investments in agricultural water in the Arab region, Fertile Ground for innovation*. [86]

French Government (2020), *France REIance*, https://www.economie.gouv.fr/plan-de-relance. [55]

Gasson, C. (2020), *Is inclusivity COVID's hidden message to water?*, https://www.globalwaterintel.com/news/2020/39/is-inclusivity-covid-s-hidden-message-to-water (accessed on 21 October 2020). [39]

Gietema, H. (2022), "Financial structuring: key tool for water sector investments", in *Investing in Water and Growth*. [10]

Gruère, G. and J. Brooks (2021), "Viewpoint: Characterising early agricultural and food policy responses to the outbreak of COVID-19", *Food Policy*, Vol. 100, p. 102017, http://dx.doi.org/10.1016/j.foodpol.2020.102017. [89]

Gruère, G. and H. Le Boëdec (2019), "Navigating pathways to reform water policies in agriculture", *OECD Food, Agriculture and Fisheries Papers*, No. 128, OECD Publishing, Paris, https://dx.doi.org/10.1787/906cea2b-en. [85]

Gruère, G. and M. Shigemitsu (2021), "Measuring progress in agricultural water management: Challenges and practical options", *OECD Food, Agriculture and Fisheries Papers*, No. 162, OECD Publishing, Paris, https://dx.doi.org/10.1787/52b4db7e-en. [81]

Gruère, G., M. Shigemitsu and S. Crawford (2020), "Agriculture and water policy changes: Stocktaking and alignment with OECD and G20 recommendations", *OECD Food, Agriculture and Fisheries Papers*, No. 144, OECD Publishing, Paris, https://dx.doi.org/10.1787/f35e64af-en. [74]

GWI (2021), "EBRD repositions as COVID changes rules on water loans", *Global Water Intelligence*, Vol. 22/7, https://www.globalwaterintel.com/global-water-intelligence-magazine/22/7/general/ebrd-repositions-as-covid-changes-rules-on-water-loans. [45]

GWI (2021), *LA Advanced Water Purification Facility, CA*, http://httpswww.globalwaterintel.com/global-water-intelligence-magazine/project-trackers/la-advanced-water-purification-facility-ca (accessed on 14 February 2022). [41]

GWI (2021), "Philippines looks to nationwide water reform", *Global Water Intelligence*, Vol. 22/10, https://www.globalwaterintel.com/global-water-intelligence-magazine/22/10/general/philippines-looks-to-nationwide-water-reform (accessed on 14 February 2022). [42]

GWI (2021), "Water tariffs back on the rise again as utilities seek to claw back lost revenues", *Global Water Intelligence*, Vol. 22/9, https://www.globalwaterintel.com/global-water-intelligence-magazine/22/9/general/water-tariffs-back-on-the-rise-again-as-utilities-seek-to-claw-back-lost-revenues. [44]

GWI (2020), *Rate decreases introduced as COVID-19 hits Asia Pacific*, https://www.globalwaterintel.com/global-water-intelligence-magazine/21/9/general/rate-decreases-introduced-as-covid-19-hits-asia-pacific-9-2020 (accessed on 21 October 2020). [40]

GWI (2020), "Water utilities count the cost as COVID-19 hits income from tariffs during pandemic", *Utility Finances, Global Water Intelligence*, Vol. 21/5, https://www.globalwaterintel.com/global-water-intelligence-magazine/21/5/water-leaders/water-utilities-count-the-cost-as-covid-19-hits-income-from-tariffs-during-pandemic. [36]

GWI (2019), *The Global Water Tariff Survey.* [64]

Haasnoot, M. et al. (2019), "Investments under non-stationarity: economic evaluation of adaptation pathways", *Climatic Change*, pp. 1-13, http://dx.doi.org/10.1007/s10584-019-02409-6. [34]

Haasnoot, M. et al. (2019), "Investments under non-stationarity: economic evaluation of adaptation pathways", *Climatic Change*, http://dx.doi.org/10.1007/s10584-019-02409-6. [28]

Hertel, T. and J. Liu (2016), "Implications of water scarcity for economic growth", *OECD Environment Working Papers*, No. 109, OECD Publishing, Paris, https://dx.doi.org/10.1787/5jlssl611r32-en. [76]

Huntington, T. (2006), "Evidence for intensification of the global water cycle: Review and synthesis", *Journal of Hydrology*, pp. 83-95, https://reader.elsevier.com/reader/sd/pii/S0022169405003215?token=C9769A611E50997FB8A0F36A61AA56C48767A51875EA9120F2A2E4452810471185F3663A6C67BA2597886C5A16A8F3A0&originRegion=eu-west-1&originCreation=20210629132315 (accessed on 29 June 2021). [27]

Hutton, G. and M. Varughese (2016), *The Costs of Meeting the 2030 Sustainable Development Goal Targets on Drinking Water, Sanitation, and Hygiene*, http://www.worldbank.org/water. [57]

IPCC (2021), "The Physical Science Basis Summary for Policymakers Working Group I contribution to the Sixth Assessment Report of the Intergovernmental Panel on Climate Change". [70]

Leflaive, X. and M. Hjort (2019), "Addressing the social consequences of tariffs for water and sanitation", OECD Publishing, Paris. [20]

Linkov, I. et al. (2019), *The business case for resilience in water infrastructure investments*, http://dx.doi.org/10.1080/02626667.2018.1426858. [32]

MAFF (2029), *Annual Report on Food, Agriculture and Rural Areas in Japan FY 2018*, Ministry of Agriculture, Food and Forestry (MAFF), Tokyo, https://www.maff.go.jp/e/data/publish/attach/pdf/index-177.pdf. [73]

Masson-Delmotte, V. et al. (2018), *Global warming of 1.5°C An IPCC Special Report on the impacts of global warming of 1.5°C above pre-industrial levels and related global greenhouse gas emission pathways, in the context of strengthening the global response to the threat of climate change, sustainable development, and efforts to eradicate poverty Summary for Policymakers Edited by Science Officer Science Assistant Graphics Officer Working Group I Technical Support Unit*. [25]

Matthews, J. (2019), *New financing modalities for climate adaptation: Towards Resilient Finance*. [33]

Money, A. (2017), *Projects, investors, risks and returns*, https://www.oecd.org/env/resources/Money%20(2017)%20Projects,%20investors,%20risks%20and%20returns.pdf (accessed on 27 July 2021). [1]

Money, A. (2017), *Scaling-up financing through an attractive risk-return profile*, https://www.oecd.org/environment/resources/RT-Financing-Water-background-paper-session-A-Money-Oxford.pdf (accessed on 2 June 2020). [11]

OECD (2021), *Agricultural Policy Monitoring and Evaluation 2021: Addressing the Challenges Facing Food Systems*, OECD Publishing, Paris, https://dx.doi.org/10.1787/2d810e01-en. [79]

OECD (2021), *Losses and Damages from Climate Change*. [30]

OECD (2021), *OECD Economic Outlook, Volume 2021 Issue 1: Preliminary version*, OECD Publishing, Paris, https://dx.doi.org/10.1787/edfbca02-en. [48]

OECD (2021), *OECD Economic Outlook, Volume 2021 Issue 2, No. 110*, OECD Publishing, Paris, https://doi.org/10.1787/66c5ac2c-en. [49]

OECD (2021), *Sixth meeting of the Roundtable on Financing Water regional meeting Europe: Summary and discussion highlights*, https://www.oecd.org/water/6th-Roundtable-on-Financing-Water-in-Europe-Summary-and-Highlights.pdf (accessed on 28 June 2021). [23]

OECD (2021), *Watered down? Investigating the financial materiality of water-related risks in the financial system; Background Paper Session 3 of the 8th Roundtable on Financing Water, 23-24 September*, https://www.oecd.org/water/Background-paper-RT-on-Financing-Water-and-Climate-Action-Session-3.pdf. [91]

OECD (2020), "Agricultural support estimates (Edition 2020)", *OECD Agriculture Statistics* (database), https://dx.doi.org/10.1787/466c3b98-en (accessed on 3 August 2021). [84]

OECD (2020), *Financing Water Supply, Sanitation and Flood Protection: Challenges in EU Member States and Policy Options*, OECD Publishing, https://doi.org/10.1787/6893cdac-en. [24]

OECD (2019), *A Typology of Water-related Investments, Background paper for the 4th Roundtable meeting on Financing Water, 26-27 June.*, https://www.oecd.org/water/Session1.A-typology-of-water-related-investments.pdf (accessed on 2 June 2020). [12]

OECD (2019), *Making Blended Finance Work for Water and Sanitation: Unlocking Commercial Finance for SDG 6*, OECD Studies on Water, OECD Publishing, Paris, https://dx.doi.org/10.1787/5efc8950-en. [7]

OECD (2018), "Financing Water, Investing in sustainable growth, Policy Perspectives", *OECD Environmental Policy Paper No. 11*, https://www.oecd.org/water/Policy-Paper-Financing-Water-Investing-in-Sustainable-Growth.pdf. [14]

OECD (2018), *Third meeting of the Roundtable on Financing Water, 12 November, Paris Summary and Discussion Highlights*, http://www.oecd.org/water/roundtable-financing-water-2018-summary-and-highlights.pdf (accessed on 2 June 2020). [35]

OECD (2017), *Diffuse Pollution, Degraded Waters: Emerging Policy Solutions*, OECD Studies on Water, OECD Publishing, Paris, https://dx.doi.org/10.1787/9789264269064-en. [78]

OECD (2017), *The Gap Between the Econonmic Case for Investment in Water Security and the Financial Case*. [6]

OECD (2017), *Water Risk Hotspots for Agriculture*, OECD Studies on Water, OECD Publishing, Paris, https://dx.doi.org/10.1787/9789264279551-en. [66]

OECD (2016), *OECD Council Recommendation on Water*, https://www.oecd.org/environment/resources/Council-Recommendation-on-water.pdf. [17]

OECD (2015), *Drying Wells, Rising Stakes: Towards Sustainable Agricultural Groundwater Use*, OECD Studies on Water, OECD Publishing, Paris, https://dx.doi.org/10.1787/9789264238701-en. [77]

OECD (2015), *The Economic Consequences of Climate Change*, OECD Publishing, Paris, https://dx.doi.org/10.1787/9789264235410-en. [71]

OECD (2015), *Water Resources Allocation: Sharing risks and opportunities*. [8]

OECD (2014), *Climate Change, Water and Agriculture: Towards Resilient Systems*, OECD Studies on Water, OECD Publishing, Paris, https://dx.doi.org/10.1787/9789264209138-en. [72]

OECD (2013), *Water and Climate Change Adaptation: Policies to Navigate Uncharted Waters*. [29]

OECD (2010), *Innovative Financing Mechanisms for the Water Sector*, OECD Studies on Water, OECD Publishing, Paris, https://dx.doi.org/10.1787/9789264083660-en. [16]

Pories, L., C. Fonseca and V. Delmon (2019), *Mobilising Finance for WASH: getting the foundation right*, Water.org, IRC and The World Bank, http://documents1.worldbank.org/curated/en/725521553154723194/pdf/Mobilising-Finance-for-WASH-Getting-the-Foundation-Right.pdf. [21]

Rosegrant, M. et al. (2017), *Quantitative foresight modeling to inform the CGIAR research portfolio*, http://ebrary.ifpri.org/cdm/ref/collection/p15738coll2/id/131144. [61]

Rozenberg, J. and M. Fay (2019), *Beyond the Gap: How Countries Can Afford the Infrastructure They Need while Protection the Planet.*, World Bank, Washington, D.C. [60]

Sadoff, et al. (2015), *Securing water, sustaining growth : report of the GWP/OECD task force on water security and sustainable growth.* [3]

Scotney, T. (2021), "What do the Global Water Awards tell us about COVID?", *Global Water Intelligenve*, Vol. 22/2, https://www.globalwaterintel.com/global-water-intelligence-magazine/22/3/opinion/what-do-the-global-water-awards-tell-us-about-covid (accessed on 14 February 2022). [43]

Shrivastava, A. (2016), *Climate change and Indian agriculture, International Policy Digest*, https://intpolicydigest.org/2016/08/22/climate-change-and-indian-agriculture/ (accessed on 11 January 2021). [75]

Smith, M. et al. (2019), *ADAPTATION'S THIRST: ACCELERATING THE CONVERGENCE OF WATER AND CLIMATE ACTION*, Global Commission on Adaptation, http://www.gca.org. (accessed on 29 June 2021). [31]

Streeter, W. (2017), *Financing Water and Sewer Infrastructure in the Developing World*, Taylor & Francis. [15]

Strong, C. et al. (2020), *Achieving Abundance: Understanding the Cost of a Sustainable Water Future*, https://www.wri.org/research/achieving-abundance-understanding-cost-sustainable-water-future (accessed on 7 February 2022). [56]

UN Water and WHO (2019), *National systems to support drinking-water, sanitation and hygiene: GLobal status report 2019. UN-Water global analysis and assessment of sanitation and drinking water (GLAAS) 2019 report.* [62]

UNCTAD and Convergence (2020), *Blended Finance*, http://https ://www.convergence.finance/blended-finance. [58]

UNESCO (2020), *World Water Assessment Program, Facts and Figures*, http://www.unesco.org/new/en/natural-sciences/environment/water/wwap/facts-and-figures/all-facts-wwdr3/fact-24-irrigated-land/#:~:text=Rainfed%20agriculture%20covers%2080%25%20of (accessed on 18 March 2021). [67]

UN-Water (2021), *Summary Progress Update 2021: SDG 6-water and sanitation for all*, https://www.unwater.org/publications/summary-progress-update-2021-sdg-6-water-and-sanitation-for-all/. [4]

UN-Water (2019), *GLAAS 2019: National systems to support drinking-water, sanitation and hygiene - Global status report 2019 | UN-Water*, https://www.unwater.org/publications/un-water-glaas-2019-national-systems-to-support-drinking-water-sanitation-and-hygiene-global-status-report-2019/ (accessed on 6 September 2021). [19]

Waalewijn, P. et al. (2020), *Examining the pandemic's impact on the irrigation and drainage sector and opportunities for recovery*, https://blogs.worldbank.org/water/examining-pandemics-impact-irrigation-and-drainage-sector-and-opportunities-recovery (accessed on 26 November 2020). [38]

World Bank (2020), *Water in Agriculture*, https://www.worldbank.org/en/topic/water-in-agriculture#1 (accessed on 18 March 2021). [68]

World Bank (2019), *Debt Sustainability Database*, https://www.worldbank.org/en/topic/debt-sustainability. [65]

World Bank (2017), *Easing the transition to commercial finance for sustainable water and sanitation*, http://documents.worldbank.org/curated/en/182521503466225465/pdf/119048-WP-REPLACEMENT-PUBLIC.pdf. [13]

World Bank Group (2020), *Opportunities for Investments in Agricultural Water Contributing to Resilient Recovery, Presentation for the 7th Roundtable Meeting on Financing Agricultural Water*, https://www.slideshare.net/OECD_ENV/presentation-seventh-roundtable-on-financing-agricultural-water-pieter-waalewijn. [87]

Yu, W. et al. (2021), *Can water productivity improvements save us from global water scarcity?*, White paper . FAO, Rome, http://www.fao.org/3/cb3896en/cb3896en.pdf. [82]

Notes

[1] The survey was carried out in May 2020 by the Global Water Leaders Group. It is based on responses from 44 utilities around the world.

[2] Comprised of the recovery instrument *Next Generation EU* (EUR 750 billion) and the reinforced long-term budget for 2021-2027 (EUR 1,100 billion)

[3] The selected directives are the Drinking Water Directive, the Urban Waste Water Treatment Directive and the Floods Directive.

[4] EU-13 countries are Bulgaria, Croatia, Cyprus, Czech Republic, Estonia, Hungary, Latvia, Lithuania, Malta, Poland, Romania, Slovak Republic and Slovenia. EU-15 countries are Austria, Belgium, Denmark, Finland, France, Germany, Greece, Ireland, Italy, Luxembourg, Netherlands, Portugal, Spain, Sweden as well as the United Kingdom (which was part of the EU when the analysis was undertaken)

[5] Considered as a situation when households spend more than 3-5% of their disposable income on water supply and sanitation

[6] The impact of the pandemic on the financial health of WSS utilities may constrain opportunities to mobilise commercial finance for the sector in some member countries.

[7] Note by Turkey: The information in this document with reference to "Cyprus" relates to the southern part of the Island. There is no single authority representing both Turkish and Greek Cypriot people on the Island. Turkey recognises the Turkish Republic of Northern Cyprus (TRNC). Until a lasting and equitable solution is found within the context of the United Nations, Turkey shall preserve its position concerning the "Cyprus issue". Note by all the European Union Member States of the OECD and the European Union The Republic of Cyprus is recognised by all members of the United Nations with the exception of Turkey. The information in this document relates to the area under the effective control of the Government of the Republic of Cyprus.

[8] The estimate is derived from the gap in access to services as of 2015 and the cost of connecting those without access as well as improving level of service for those with access to reach SDG 6.1 and SDG 6.2 targets. It includes capital, maintenance and operation costs.

[9] Note that irrigation expansion may not be suitable where irrigation is already taking place, calling for potentially significant and costly redirections of investment and finance.

[10] Estimates provided in this section were derived from the OECD agriculture support database, updated until 2019 (OECD, 2020[84]). The full dataset is available at https://www.oecd.org/agriculture/topics/agricultural-policy-monitoring-and-evaluation/. Reported data only include water-related agricultural government expenditures in the covered countries and the EU. Support to agricultural production and price distorting measures that impact production choices and may indirectly affect water use, are not included. Implicit water price subsidies, such as pricing for water that does not cover fully irrigation costs, are not systematically reported, and may therefore not all be included.

[11] This analysis presents time series, which includes the United Kingdom prior to its withdrawal from the European Union on 31 January 2020 at 23:00 GMT. The EU aggregate presented here therefore refers to the EU including the UK.

[12] The 13 emerging economies include Argentina, Brazil, China, India, Indonesia, Kazakhstan, the Philippines, Russia, Ukraine, South Africa, and Viet Nam.

[13] Data presented in this section were compiled from the OECD QWIDS database, available at https://stats.oecd.org/qwids

[14] OOF includes official assistance that does not fit the ODA definition. For more information, please see: http://www.oecd.org/dac/financing-sustainable-development/development-finance-standards/officialdevelopmentassistancedefinitionandcoverage.htm

[15] "Rio makers" are used to determine if an ODA flow is designated for a specific objective. The emphasis of the markers is on the objective pursued in providing support for a particular activity, as described in the activity documentation (e.g. primarily the written material which forms the basis for the agreement to provide funding).
In this exercise, of the flows screened, we have presented the percentage of flows that were determined to be "principle" or "significant" in their respective marker.

[16] OECD work on the financial materiality of water-related risks is currently ongoing. A forthcoming paper will look at the framing of risks in the global financial sector and how it takes into account water related risks.

[17] From a total of 2 934 reporting companies, 1 471 companies disclosed their responses publically.

[18] Companies from the materials sector represent 15% of all responding companies.

[19] Companies from the manufacturing sector represent 47% of all responding companies.

[20] Note that neither agriculture nor housing are covered in the survey.

[21] Note that corporates in other countries could be exposed to high risks, where disclosure rates might be low.

3 Options to address the financing challenge

This chapter presents options to address the financial challenge through a multi-pronged approach. It sets out the key components of the enabling environment for investment, consisting of policies, regulations and institutional arrangements for both the water and the financial sector. It highlights the need for making the best use of existing sources of finance and assets to minimise overall investment needs. Finally, the chapter discusses how strategic investment planning can help to optimise future investment needs, including through nature-based solutions.

Mobilising capital for investment in water security requires urgent attention and action. Ensuring that water-related expenditures deliver value for money and tangible benefits in terms of water security and sustainable growth matters as well.

The scale of investment needs is a testament to inadequacy of prevailing policies, financing strategies and mechanisms. Public finance (supplemented by official development assistance in developing countries), although an essential contribution to financial sustainability of the sector, is not available at scale to cover current and projected investment needs. Moreover, individual investments and projects must form part of a robust pathway towards a resilient water management system if the multiple benefits are to materialise.

The challenge is not merely about mobilising more capital. A multi-pronged approach is required. Four key action areas discussed in turn below can guide efforts to improve the effectiveness and efficiency of water-related investments.

3.1. Strengthen the enabling environment for investment

3.1.1. Why a strong enabling environment is needed to facilitate investment

It is widely recognised that the water sector needs robust public policy and institutional frameworks to function effectively, given the common pool nature of water resources and the public good dimensions of selected water policies and services (OECD, 2019[1]). Such frameworks also have a profound influence on the water sector's attractiveness to investors and its ability to recover costs and secure sustainable financing. As noted above and further examined in Chapter 4, the huge investment needs of the water sector over the coming decades demand increased volumes of sustainable finance drawn from a more diverse range of public and private sources (Money, 2017[2]; Pories, Fonseca and Delmon, 2019[3]; OECD, 2019[4]). To meet the financing challenge, governments should consider how existing policies and institutions might be enabling or impeding water-related investments.

A strong enabling environment for water-related investment can be broadly characterised as a set of policies, regulations and institutional arrangements that facilitate investment in activities that contribute to water security. This includes sector-specific policies, regulations and institutional arrangements as well as those relating to the regulation of the financial sector and capital markets. Well-designed policies and institutions are important for not only attracting investors, but also for ensuring that individual investments deliver their intended benefits and contribute to the sustainable financing and management of water resources and the delivery of water and sanitation services. Such conditions can therefore also play a pivotal role in minimising countries' water-related investment needs over the long term, by contributing to policy coherence and ensuring the sector adapts to changing conditions, including climate change. A robust enabling environment is critical for allowing governments and investors to situate individual investments within their broader policy context, and to develop new projects and markets not as isolated, standalone investments conducted for their own sake, but instead as part of a holistic approach to achieving water policy aims (OECD, 2020[5]). Further, clearly defined policy orientations for water-related investment help governments to articulate both the benefits and the risks of different investment proposals (World Bank, 2017[6]).

By assessing the policy and institutional arrangements that create the settings for water-related investments, governments and investors can adopt a systemic perspective on the financing challenge and identify how such frameworks may be supporting or undermining efforts to scale up and diversify finance for the water sector. This applies to both public and private finance sources, but is especially critical in the context of efforts to secure commercial finance; the enabling environment can be a key determinant in the creditworthiness of potential borrowers and the "bankability" of proposed water projects (Pories, Fonseca and Delmon, 2019[3]; Streeter, 2017[7]).

This section examines various components of the enabling environment for investment to identify some of the main levers of influence available to governments seeking to increase water-related investment. These include the evaluation of policy settings (legal and regulatory, economic and financial, and information-based policy instruments) as well as the coherence of policies across different sectors and domains (e.g. water, agriculture, land use, urban planning, energy, and finance). An assessment of the structure and operation of the institutions that design, implement and evaluate policies and activities in the water sector is equally vital for ensuring accountable and efficiently functioning investment environment. Finally, adequate resources and capacities are needed for policies to be delivered and institutions to function as intended.

3.1.2. Policies and institutional settings define the conditions for water-related investment

A country's public policy and institutional settings create a set of multi-layered conditions for water-related investments that can be complex for governments, service providers and investors alike to grasp and navigate. As outlined in Chapter 2, water-related investments have characteristics that challenge conventional approaches to public and private financing, including long payback periods and often complex risk-return profiles and project attributes. This reflects the fact that water policies and institutions are focused on ensuring access to water as a dynamic resource managed across jurisdictional boundaries and is essential for life. This demands sustainable management over decades-long time frames, and has strong interdependencies with other policy domains (e.g. agriculture, energy, urban planning) (OECD, 2016[8]). The inherent complexity of many water-related policy interventions has contributed to investors' perception of water-related investments as more risky and generally less attractive than those in other sectors (Streeter, 2017[7]).

Strengthening the enabling environment for investment requires governments to recognise this diversity of potential projects and investors as well as the spectrum of diverse types of water-related investments and consider how adjustments to policies and institutions could help to facilitate the types of investments and investors that are most needed in their water sector.

3.1.3. Key components for improving the enabling environment

Table 3.1 summarises key elements of the enabling environment for investment, including policy frameworks and institutional arrangements related to water. In addition to the elements included in the table, financial policies, regulations and markets need to be conducive to providing long term, low cost capital to fund infrastructure investments (see discussion in the section on blended finance). These elements are discussed in more detail in the section below.

Table 3.1. Key elements of the enabling environment for investment

Component	Examples of instruments, mechanisms or interventions	Selected examples relevant to the water sector that can influence the investment environment
Policy settings	Legal and regulatory policy instruments	Legal status for water resources Legal recognition of the human right to water Clear legal status for WSS service providers Laws and regulations for managing water resources allocation (e.g. abstraction limits, enforcement mechanisms, entitlements to use water) Laws and regulations related to water quality standards (for drinking water, wastewater treatment, pollution loads in water bodies, etc.)> Laws governing infrastructure and services for e.g. drinking water supply, wastewater collection and treatment
	Economic policy instruments	Tariffs for WSS services Targeted subsidies to address household affordability constraints in accessing WSS services Charges or taxes for water abstraction or pollution (Polluter Pays principle) Markets to trade for abstraction entitlements and pollution rights Payments for ecosystem services Insurance for water related risks (drought, flood protection)
	Information-based policy instruments	Information systems (e.g. data collection, monitoring and early warning systems on water quality/quantity, service quality and efficiency, asset status, etc.)[1] Public registers and information schemes (e.g. disclosure requirements on WSS service operations or service provider finances) Education and training programmes for WSS service providers Communication strategies and campaigns (e.g. for households, farmers)
	Mechanisms to facilitate policy coherence across domains/sectors	Systems for tracking and monitoring shared policy objectives in a given sector (e.g. checklists, tracking finance for activities with multiple objectives) Policy mainstreaming processes (e.g. climate policy mainstreaming across sectors) Designating coherence objectives as part of central government processes (e.g. budgeting) Intra- and inter-governmental water policy co-ordination mechanisms
Institutional arrangements and provisions	Independent oversight	Regulation of the WSS sector (e.g. WSS tariff-setting) by an independent economic authority
	Devolution or decentralisation reforms for service delivery	Devolution of authority for WSS service delivery to municipal/local level Reconfiguration of service provision boundaries to consolidate service delivery at a defined scale
	Mechanisms for accountability to e.g. citizens, service users	Public consultation and participation requirements for water tariff reforms WSS service user feedback and complaint mechanisms
	Mechanisms to improve services	Performance incentive structures and monitoring for WSS service providers (economic regulation of service provision)
Supporting resources and capacities	Finance for policy implementation	Resourcing for effective auditing and enforcement of water regulation (infringement proceedings, etc.)
	Capacity building measures	Technical assistance, education and training to improve the technical, human resource and financial capabilities of WSS service providers

Note: The examples in this table illustrate some relevant settings and conditions, but cannot provide a comprehensive or fully accurate depiction of the enabling environment across all countries. Governments combine various instruments and interventions to support and reinforce each other to meet policy objectives.
Source: Authors

Strengthening policy settings

Legal and regulatory instruments

Legal and regulatory policy instruments set the fundamental rules and parameters for a well-functioning water sector. Governments use them not only to establish their long-term water policy goals and plans, but also to ensure the accountability and cost-effectiveness of the activities and investments undertaken to achieve those goals. Relevant laws and regulations range from instruments that define water quality standards, allocation regimes, flood protection standards, to legal frameworks governing the design and implementation of and the delivery of WSS services.

A well-designed regulatory framework is particularly critical in the water sector because of water's fundamental role in ensuring the well-being of people and ecosystems and the function of many economic sectors (OECD, 2009[9]). Given the monopolistic nature of the market for WSS services, a strong regulatory regime is important to ensure the cost-effectiveness and efficiency of policy measures, and to provide assurance to financiers which seek both predictability and transparency in the regulation and design of services (World Bank, 2017[6]). A regulatory regime is only strong if and when compliance is monitored and enforced.

The regulation of water pricing and charges such as WSS service tariffs offers an insight into the interplay between water laws, public and political expectations for water policy and services, and the sustainability of water sector financing. Considering that WSS are essential services, the public often has the expectations for keeping WSS tariffs low, with accompanying political pressure to regulate to keep tariffs low, sometimes also due to concerns about service affordability[2]. This can directly inhibit adequate cost recovery, which WSS service providers need to work towards to enable the delivery of reliable, sustainable services

Laws and regulations focused in other policy domains – such as those governing competition policy and financial markets – also influence the conditions for water-related investment. In low- and middle-income countries in particular, underdeveloped financial sectors and markets are a widely recognised challenge for increasing water-related investment, particularly from commercial investors (Pories, Fonseca and Delmon, 2019[3]). For example, some countries have legal restrictions in place that limit the scope for both potential borrowers and lenders to engage in new water-related investments and do not facilitate the water sector's participation in markets. Further, some countries require banks to lend certain percentages of their portfolios to local infrastructure projects in defined areas, which may not encompass water sector priorities (World Bank, 2017[6]). Similarly, there may be rules in place that confine service providers to borrowing from government sources or prohibit them from issuing corporate bonds, or banks may only be permitted to invest a limited percentage of their capital in securities sold by service providers (World Bank, 2017[6]). In the case of improving catchment management via payments for ecosystem services, financial transfers to farmers can be restrained by regulations designed to promote fair competition and trade (e.g. WTO or EU law).

Economic and financial instruments

Governments use a variety of economic and financial policy instruments to influence the behaviour of individuals, communities and organisations to help achieve water policy goals. Such measures generally aim to account for the costs or benefits that different actors incur from using services or from polluting or abstracting water resources[3]. Examples include instruments such as WSS tariffs, taxes, charges and fiscal transfers (e.g. subsidies), along with mechanisms such as markets for trading water entitlements or pollution permits, and conditional and voluntary incentive schemes such as payments for ecosystem services.

Economic and financial measures not only provide important price signals of the value of water and provide incentives for water-wise decisions, but are also a vital means for providing revenue streams. In the case of WSS, service providers' ability to generate revenue is derived from tariff levels and structures, bill collection and the associated incentives they create; typically, the WSS service providers should aim to achieve sustainable cost recovery, efficiency in the provision and use of water, and service affordability (World Bank, 2017[6]). In both emerging and developed markets, low WSS tariffs are the main constraint to sustainable cost recovery and reliable revenue streams for WSS service providers (World Bank, 2017[6]; Pories, Fonseca and Delmon, 2019[3]). Tariffs are often fixed at a level that is well below what is needed to recover the costs of operations and maintenance (O&M) ((Leigland, Trémolet and Ikeda, 2016[10]) in (Pories, Fonseca and Delmon, 2019[3])). Figure 3.1 illustrates that average annual water bills (for a representative household) remain relatively low, even in many higher income countries.

Figure 3.1. Average Gross National Income vs. Average Annual Water Bill

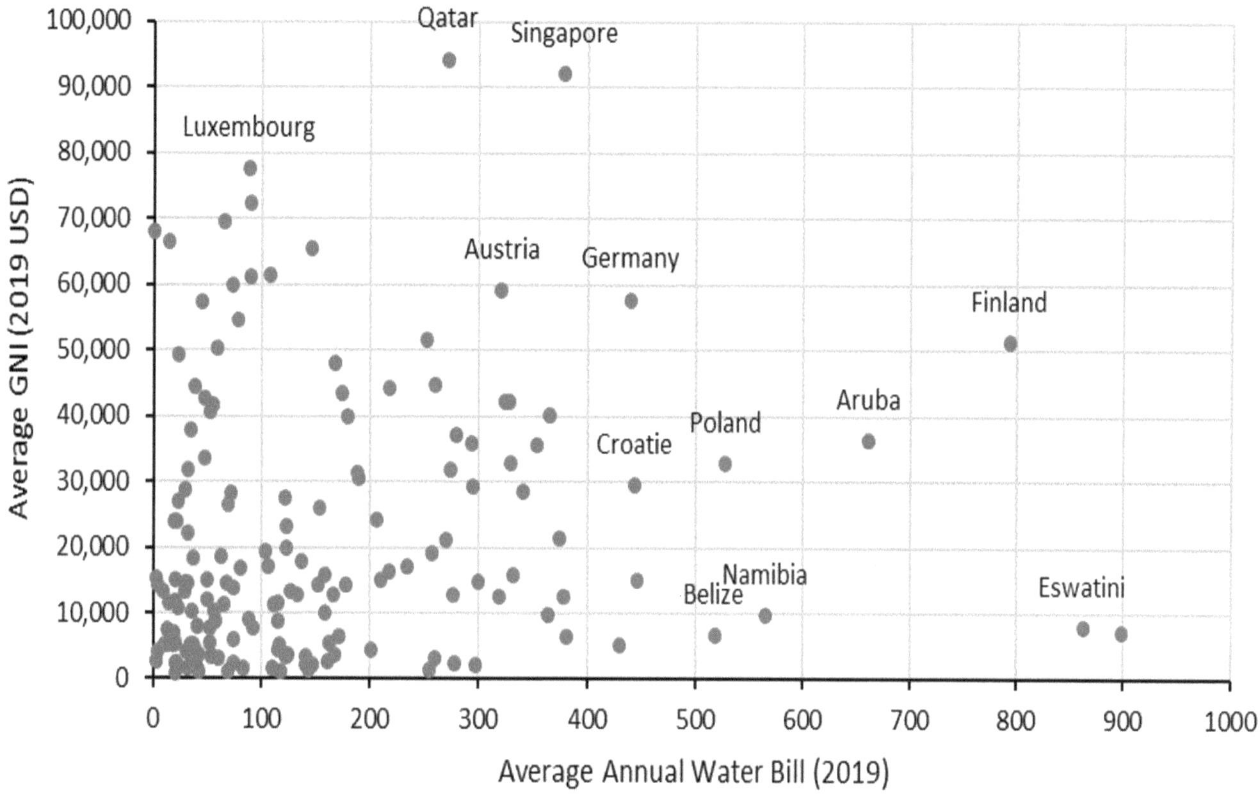

Source: Authors, based on World Bank for GNI data and GWI for average annual water bill

To attract investors' interest, tariffs need to be set in a predictable and transparent way with the aim of covering O&M costs, the cost of debt service and a progressive share of capital expenditure (CAPEX) where feasible. A lack of sustainable cost recovery can leave commercial lenders hesitant to provide loans as they need an assured sufficient and constant operating surplus that can service the debt over the maturity period (Pories, Fonseca and Delmon, 2019[3]).

While water tariffs provide a stable revenue stream for water supply and sanitation investments, it is more challenging to quantify and monetise the benefits of other water-related investments, such as for flood protection or water resource management. Dedicated economic instruments are needed to help internalise externalities and to create revenue streams to capture the benefits of such investments. Further, combining water-related investments with objectives from other domains, such as agriculture, energy, tourism and urban planning can help to exploit synergies, creating opportunities to capture additional revenues and can unlock investment by applying an integrated approach across the value chain of water-related investment (OECD, 2019[1]; OECD-WCC, 2017[11]; OECD, 2018[12]). Examples include pollution taxes, which can provide funding for investments in water quality or wastewater treatment. Taxes on urban development in floodplains or impervious surfaces generate revenues for flood protection measures. Abstraction charges can fund water resource management interventions and can help cover some of the costs related to droughts or water scarcity. Reduced storm water fees for non-residential customers can encourage direct investment by private property owners and thus reduce the burden on public budgets. (OECD, 2020[13]; OECD-WCC, 2017[11]).[4] However, highlighting opportunities for synergies should not overlook the reality that there will inevitably be trade-offs among policy objectives that must be addressed. Table 3.2. summarises selected examples which generate funding for various water security interventions. Box 3.1 discusses cost recovery for water in the agriculture sector.

Table 3.2. Selected policy instruments to generate revenue for water-related investments

Policy instrument	Type of costs to recover
Pollution taxes	Wastewater treatment costs, investments in water quality improvements
Taxes on urban development in floodplains or impervious surfaces	Flood protection costs
Abstraction charges	Water resource management and allocation, costs related to drought or water scarcity
Reduced storm water fees for non-residential customers	Encourages direct investment by private property owners, reduces burden on public budgets
Charges or fees on resources recovered from wastewater treatment	Revenue generated from energy or nutrient recovery from wastewater treatment

Source: Authors, based on OECD (2020) *Financing Water Supply, Sanitation and Flood Protection, Challenges in EU Member States and Policy Options* and OECD-WCC (2017) *Session 3. Converting economic benefits of water security investments into financial returns.* Background paper for OECD-WWC-Netherlands Roundtable on Financing Water, 12-13 April 2017, Paris.

Box 3.1. Cost recovery for water in the agriculture sector

Like the WSS sector, the agriculture sector also faces challenges in recovering the costs of O&M and capital. Irrigating farmers generally do not cover the costs of the water they access. Only nine of 39 respondents to a recent survey of countries that adhere to the OECD Council Recommendation on Water indicated that they have full cost recovery in place for both capital and O&M costs for irrigation. In Germany, for example, operators bear the full costs of capital and O&M, and the federal states set different abstraction fees, some of which internalise a portion of the environment and resource costs. Under the EU Water Framework Directive, countries are required to ensure that the water prices charged reflect the full costs (e.g. operation and maintenance costs, capital costs, environmental and resource costs), although full recovery is not required and derogations are possible for less-favoured areas or on grounds of social welfare.

Most country adherents to the OECD Council Recommendation on Water only partially recover the costs of capital and/or O&M. A limited number of countries responding to the survey (Austria, Denmark, Finland, New Zealand, Sweden and the United Kingdom) indicated that they are covering a progressive proportion of the capital costs of infrastructure in addition to O&M costs.

Cost recovery is even less common for groundwater, though the situation differs from surface water as costs are often borne by users of individual wells.

Source (OECD, 2021[14]) (Gruère, Shigemitsu and Crawford, 2020[15])

Information-based instruments

Information-based policy instruments can help to achieve water policy goals and create strong conditions for investment in two vital ways: as standalone information systems and products (e.g. monitoring databases, communication campaigns) and as an input and support to other policy measures and investments (e.g. to inform water resource allocation reforms, or WSS tariff restructuring). Information systems (including accounting and measurement frameworks) are a key example of information-based instruments (such as for data collection, monitoring, and early warning systems on water resource quality/quantity; water-related risks; water infrastructure assets; WSS service efficiency, quality and quantity). Other examples include public registers and information schemes (e.g. disclosure requirements for WSS service operations or provider finances), education and training programmes (e.g. for WSS service providers or new investors), and communication strategies and campaigns (e.g. targeted at key audiences to facilitate or accompany other policy measures). Each of these play a role not only in ensuring access to salient information for decision makers, but also in creating a transparent and accountable water sector in which the public (including investors) can have confidence.

A prominent challenge is the lack of detailed knowledge in most countries of the current state of water infrastructure and assets across multiple water sub-sectors. For example, in the European Union, member states lack a detailed knowledge of the rate of asset renewal in the WSS sector (OECD, 2020[13]). Where the rate of renewal is known, it is usually below a level that would be consistent with assets' life expectancy, which suggests an urgent need for increased renewal efforts to avoid the rapid decay of built infrastructure and declining service quality. The deterioration of assets also results in water leakage and reduced water quality, creating greater challenges for WSS service providers while affecting the health of humans and ecosystems and increasing downstream treatment costs (OECD, 2020[13]).

Countries face similar data challenges for flood protection: only a few countries monitor financial flows for this purpose, making it difficult to project further investment needs (OECD, 2020[13]). Limited knowledge and data on both the state of infrastructure and existing financial flows make it difficult to identify or monitor problems and properly plan improvements, and are thus a major barrier to investment. In some countries, ageing networks are expected to be the single biggest driver for investment in water supply and sanitation (OECD, 2020[13]).

Box 3.2. Information-based instruments for accurate knowledge of WSS assets

In recognition of the vital need for better access to robust water data (observations, processed data and model output), the international High Level Panel on Water (2016-18) endorsed the World Water Data Initiative. In its first phase the initiative resulted in the production of good practice guidelines for water data policy by the Australian Government and the World Meteorological Organization (WMO). The High Level Panel on Water recommended that the subsequent second phase, directed by the WMO, should *inter alia* support the dissemination of guidance for improving water data policy and secure funding for new innovations in water data (United Nations, 2018[16]).

A key area of innovation in information-based instruments for water management is in the use of artificial intelligence (AI), including for more accurate knowledge of WSS assets. A recent report estimates that AI-enabled innovation for the water sector will contribute USD 200 billion in value to the global economy by 2030 (Mehmood et al., 2020[17]). AI is already being used in countries such as Singapore, Kenya and the United States to support the predictive maintenance of water supply and wastewater assets and to track non-revenue water. These developments are occurring as part of a shift away from traditional scheduled inspection and maintenance approaches towards the use of intelligent sensor-physical systems that monitor the condition of assets (e.g. identifying leaks, blockages and damage) to inform the scheduling and prioritisation of maintenance. Machine learning algorithms are also being used to calculate the likelihood of failure of water infrastructure. Countries are also using AI to forecast water demand and consumption, monitor water reservoirs and dams, track water quality, and monitor and predict water-related disasters.

On the regulatory side, France has embarked on a programme that aims to contribute to better knowledge of the state of the assets for water services, thus supporting more accurate planning and decisions for operation, maintenance and renewal. A regulation issued in 2020 requires local authorities to inventory public networks for water supply and sanitation. An index was set to assess compliance with this requirement. When an authority scores below 40 (out of a maximum score of 120), the abstraction charge aid to the water agency is multiplied by two. There is no such incentive for sanitation. In 2014, two thirds of water services in France failed to comply with this regulation (*figure provided by Canalisateurs de France, based on SISPEA data*).

Sources: (OECD, 2020, p. 66[13]; Mehmood et al., 2020[17]; United Nations, 2018[16]; WMO, 2018[18])

Mechanisms to support policy coherence

As noted above, water's essential role across many sectors means that governments should aim to continually assess and improve the coherence of water policies with those of related domains to ensure that priorities, measures and investments support, rather than undermine, one another. Some prominent examples of policy domains that intersect directly with water include agriculture, climate, energy, health, industry, urban planning and land use policy (OECD, 2016[8]). Common mechanisms for policy coherence include processes by which governments systematically assess how a given sector integrates other sectors' objectives in its policies and measures (e.g. checklists for new policy proposals, finance tracking and monitoring, such as for water-related finance as a share of dedicated climate finance). Processes that centralise certain policy priorities in decision-making are another example (e.g. mainstreaming, central government budgeting). Effective cooperation both within and between governments and non-state actors

– i.e. at horizontal and vertical scales – can enhance coherence among different institutions. Address potentially competing policy aims will require identifying and addressing trade-offs.

Improved policy coherence can help to ensure that water-related investment decisions are taken with a systems perspective and are not isolated from broader government decision making and priority setting. In the absence of such coherence efforts, water projects and investments can be left exposed to significant risk as a result of unforeseen or inadequately considered influences from other policy domains.

Strengthening institutional arrangements

Alongside the policy settings outlined above, the institutional arrangements that govern and facilitate the operation of a country's water sector can have a considerable influence on the enabling conditions for water-related investment. It is important that the institutions that are part of the water policy landscape are designed and fully adapted according to each country's specific context, governance systems and structures, and policy priorities, as underscored in the OECD Water Governance Principles (OECD, 2016[19]). Overall, investors are attracted to working with institutions that have established autonomy and leadership at the right levels to deliver on their mandates, offer confidence in their financial management capabilities, and are well equipped to help ensure transparency, accountability and predictability (World Bank, 2017[6]; Streeter, 2017[7]).

The devolution of authority for water sector functions – particularly decentralisation processes for local-level WSS service provision or water resources management at basin level – are a key example of institutional water sector reforms that aim to improve economies of scale and the conditions for investment. The devolution of WSS service delivery needs to be to the right level to ensure sufficient scale of operations, reduce operating costs, and support economic viability (Streeter, 2017[7]). In many countries, decentralisation processes are fragmented or incomplete. In emerging market countries in particular, municipal and local-level institutions often have weaker capacities and need significant support to improve their administration, planning and operations if they are to be deemed creditworthy (Streeter, 2017[7]). While decentralising service delivery can increase accountability by devolving responsibility to a level that is closer to the service user, it can also allow for greater variation in the design and enforcement of policies, make central oversight more onerous and complex, and introduce financial sustainability issues (World Bank, 2017[6]).

To address issues such as these in decentralisation processes, there are a number of options and imperatives. WSS service providers require clear mandates to support their financial self-sufficiency and autonomy. This requires sufficient capacity and independence to develop accurate projections on costs to inform tariff setting as well as long-term planning for infrastructure O&M and service delivery, with adequate consultation with connected authorities and the public (service users/customers), and without undue influence from political cycles and interests (Streeter, 2017[7]). Processes and mechanisms that support accountability and transparency in WSS service provision include requirements for systematic public consultation in decision making, as well as standardised, publicly available financial information and disclosure requirements for contractual processes (Streeter, 2017[7]).

Many countries opt to establish designated institutions with a mandate to independently oversee water sector operations, facilitating economic regulation and creating incentive structures to improve the performance of service providers. The independent regulation of public WSS service providers has been an increasingly common government response to deteriorating quality of WSS service delivery and, when well-designed, can help to reduce political interference in implementing key economic instruments such as tariffs (Mumssen, Saltiel and Kingdom, 2018[20]). Independent economic regulation can take various forms according to countries' governance structures and priorities, and is examined in more detail below. While independent local- or national-level regulators can be instrumental in reducing political influence and financial mismanagement in service provision, they are not a silver bullet, and local circumstances should inform the appropriate solution that supports adequate oversight of service provision by a properly resourced and autonomous regulator (Pories, Fonseca and Delmon, 2019[3]).

Ensuring adequate resources and capacities to support policies and institutions

As noted in the above, two vital underlying components of a strong enabling environment for water-related investment are sufficient resourcing and capacities to enable policies to be implemented and institutions to function as intended. This reflects the principle that policy and institutional plans for the water sector should be backed by sustainable financing and resourcing strategies adapted to the specific context (OECD, 2020[13]). Naturally, adequate resourcing entails ensuring appropriate levels and structures of funding and financing are available to support policy implementation and institutional operations – for example, sufficient resources to carry out audits and enforce water regulations (and e.g. to undertake infringement proceedings when regulations are breached). These fundamental resources should be accompanied by efforts to ensure that institutions have appropriate levels and types of capacity and expertise. Stronger capacity is typically pursued through measures such as technical assistance, education and training aimed at improving the technical, human resource and financial capabilities of WSS service providers.

Water sector institutions need adequate capacities in order to attract investors, maximise existing finance, and increase their potential to attract, manage and sustain new and innovative investments into the future (Streeter, 2017[7]). In some cases, a commitment from institutions to undertake capacity improvement reforms may be a condition for receiving finance, as it will help to maximise the sustainability of that investment over the long term (Streeter, 2017[7]).

To improve the enabling conditions for investment, capacity building measures can target different types of institutions. For example, WSS service providers might receive technical assistance to reduce non-revenue water or improve billing and collection, and through this, improve their creditworthiness (OECD, 2019[11]). To increase local banks' capacity to evaluate the profitability of water-related investments, financial providers might be provided with technical assistance and training to assess the financial viability of investments in the sector. Capacity building measures that are well designed and embedded in institutions over time can help to ensure that staff have the right skill sets and are motivated to achieve sector strategies and policies and participate in organisational change processes (World Bank, 2017[6]). This better positions them to meet minimum performance standards and supports staff to recognise incentives for improved performance (e.g. in service delivery, in financial management).

Capacity considerations such as these are vital for governments seeking to improve the conditions for investment and support investor confidence in local-level institutions. Ideally, local governments' and WSS service providers' capacities should be addressed as a pre-condition for introducing local borrowing (Streeter, 2017[7]). Investors seek evidence that providers have a strong ability to manage taxes and tariffs, collect revenues, prepare and manage transparent budgets, devise capital plans, co-ordinate contracts and tender processes, and conduct accountable consultation processes with the public and investment partners (Streeter, 2017[7]). Such capacities at the provider level are also important to enable national and sub-national governments and independent regulators to access the information they need to carry out their own responsibilities in determining and reforming water policy.

3.2. Make the best use of existing sources of finance and assets

Structural and operational inefficiencies limit the optimisation of available funding and existing assets in the water sector. The water sector has traditionally relied heavily on public finance (and concessional loans in developing countries), which in many cases has contributed to the inefficient allocation and use of existing funding. This section explores five options that governments can consider to focus their efforts to make better use of existing sources of finance and assets, and lay the groundwork for increasing access to more diverse sources of finance across the water sector. A focus on both the supply and demand side of finance provides two distinct entry points to address the financing challenge. Options to consider include:

- improving timely asset management to reduce operational inefficiencies
- sound capital expenditure planning
- targeted allocation of public subsidies
- seizing opportunities to improve economies of scale, and
- creating and maintaining incentives for performance.

Action in these areas can generate efficiency gains and financial savings that can be used to provide better services and contribute to broader policy objectives (such as more secure, less polluted water resources and healthier ecosystems). WSS service providers and related institutions with transparent and efficient operations benefit not only from an increased and more reliable revenue base, but also from increased credibility that reinforces customers' willingness to pay for quality services and encourages investor confidence. This helps to ensure a sustainable stream of finance to meet the full scope of a country's service needs, address emerging challenges for the sector, and free up scarce public funds to be deployed to other policy priorities (World Bank and UNICEF, 2017[21]).

3.2.1. Improving timely asset management to reduce operational inefficiencies

Timely management of water assets – such as reservoirs, pipes and wastewater treatment facilities – supports efficient operations and maintenance (O&M) that in turn strengthens the sustainability of water services and supports water security (OECD, 2016[22]). When timely asset management is prioritised, asset owners and managers are able to identify and address O&M needs in the present – rather than deferring them to be borne by future water managers or service users – and ensure that deteriorating assets do not increase overall water-related investment needs. Timely asset management adequately accounts for assets' economic life spans as well as the emerging challenges that the water sector will face over the coming decades. This involves a focus on sustaining assets throughout their full life cycles – from their design and construction to O&M and continuous monitoring and evaluation to facilitate necessary improvements in response to future risks (Kingdom et al., 2018[23]; World Bank, 2017[6]). As such, timely asset management can facilitate the supply of finance by ensuring cash flow reliability.

Conversely, insufficient investment in asset management reduces existing assets' value and increases the risk that assets will need to be prematurely replaced. It can also mean that maintenance efforts are preoccupied with fixing asset breakdowns, rather than upgrades that have been strategically prioritised (ADB, 2013[24]). While this section focuses on the need for timely asset management, this issue is closely interlinked with the need for robust capital expenditure planning, which is examined in the next section.

As outlined above in Section 1 on the enabling environment for investment, a number of conditions are needed to support strong O&M – notably sustainable cost recovery based on an appropriate mix of revenue from the "3Ts" (tariffs, taxes and transfers) (OECD, 2009[25]). For WSS, low tariff levels are typically the primary factor preventing the recovery of O&M costs and thereby inhibiting adequate maintenance, reducing assets' performance and shortening overall asset life (World Bank and UNICEF, 2017[21]). Where revenues from tariffs are insufficient to recover O&M costs, the gap needs to be filled using tax revenues that are carefully targeted, predictable and transparent to facilitate rigorous O&M (World Bank and UNICEF, 2017[21]).

Timely asset management is only possible when it is informed by accurate, sufficiently detailed data on the state and renewal rates of assets, yet as noted above, many countries lack this information (OECD, 2020[13]). A clear, well-articulated vision of asset renewal needs and accurate forecasts of water demand and risks allows WSS service providers and water management authorities to rigorously plan O&M and future investments (OECD, 2016[22]). This information can also support transparency about the effectiveness of services, and act as a basis for establishing precise, secure service contracts, reducing information asymmetries and rent-seeking behaviour (OECD, 2016[22]). Box 3.3 illustrates how various tools and technologies are being used to gather more precise data on assets and inform their sound management.

Box 3.3. Technologies and methodologies for data gathering and analysis to inform water asset management

Urban WSS service providers in developed countries have been increasingly relying on remote sensing and imaging technologies to acquire precise knowledge of assets' status and performance levels, particularly those that are located underground (see, for example applications of AI discussed in Box 3.2). This information supports better planning of investments in maintenance and renewal to improve system reliability (e.g. to repair damaged pipes). Innovative and emerging tools and technologies expand the scale and scope of infrastructure monitoring, and extend the time horizon for asset management.

In New Zealand, the city of Auckland has used geographical information systems to overlay actions and investments that have a direct or indirect effect on freshwater quality, including those targeting storm water asset maintenance, renewal and development, cycleway and road construction, and network infrastructure development (e.g. broadband rollout).

In the United States, the Massachusetts Water Resources Authority developed a predictive maintenance strategy based on condition monitoring, and the probability and consequences of failure of each component. The programme increased equipment availability to 99%; it achieved cost savings by eliminating unneeded and low-value preventive maintenance work, and shifting the freed-up resources to predictive tasks and actual maintenance work. Predictive and probability-based maintenance illustrates a shift from zero-risk asset management (which translates into high degrees of infrastructure redundancy) to more thorough risk analysis, allowing more strategic and cost-effective asset management.

Sources: Adapted from (OECD, 2016[22]; OECD, 2015[26]; OECD, forthcoming[27])

Where the renewal rates of water assets are known, they often reflect a significant backlog of investment in O&M for existing assets. In the WSS sector in European Union countries, renewal rates are typically below levels that would be commensurate with assets' life expectancy (OECD, 2020[13]). Other parts of the water sector – such as agricultural water – face similar challenges with ageing and deteriorating assets: for example, while Japan has invested heavily in its irrigation infrastructure over the last 50 years, more than 20% of the core irrigation facilities have now exceeded their expected lifespan (OECD, 2019[28]).

Failure to monitor assets, resolve problems or implement upgrades in a timely way can lead to excessive water losses, including non-revenue water, which undermines the efficiency and effectiveness of water services and raises costs. High rates of non-revenue water are often a sign of operational inefficiency and can provide a partial insight into the extent of backlogs of investment in O&M (OECD, 2020[13]). As non-revenue water can be driven by a combination of issues arising from key operational aspects of service provision – such as water production and distribution, asset maintenance, management of service users, and billing – timely asset management is just one of the possible solutions[5] (Sy and Ahmed, 2016[29]). A recent OECD study found that there is significant potential to reduce non-revenue water in EU countries including Bulgaria, Poland, Cyprus[6] and Romania, including through targeted maintenance of assets to improve leakage control and drive asset renewal and modernisation (OECD, 2020[13]). Such asset-focused interventions can be accompanied by measures such as performance based contracts to improve incentives for higher O&M performance, or capacity building programmes to build service providers' skills in managing the technical dimensions of O&M. Indeed, in some cases, such measures can reduce or fully avoid the need for capital-intensive asset upgrades by minimising non-revenue water through other means (Kingdom et al., 2018[23]).Figure 3.2 illustrates the position of select countries with respect to the operating expenditure (OPEX) ratio (total annual operational revenue over total annual operating cost) and the share of non-revenue water (NRW). A higher OPEX ratio reflects a higher share of cost recovery for OPEX, providing more stable financing for timely maintenance of infrastructure assets. However, it is notably that there is significant scope for improvement to reduce non-revenue water, irrespective of the OPEX ratio.

Figure 3.2. Operational Ratio vs. Percentage of Non-Revenue Water, by Country

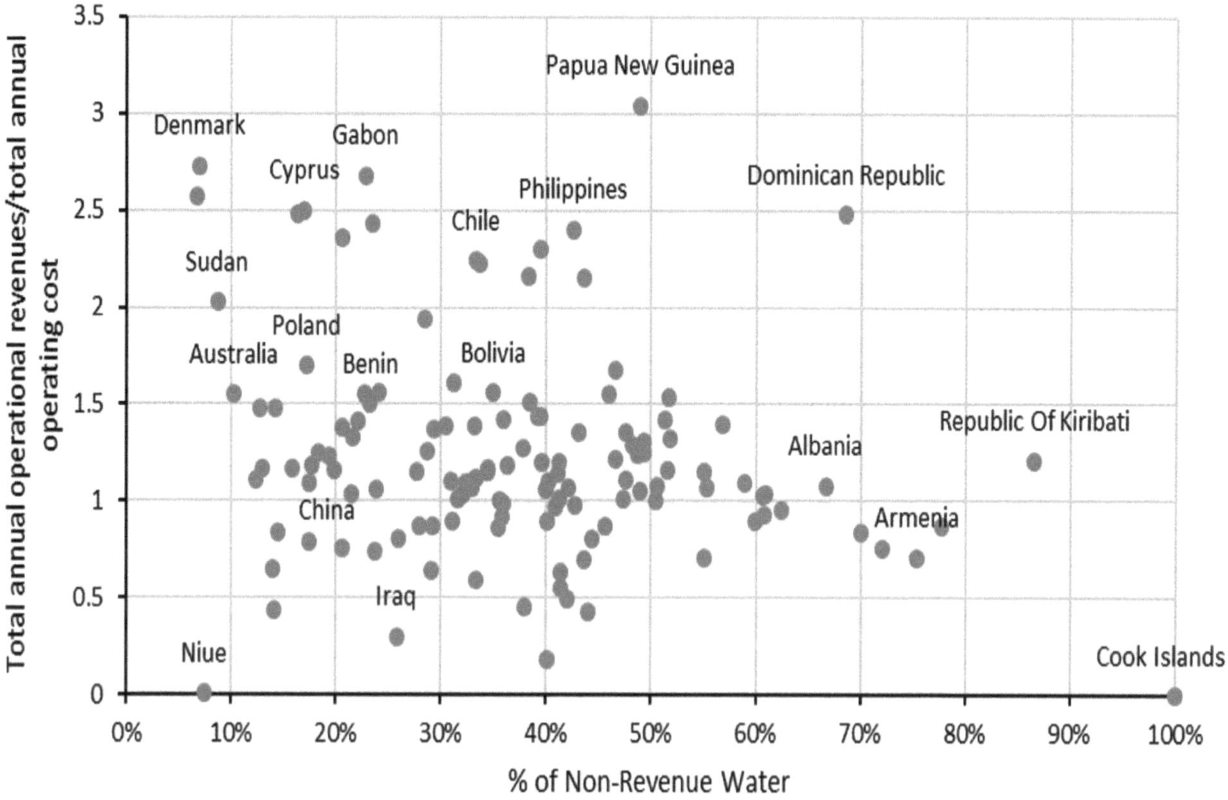

Source: Authors, based on IBnet The International Benchmarking Network https://ib-net.org

3.2.2. Sound capital expenditure planning

CAPEX in the water sector should be carefully planned to ensure that finance is used to maximise economic, social and environmental benefits and improve overall capital efficiency. As noted in the above section, the need for well-planned, efficient CAPEX is interlinked with the need for investment in robust O&M; both are critical to making the best use of existing sources of finance and assets over their full life cycles (Kingdom et al., 2018[23]). This interconnection is illustrated by the WSS sector's emphasis on the need to move away from the *"design, build, neglect, rebuild"* approach that has traditionally characterised capital expenditure in many countries and shift to a more cost-effective *"design, build, maintain"* model (Kingdom et al., 2018[23]). While the imperatives for operational efficiency have been gaining attention in the WSS sector, capital costs amount to around 50% of the total costs of service provision, which suggests that it is equally important to identify and exploit opportunities to reduce wasteful capital spending and make better use of existing finance and assets (Kingdom et al., 2018[23]).

Sound CAPEX planning should focus on reducing capital costs and minimising the associated long-term costs of O&M (World Bank and UNICEF, 2017[21]). This can be done in various ways. For example, planners should ensure that demand management options have been fully explored and new infrastructure is actually needed; policies are coherent across sectors, and exposure and vulnerability to water-related risks are considered; lower cost options have been considered in determining selected approach; robust design standards are in place; overpricing is mitigated (with costs and contract awards adequately regulated and monitored and transparently benchmarked); and communities are involved to provide local oversight (World Bank and UNICEF, 2017[21]). They should also conduct cost-benefit analyses with a view to supporting policy coherence and solutions that generate multiple benefits, including those that are difficult to monetise (such as nature-based solutions, potentially in combination with more traditional "grey" infrastructure) (see discussion on NbS in Section 3). Addressing trade-offs across geographic scales needs to be considered, though this can add significant complexity.

Investment in the water sector has traditionally focused on large-scale CAPEX, while commonly overlooking smaller investments that could improve performance or maximise local capacities and increase operational efficiency over the longer term. Planning that over-emphasises large-scale CAPEX can result in expensive yet underused infrastructure: a considerable share of WSS infrastructure, particularly in low- and middle-income countries, is oversized and fails to be used to capacity, or is not connected to sewerage networks at all (World Bank, 2017[6]). This sometimes occurs when technical standards are imported from high income countries and insufficiently adapted to the local context (World Bank, 2017[6]). Unnecessary costs can also arise in the design, selection and implementation of new infrastructure due to inefficient procurement processes, limited competition, or vested interests and biases towards the use of certain (and often more expensive) technologies (World Bank, 2017[6]). A lack of capacity and/or sufficient performance incentives for planners and operators can also drive poor CAPEX decisions. All of these issues not only undermine well-planned CAPEX, but also diminish the credibility and creditworthiness of service providers, limiting their ability to attract commercial finance (OECD, 2018[30]).

A bias in CAPEX planning towards large-scale "grey" and networked solutions can also impede the consideration and adoption of alternative options that may cost less now or in the future offer the same levels of service, often with other social and ecological benefits. This is an especially critical issue in countries that still have sizable populations lacking access to safe, reliable WSS services. Decentralised WSS systems can sometimes have lower costs and offer greater flexibility in hard-to-reach or rapidly changing environments (such as informal settlements), and avoid the need for large investments in piped infrastructure (Kingdom et al., 2018[23]). Experience in Dakar, Senegal, offers one example: a 2012 study found that the estimated annualised cost for sewerage services was almost USD 55, while the cost of on-site sanitation with faecal sludge management was estimated at less than USD 12 ((Dodane et al., 2012[31]) in (World Bank, 2017[6])). These decentralised systems can deliver cost savings relative to conventional networked infrastructure, although should be accompanied by reliable monitoring and enforcement capacity.

Nature-based solutions (NbS) are another example of interventions with strong potential cost-benefit ratios. They are generally less capital-intensive - with lower O&M and replacement costs, can avoid lock-in associated with capital-intensive grey infrastructure, and appreciate in value over time with the regeneration of ecosystems and their associated services (OECD, 2020[13]). NbS can also present distinctive challenges in terms of investment design, funding and financing (further details in the following section).

A disconnect between the accountability and incentive structures of asset financiers and asset operators can also undermine cost-efficient capital expenditure. This is particularly the case in low- and middle-income countries, where WSS service providers are often public entities that pay either nothing or a minimal cost for the infrastructure they use for service delivery (i.e. it is highly subsidised) (World Bank, 2017[6]; Kingdom et al., 2018[23]). This can directly constrain service providers' accountability for asset use and management, and limit their incentives to pursue adequate cost recovery. Experience in some higher income countries, where the full cost of service delivery is accounted for, reflects that the debt service to repay loans for capital costs can be significant. For example, capital costs amount to an average of 49% of total costs for water utilities in England and Wales in the United Kingdom (Kingdom et al., 2018[23]).

3.2.3. Targeted allocation of public subsidies

Funding from public budgets is a significant source of funding of water services and water resources management. Yet in many countries the allocation of public funding could be better designed and allocated to improve equity and ensure the best use of available finance. Public subsidies refer to transfers that fill the gap that results from inadequate cost recovery through pricing. In the context of water supply and sanitation services, a subsidy[7] occurs when a water user pays less for a product or service than the cost to the service provider, and the responsibility for covering the difference is shifted onto a third party, such as the government, other water users, or future generations (Andres et al., 2019[32]). Subsidies may be direct financial transfers from one entity to another (e.g. from a government to a service provider) or implicit transfers, such as non-payment for services or delayed maintenance (Andres et al., 2019[32]).

When well designed and deployed, public subsidies can be an important means for extending access to water resources and services for groups that may otherwise struggle to access them (e.g. due to affordability constraints), and need to be carefully targeted, transparent and predictable (World Bank, 2017[6]). Subsidies often fail to meet these criteria, instead distorting prices or creating perverse incentives that negatively affect water availability, quality or demand, including generating impacts beyond the water sector, for example through detrimental impacts on biodiversity via the intensification of agriculture. In such cases, governments should reform subsidies to ensure they meet their intended purpose, or phase them out where appropriate, using transition plans that avoid adverse impacts on vulnerable groups (OECD, 2016[8]).

This section focuses on examples of subsidies in the WSS and agricultural water sectors to identify some of the available options for fairer allocation that can support the best use of available resources. Table 3.3. outlines further examples of subsidies in the different parts of the water sector.

Table 3.3. Examples of subsidies in water services and water resources management

Transfer mechanism	Example
Direct transfers of funds	Capital investment subsidies for water supply and sanitation providers
Foregone tax revenue	Environmental pollution charges that do not cover the cost of pollution, as well as special reductions or exemptions
Foregone user charge revenue	Water supply and sanitation tariffs that do not cover the cost of service provision; lack of abstraction charges; reduced electricity tariffs for irrigation pumps
Transfer of risk to government	Government compensation to households and firms for property damage due to water-related disasters
Induced transfers	Cross-subsidies for water supply and sanitation services (industrial vs. household tariffs)
Economic advantage due to unequal regulation or policy	Different regulations or charges for industry discharging pollutants to sewer systems or directly to water bodies

Note: These are illustrative examples and not an exhaustive list of all subsidies that may exist in the water sector.
Sources: (OECD, forthcoming[27]) adapted from (EAP Task Force, 2013[33]).

Subsidies in the water supply and sanitation sector

Governments have traditionally heavily subsidised the WSS sector, usually with the overarching aim of expanding access to safe WSS services and capturing the positive externalities of access to WSS services (e.g. benefits for public health, productivity or educational outcomes). A recent study finds that subsidies are prevalent across countries, regardless of their region or income level (Andres et al., 2019[32]). This is not only because of the fundamental need for governments to support access to safe WSS services, but also because of the networked nature of many WSS services. Approximately 65% of the cost of supplying piped water and 80% of the cost of sewerage systems are for long-lived capital assets; this can allow service providers to use pricing structures in the short- to medium-term that do not cover capital or O&M costs, relying on subsidies that are often driven by pressure to keep prices low for users (Andres et al., 2019[32]).

Most existing WSS subsidies are costly, non-transparent and distortionary: they typically fail to benefit users through better services or lower prices, can allow rent-seeking by governments and service providers, and can limit service efficiency and sustainability (Andres et al., 2019[32]). They are also often poorly targeted and regressive. For example, subsidies commonly focus on networked services that poorer communities cannot access or afford, and ultimately disproportionately benefitting wealthier segments of the population that are already connected to services (see Box 3.4) (Andres et al., 2019[32]; Leflaive and Hjort, 2020[34]).

Box 3.4. Potential limitations of WSS subsidies that are delivered through tariff mechanisms

Subsidies that are delivered through tariffs for WSS services tend to be poorly targeted and regressive, as the most common tariff structures are unable to effectively direct subsidies to poor households. Studies have shown that such subsidies in fact lead to more unequal distribution of resources as compared to if subsidies were equally distributed among the population, due to errors of inclusion as well as of exclusion from the subsidies (Fuente et al., 2016[35]).

In Lima, Peru, 20-30% of the population faces water affordability issues (the critical share of total water expenditure in income is set to 2%). As many as 90% of poor connected customers receive a WSS subsidy; however, 91% of the subsidy beneficiaries, or 78% of the connected population, are non-poor (Barde and Lehmann, 2014[36]). A similar situation is observed in Nairobi, Kenya, where households in the lowest wealth quintile receive 15% of the total WSS subsidies delivered.

Source: (Leflaive and Hjort, 2020[34])

Subsidies in the WSS sector need to be more carefully designed and targeted if they are to facilitate access to sustainable services and efficiently address equity and affordability issues. This means accurately identifying and aiming subsidies at priority groups (e.g. poor and vulnerable populations) and priority types of services (e.g. avoiding a disproportionate focus on urban, networked water services and duly addressing other areas of need, such as for rural sanitation services) (Andres et al., 2019[32]). Subsidies may target either connection fees (e.g. one-off financial support to expedite connection to existing or new networks, or the recurrent part of water bills (when there is one). Rather than being tied to individual expenditures, subsidies can also be made conditional on improved performance by service providers, using transparent key indicators and targets for better service results (Andres et al., 2019[32]).

Subsidies for WSS services tend to be most effective when they are decoupled from service access and consumption charges, and are instead provided as separate, targeted measures – for example, through dedicated funds for payment relief to poor households, or via rebates, vouchers or lump sum transfers to water users. Subsidies that are based on the volume of water consumed can distort consumption and, as a result, hamper efficient allocation of water resources ((Reynaud et al., 2016[37]) and (OECD, 2011[38]) in (Leflaive and Hjort, 2020[34])). This implies that measures should be designed in order to secure basic needs, rather than be based on measured consumption at the household level. In Chile, policymakers have created a clear distinction between basic water needs and optimal consumption. Eligible poor households are provided with vouchers that help them cover a smaller or larger share (depending on their assessed needs) of the bill for basic water volumes, but never for volumes above this level. This guarantees that the social measures never cover water for profligate use (Leflaive and Hjort, 2020[34]).

Whether they are phasing out an existing subsidy or considering the introduction of a temporary one, governments should prepare well-considered "exit strategies" for subsidies' eventual removal. These should be informed by whether the conditions driving the need for the subsidy are long-standing, permanent, or will change or disappear over time. Proposals to remove subsidies should be transparently consulted upon and communicated, with phase-outs accompanied by complementary measures such as legal reforms and transitional measures that account for the impacts of lost benefits (Andres et al., 2019[32]).

Subsidies for agricultural water

Governments often provide public subsidies for agricultural water; as is the case in the WSS sector. This can create perverse incentives and distortions that harm the efficiency, equity and/or sustainability of water resources management. One example is water-related input subsidies (e.g. of the costs of irrigation, fertilisers, pesticides or groundwater pumping): by lowering input costs, they can directly undermine water allocation regimes or harm water resources in certain contexts (Gruère and Le Boëdec, 2019[39]). Other examples include forms of support for agricultural activities that indirectly affect water resources, for example by encouraging the use of water, fertiliser, pesticides, or livestock intensification. Both types of subsidies can harm water resources by encouraging the overuse, overconsumption and/or pollution of surface water and groundwater (Gruère and Le Boëdec, 2019[39]).

Farm subsidies that negatively affect water resources are often designed with a different policy objective in mind – for example, they may effectively raise agricultural production or profitability, yet trigger inefficient or unsustainable water use or pollution of water resources (OECD, 2007[40]). When a subsidy has unintended negative consequences for water quality and quantity, it is sometimes highly politically sensitive or controversial to attribute the consequences to the subsidy, and this can be an early stumbling block for governments seeking to reform or remove it. For example, support for irrigation efficiency technologies might increase water consumption, to the detriment of other users and water ecosystems, due to a misrepresentation of the local hydrology or farmers' response ((Grafton et al., 2018[41]) in (Gruère and Le Boëdec, 2019[39])). Long-standing subsidies can sometimes be viewed by certain groups as entitlements.

Subsidies that negatively affect water resources can also further entrench existing inequalities. For instance, if the size of a subsidy is proportional to the amount of land owned, it will likely benefit wealthy farmers with larger farms. Subsidies' impact on equity can also be indirect: irrigation subsidies can exacerbate existing operations and maintenance deficits by encouraging more water use, which in turn deteriorates the quality of the service and the availability of the resource (Gruère and Le Boëdec, 2019[39]). This can affect poor farmers the most, as they are often downstream users at the end of irrigation systems and cannot afford to invest in alternative sources of water or cope with the degradation of water quality (e.g. due to salinisation) (Gruère and Le Boëdec, 2019[39]).

As in the WSS sector, to improve equity and ensure that any agricultural water subsidies are fair and consistent with water policy objectives, governments can use packages of measures to reform the subsidies (e.g. through better targeting) or, as appropriate, phase them out over time. These measures can be combined to complement each other, and may include, for example (Gruère and Le Boëdec, 2019[39]):

- pilots and demonstration projects that allow governments to test and make a case for the adjustment or removal of subsidies in certain locations before they are scaled up
- legal or governance reforms that increase transparency around subsidies
- engagement and consultation with key stakeholders to foster transparency and build trust in reform processes, and
- purposefully designed and targeted transfer payments to certain groups, to protect or insulate them from short-term shocks or negative impacts from the reform.

To be effective, these actions typically require a lengthy but clearly time-bound implementation period, fortified by a continual effort to sustain political buy-in throughout the process of the reform.

Data and tools to improve the equity of water sector subsidies

The importance of access to accurate information and tailored methods for improving the fairness of water sector subsidies cannot be overstated. Governments should be attuned to how technological development and data innovation are creating new opportunities to better tailor and target subsidies.

For example, in the WSS sector, relevant data is indispensable to inform the tariff-setting process as well as the design of accompanying social measures, yet decision makers and service providers' reform efforts can be hampered by data restrictions. For example, an absence of metering limits detailed documentation of water use, and in some countries, privacy laws prevent service providers from accessing data on the households "behind" the meters (Leflaive and Hjort, 2020[34]). However, when affordability and equity issues are addressed through separate measures outside of the water bill, relevant data – such as on household incomes and health – can be more readily available. The World Bank has piloted the use of remote sensing and street view data along with machine learning algorithms to map poor communities in Luanda, Angola, to inform the targeting of subsidies (Andres et al., 2019[32]). Analytical tools such as these can be instrumental in supporting governments to accurately identify which groups benefit or lose as a result of existing subsidies, as well as how subsidies may be better tailored to reach those groups as needed. Such analysis is fundamental to any rigorous effort to more fairly allocate subsidies in support of overall water policy objectives.

3.2.4. Seizing opportunities to improve economies of scale

Governments may consider institutional and market reforms to improve economies of scale, and through this, reduce operational costs and investment needs in the WSS sector. Aggregation reforms in the WSS sector are one option for reducing fragmentation in service delivery and optimising the use of existing sources of finance and assets.

As discussed above in Section 1 on the enabling environment for investment, the authority for WSS service provision in many countries is decentralised and devolved to the municipal or local level. While this is typically driven by the recognition that WSS services are intrinsically local and therefore best managed at that level, poorly designed or incomplete decentralisation can result in the creation of small, under-resourced WSS service provider institutions with inadequate capacities for administration and financial management, planning, and/or technical operations (Streeter, 2017[7]; OECD, 2010[42]). Decentralisation reforms can be particularly challenging for countries that need to provide WSS service coverage in areas with low density and/or hard-to-reach populations (e.g. rural areas, remote areas, or informal settlements). In such contexts, WSS services are often provided via devolved, dispersed networks of small providers that struggle to efficiently allocate their limited resources over large and sometimes technically complex service areas. This can create a varied and fragmented landscape for WSS service provision that is difficult to coherently oversee and sustainably finance.

To address these fragmentation challenges, some countries opt to adjust the scale and scope of WSS service provision by aggregating service provider institutions (OECD, 2010[42]). For example, aggregation reforms may seek to deliver WSS services at a more appropriate scale by creating a single institution that is responsible for services across multiple municipalities or within a given region. They may also adjust the scope of a provider's responsibilities by either reducing or expanding the range of WSS services it delivers. Aggregation reforms generally aim to reduce perceived inefficiencies and low capacities in WSS service delivery by ensuring that providers have a customer base of appropriate size and a staff with the necessary capabilities to cost-effectively deliver WSS services (ERM, Stephen Myers and Hydroconseil, 2005[43]). This can in turn make WSS service providers financially viable, improving their creditworthiness and attractiveness to investors.

Currently, work is underway in Estonia and Lithuania on these issues, in the context of policy dialogues led by the OECD in co-operation with the European Commission DG Reform. The work will examine options for different modalities of water utilities sector consolidation, increasing social equity in access to - and prices for - WSS services in these countries. It will consider different scenarios of consolidation, including consolidation based on the principles of scale (national, regional, basin level) or/and scope (aggregation of such functions as technical maintenance, customer relation, revenue collection, etc.).

Aggregation reforms can have a variety of drivers and take different forms, depending on countries' legal, regulatory and institutional frameworks. Like reforms of WSS tariffs or subsidies, aggregation processes can also be influenced by political cycles and interests, given their potential implications for different institutions' roles and responsibilities, mandates and resources. Aggregation reforms might be locally-led and voluntary (e.g. arising from local governments' initiative), incentivised and supported by a higher level of government and locally implemented, or wholly mandated and led by a higher level of government (ERM, Stephen Myers and Hydroconseil, 2005[43]). These drivers can be an important determinant of the willingness of existing service providers and other government institutions to support or participate in aggregation. For example, authorities at the local level may sometimes be reluctant to engage with aggregation reforms, due to concerns about losing their ability to oversee and adequately respond to customers' demands and concerns, or losing access to and oversight of existing sources of finance, or where local utilities perform multiple functions. Factors such as these have delayed some countries' reforms (OECD, 2020[13]). Governments also need to consider whether their aggregation process will be accompanied by a transfer of asset ownership to the level of service provision – this depends on the country context and identified service needs, and can be another sensitive factor (ERM, Stephen Myers and Hydroconseil, 2005[43]). Regardless of aggregation reforms' main drivers, these considerations underscore the need for thorough scoping, consultation and negotiation processes for aggregation reforms among different levels of government and institutions.

Countries' various experiences with aggregation to date reflect that while they require a strong grasp of institutional incentives and potentially extensive or lengthy negotiations, they can be most effective when they combined with complementary measures aimed at improving services (such as independent regulation or programmes to strengthen performance). Indeed, aggregation commonly leads to a need for governments to reform existing mechanisms for the oversight of service provision (ERM, Stephen Myers and Hydroconseil, 2005[43]). Aggregation of service providers can also be important in facilitating cross-subsidies between water users and territories, such as between rural and urban areas. This is the case in Romania and Bulgaria, and to a lesser extent in Lithuania, Latvia and Poland (OECD, 2020[13]).

3.2.5. Creating and maintaining incentives for performance

Strong administrative and operational performance within the institutions that manage water resources and deliver WSS services is vital to ensuring the best use of existing finance and assets. In the WSS sector, inadequate performance requirements and incentives for service provision can have various drivers – such as insufficient institutional accountability structures, a lack of well-defined and attainable performance standards, and/or insufficient institutional resources and capacities to enable good performance. Such conditions can translate to low motivation and poor standards for O&M, deteriorating assets, and low service quality. In turn, this reduces providers' credibility and public trust in their ability to provide high quality WSS services – and can result in, for example, low user willingness to pay for local WSS services, or decisions by central government authorities to allocate much-needed finances to other purposes that are deemed more worthy or valuable. These issues also limit service providers' creditworthiness and attractiveness to investors.

The section above on the enabling environment outlined the importance of policy and institutional settings – supported by the necessary resources and capacities – in creating the conditions for accountable, effective and efficient water service provision and ensuring reliable, financially sustainable institutions.

Mechanisms for the independent regulation of services and information-based instruments are two types of measures that can help to make service providers' performance transparent and set standards and incentives to further improve it. This section briefly expands on these measures and their role in driving higher performance to optimise existing finance and assets.

The role of independent economic regulation in driving consistent performance

Service accountability and transparency can be limited when the roles and responsibilities of the different actors involved in WSS services are not delineated and structured through clear institutional arrangements (e.g. for government authorities, asset owners, and service operators). Institutional structures sometimes also fail to provide clear requirements and incentives for service providers to improve service efficiency, meaning there is limited impetus for them to address problems or strengthen services in order to confront future challenges. Governments may struggle to require or incentivise higher service provider performance where the functions and powers of policy- and decision-making (e.g. on the design of economic instruments) are not explicitly separated from operations. Where such institutional separations do exist, regulatory bodies sometimes still lack the necessary powers to ensure that service provision complies with regulations and/or other standards.

Properly resourced independent regulation can help to address these issues, providing a clear accountability structure for institutions and a basis for setting and enforcing service performance standards. The three core elements of sound water regulation are to protect the environment (water resources and broader ecosystems), protect service users' (customers') interests, and protect the quality of services (e.g. for drinking water or wastewater management) (OECD, 2020[13]). Independent regulation can be designed and implemented in different forms according to countries' specific governance contexts and needs. Regulation may be conducted by government; by contract (with regulation specified through legal instruments); by one or multiple independent regulators (e.g. with separations between decision-making, management and financing); or by outsourcing selected regulatory functions to third parties (i.e. external contractors that undertake tariff reviews or benchmarking) (OECD, 2020[13]).

The way in which a regulator acquires performance information and sets performance targets for service provision is important in bridging any gap between governments' and customers' expectations (OECD, 2020[13]). An outcome-based approach can help to ensure that service providers' focus is not simply on easily measured outputs, but also accounts for longer-term aims for WSS services and the environment. A regulator should expect the service delivery body to monitor its services, the operational performance of its assets, and how it is planning for resilient systems operation in the face of shocks, such as drought, process failures or cyber-attacks. Just as governments need to ensure adequate resourcing for the regulator, the regulator should ensure the adequate funding of service provision institutions to enable them to efficiently and effectively meet service standards.

Transparency is crucial: defined standards and targets, and service providers' performance against them, should be published and made available to customers (OECD, 2020[13]). Customers should also expect to be able to express their views on levels of service, priorities for investment and options for major infrastructure where this is proposed. The extent to which customers participate in the development of business plans can influence both their behaviour – and how much they value water and the service they receive – as well as that of the service provider.

Information-based instruments for improving performance

Producing and sharing reliable information on WSS service providers' performance is an important means for establishing and assessing their creditworthiness and transparently identifying areas for improvement (OECD and ADB, 2019[44]). Box 3.5. summarises examples of performance indicators for WSS services. Benchmarking can be a critical tool for stimulating progress and convergence towards standards and good practices. A variety of tools and mechanisms exist, using robust data collection mechanisms and various indicators which can be tailored to the priorities in a particular country or basin. The International Benchmarking Network for Water and Sanitation Utilities (IBNet) is a global mechanism, and there are others at smaller geographical scales. Another international example is AquaRating – a standard for assessing water and wastewater systems. AquaRating evaluates utilities based on key performance indicators and the adoption of best practices grouped into eight areas that include different stages and processes in the value chain ((IDB, 2018[45]) in (OECD and ADB, 2019[44])). It helps WSS service providers to accurately gauge their current status, identify opportunities for improvement, and take actions to meet international good practices. Through this, AquaRating can provide lenders with critical information on creditworthiness to enhance the commercial financial flow to the water sector (OECD and ADB, 2019[44]).

Benchmarking processes and tools such as these also underscore the need for additional complementary information-based instruments: education, training and communication materials and programmes that strengthen service providers' capacity to perform. Where WSS service providers have low capacities, this often includes a lack of performance-based management knowledge and practices and adapted business processes that can guide them in planning for the medium- and long-term (OECD and ADB, 2019[44]). Well-designed capacity building interventions can ensure that service providers are able to thoroughly understand and act on performance standards and incentives.

Box 3.5. Examples of performance indicators for WSS services

Building on international good practices, performance indicators for WSS services can focus on the following items. The relevance and relative weight of indicators would reflect local conditions.

Technical performance indicators

- Leakage performance and targets for reducing leakage and other unbilled losses, such as illegal connections
- Mains bursts (as a proxy for distribution network condition)
- Sewer collapses (as a proxy for sewer asset condition)
- Number of wastewater pollution incidents, such as from too-frequent operation of combined sewer overflows, or major failures at wastewater treatment works
- Unplanned outages (loss of supply because of bursts, contamination, etc.)

Compliance with existing regulation

- Drinking water quality compliance (integrating with and reinforcing the role of the drinking water regulator, where this is separate)
- Level of compliance with environmental permits and standards (integrating with and reinforcing the role of the environmental regulator, where this is separate); this can also be an indicator of the quality and state of assets for water supply and wastewater treatment

Customer experience

- Reducing per capita consumption for households and demand in other sectors on mains supplies
- Risk of demand restrictions in a drought
- Customer experience: how well billing queries are dealt with, information about planned outages and supply interruptions

Source: (OECD, 2020, pp. 99-100[13])

3.3. Optimise future investment needs by planning, setting priorities and sequencing investment

While financiers typically focus on the availability of a pipeline of bankable projects, government authorities and project developers should also situate these pipelines within broader strategic investment pathways to ensure they are resilient and contribute to water security and sustainable growth over the long term and preferably at the least cost. A long-term strategic approach can ensure that assets deliver anticipated benefits over their operational lifetime and avoid premature obsolescence or costly retro-fitting in the future. Such an approach would also help to secure a stable flow of investment opportunities and returns for investors.

Water-related investments need to be resilient to cope with systemic changes. A hallmark of resilience is the recognition that disruption of system functions will occur, sometimes due to expected events and other times due to unexpected ones, and thus, there is a need to plan for how to recover from them. Investment possibilities include efforts to increase system modularity, redundancy, flexibility, cohesion, adaptability, to name a few system characteristics that have emerged from ongoing research (Linkov et al., 2019[46]).

Recognising that the future is uncertain, governments can combine long-term strategic infrastructure perspectives with iterative decision making that can be adjusted over time as more information becomes available.[8] This includes taking steps in the design, operation and financing of systems to avoid inefficient path dependencies or costly infrastructure retrofits, and consider how short-term actions potentially enable or foreclose future options. Governments can signal their intention and financial ability to tender water projects over a multi-year time span. This could also include governments fostering the development of commercial finance and capital markets able to lend at an affordable cost and appropriate long term maturity to water related projects. A focus on actions that promote additional flexibility, and provide opportunities to shift among options depending on evolving trends (economic, climatic, demographic, technological, etc.) are valuable in the context of uncertainty (OECD, 2018[47]). This includes consideration of nature-based solutions, which have significant potential to lower the costs of achieving water security and related co-benefits (e.g. for biodiversity, etc.) now and in the future.

In addition to taking a long-term view, strategic investment pathways should be designed at the relevant spatial scale. Individual water projects may be bankable, but could still undermine the management of water resources. For example, a narrow focus on investments in water use efficiency for particular users may or may not improve the overall sustainable management of the resource, potentially undermining other benefits. Strategic planning can also open up the potential to exploit interdependencies among related investments, for example, where certain investments can unlock opportunities for others. A case illustration of this approach can be found in the example of the Zambezi Basin (OECD, 2020[5]). While the benefits of such pathways are better understood, operational challenges remain, that relate to the need to coordinate and align several projects, institutions and stakeholders, over a potentially long timeframe. Planning and coordination raise transaction costs. Institutional arrangements are required to address them (e.g. intermediaries and dedicated financing mechanisms).

Policy coherence is especially important for "landscape approaches", which are an increasingly common framework for creating integrated projects that pursue multiple policy goals within a given landscape. Landscape approaches recognise that the landscapes in which water management occurs are not static but instead continually adapt and evolve under the influence of interconnected social, ecological, economic and political dynamics (Cardascia, 2019[48]). By engaging different actors and mobilising capital at the scale of the landscape, these approaches can serve as pool mechanisms to channel investments with multiple objectives in different water sub-sectors. They can appeal to institutional investors such as pension funds and insurance companies by facilitating the issuance of local currency bonds in the capital markets of the countries in which those investors are already established and operating (Cardascia, 2019[48]).

3.3.1. Nature-based solutions to deliver multiple benefits in the context of a changing climate

The international community is increasingly exploring nature-based solutions (NbS) in response to deliver water security, especially in the context of a changing climate. NbS are measures that protect, sustainably manage or restore nature, with the goal of maintaining or enhancing ecosystem services to address a variety of social, environmental and economic challenges (OECD, 2020[49]; OECD, 2021[50]). The measures can include improved management practices, such as reduced fertiliser or pesticide use in agriculture, or investments reforestation or building artificial wetlands (Trémolet, S. et al., 2019[51]). NbS can also play a role as a complement to conventional "grey" infrastructure, in the form of hybrid solutions, increasing the effectiveness and operable life of infrastructure. For instance, integrating NbS into grey flood control measures can increase water absorption capacity, reduce velocity and regulate peak flows (Browder et al., 2019[52]). Wetlands can contribute to carbon sequestration, having the potential to store twice the amount of carbon as the world's forests (UNEP, 2019[53]). NbS offer new opportunities to address a number of water security risks in a cost-effective and integrated way.

More systematic consideration of NbS in strategic investment planning can deliver multiple benefits

NbS are multifunctional and have hence the potential to deliver co-benefits and to address several water security challenges simultaneously. For instance, wetlands can enhance water quality and mitigate flood and erosion risk (Cooper and Matthews, 2020[54]). Further, the use of NbS can maximise the synergies between ecosystem health, biodiversity and human well-being and increasing climate change mitigation as well as adaptation and resilience. NbS are adaptive systems, making them conducive to managing uncertainty related to climate change by avoiding or delaying lock-in to capital intensive grey infrastructure, allowing for flexibility to adapt to changing circumstances (OECD, 2020[49]; Cooper and Matthews, 2020[54]; OECD, 2013[55]). For example, a floodplain may attenuate larger volumes than can be held within a levee lined river channel, also delivering co-benefits of sustaining bird and fish species and providing recreational benefits to people (World Bank, 2017[56]).

The benefits of NbS have been found to outweigh the costs of implementation and maintenance in a range of contexts. NbS can result in substantial avoided costs. For example, investing in watershed restoration and conservation could save water utilities across the world's largest cities an estimated USD 890 million annually (Kapos et al., 2019[57]). Additionally, NbS can deliver multiple co-benefits with significant economic value, translating into a strong investment case. In Europe, for example, it was found that the restoration of rivers yielded an estimated net societal economic benefit of an estimated EUR 1 400 per hectare annually compared to unrestored rivers, in addition to increasing flood protection, enhanced agricultural production, carbon sequestration and recreation (Vermaat et al., 2015[58]).

In some cases, NbS can be more cost-effective than grey alternatives, particularly for less extreme hazards. For example, NbS were estimated to be 2-5 times more cost-effective than grey infrastructure across 52 coastal defence projects in the US, and most effective to defend against waves up to half a metre high and at increased water depths (Narayan et al., 2016[59]). Finally, investments in NbS have the potential to stimulate the economy by creating jobs. For example, in the EU, the restoration of 15% of degraded ecosystems, consistent with the EU 2020 Biodiversity Strategy, is estimated to result in between 20 000 and 70 000 full time jobs (OECD, 2019[60]). The potential for investing to receive multiple benefits rather than traditional single-purpose investments could become essential in the context of reduced public and overseas development aid budgets (Cooper and Matthews, 2020[54]).

Distinctive features of NbS create challenges for scaling up and financing

Despite opportunities and expected resilience dividends from NbS, their uptake remains limited and projects are often launched on a pilot basis and in an ad hoc way. The distinct characteristics of NbS create barriers for readily scaling up NbS. As summarised in (Dominique et al., 2021[61]) such features include difficulties in quantifying and monetizing benefits and long time lags between investment and the realisation of benefits. High transaction costs arise due to the specificity of ecosystem and climate dynamics, as well as multiple parties engaged in such projects. Other NbS-specific features that inhibit up-scaling are their large spatial scales that can cross multiple jurisdictions, limits to standardisation and barriers to funding and financing. Further, existing institutional, regulatory and financial processes are typically designed to support the development and financing of grey infrastructures, which can create a mismatch between an enabling environment that would be conducive to NbS and the status quo (Dominique et al., 2021[61]; OECD, 2020[49]; Trémolet, S. et al., 2019[51]; OECD, 2021[50]).

Monetising diffuse and non-market benefits is difficult and comparable metrics for NbS performance are lacking. This can bring a number of problems with the risk-return profile of NbS projects, deterring possible funders and financiers. Further, availability of robust performance data is limited, data may be collected inconsistently or incompletely at different times and different spatial scales. A lack of common metrics and the fact that NbS are generally unique and site-specific interventions make it challenging to compare measures and to assess the risks. (OECD, 2020[49]; Cooper and Matthews, 2020[54]; Trémolet, S. et al., 2019[51]; OECD, 2021[50]) In the absence of robust performance data for NbS, authorities charged with managing risks to communities or investors often default to better known and tested solutions (Dadson et al., 2017[62]).

Decision-making and planning processes are usually geared towards grey infrastructure and can inadvertently discourage the use of NbS. Traditional economic or financial appraisal tools, such as cost-benefit analysis (CBA) do not necessarily capture the value or full range of benefits and co-benefits from NbS projects (Cooper and Matthews, 2020[54]). Multi-criteria analysis provides a means to account for a broader range of market and non-market benefits. Various agencies are often not set up to provide the level of coordination among various partners, jurisdictions and landowners needed for NbS as they tend to operate in sectoral silos and thus favour single-purpose grey infrastructure. Further, the benefits from NbS may take longer timeframes to develop and can change over time. This might entail varying benefit-cost ratios over time, which could appear unfavourable compared to grey infrastructure during the planning and prioritisation phase (Trémolet et al., 2021[63]). A lack of short-term benefits could deter investors operating over short return periods. Moreover, investors often evaluate projects over the lifetime of the financing vehicle rather than the operational lifetime of the projects, which limits access to finance for NbS. (OECD, 2020[49]; Cooper and Matthews, 2020[54]).

Options for scaling up NbS and their financing

In order to increase their uptake, NbS need to be considered on an equal footing with grey infrastructure. Thus, decision-making processes around planning, implementing, operating and financing infrastructure need to be adapted through regulatory and legislation changes and the development of new appraisal tools (Cooper and Matthews, 2020[54]; OECD, 2020[49]). Beyond a focus on pilot projects and dedicated programmes, NbS would benefit from explicit inclusion in strategic policy and planning processes and documents, such as National Water Strategies, National Adaptation Plans, National Determined Contributions related to the UN Framework Convention on Climate Change, National Biodiversity Strategies, among others (Dominique et al., 2021[61]).

A more conducive enabling environment can be supported by shifting from an output-based approach focused on building infrastructure to an outcome-based approach focused on delivering services, such as water flow regulation, flood prevention and control, water quality improvement and so on. This promotes a shift from a focus from delivering infrastructure (typically conventional grey infrastructure) to delivering services, widening the range of possible solutions that can do so in a cost-effective way. For example, an economic regulator can promote specific service quality targets through the use of performance indicators while allowing utilities the flexibility to reach those targets in the most cost-efficient manner (Dominique et al., 2021[61]).

Expanding the traditional understanding of what constitutes an "asset" in the realm of water management would help to more broadly legitimize the use of NbS to deliver water services and expand their uptake (Cassin, Gunn and Matthews, 2021[64]). This requires ensuring that the regulatory, legislative and policy context recognise the services that NbS can deliver, and allowing for their use in the course of delivering regulated public services. The role of water sector regulators is especially crucial here. For example, when SABESP in São Paulo, Brazil, one of the leading water and sewage service providers in Latin America, faced a crisis of water shortage during the historic drought of 2014-15, it had to drastically re-adjust investment planning to strengthen the system's resilience. The regulator's role in allowing for the inclusion of these investments to increase resilience in the regulated asset base was decisive (OECD, 2019[65]).

Methods are needed which can evaluate and mainstream CBA for multi-purpose infrastructure, by adjusting discount rates as appropriate and evaluating projects over their operational lifetime rather than over their finance period. Projects in Bulgaria and Romania to implement flood risk management measures and have applied a broader range of appraisal tools, including multi-criteria analysis to better assess NbS compared with traditional approaches (OECD, 2021[66]). France, as another example, has launched a national programme to support the quantification and monetisation of the value of ecosystems and ecosystem services in 2012. The programme's 2018 report estimates that the value of the capacity of French rivers to retain nitrogen exceeds EUR 2 billion annually. However, no monetary value could be attributed to nearly half of the ecosystem services analysed due to a lack of available data or appropriate methodologies (EFESE, 2018[67]).

Improving the evidence base to quantify benefits and the performance of NbS can provide a more robust basis for funding and financing. Some well-established initiatives have made important strides in quantifying benefits related to NbS. For example, the Water Fund in Quito Ecuador (FONAG) has promoted catchment protection for 20 years. It devotes significant effort to monitoring the impact of the interventions. Impact monitoring entails the quantification of benefits in terms of water quality and quantity, with feedback on the design of the portfolio, and as an input for return-on-investment studies. These efforts are fundamental to promoting trust in the Fund and sustaining financial contributions that support its operations (De Bièvre and Coronel, 2022[68]).

Dedicated funding arrangement and financial incentives can scale up the use of NbS and have already been used in a number of countries (Trémolet et al., 2021[63]). In Peru, the Sanitation Sector Law requires utilities to use 1% of their collected tariffs to support NbS for water quality (Cooper and Matthews, 2020[54]). Further, governments can offer direct financial support for pilot projects and technical capacity building, such as seen in the United Kingdom, Canada, the United States and the European Union. In Europe, the EU Horizon 2020 programme has allocated approximately EUR 185 million to research and pilot the applications of NbS between 2014 and 2020 (OECD, 2020[49]). New project finance models that fit the characteristics of NbS' cash profiles need to emerge. Box 3.6 describes how the clustered approach has been used for water-related investments in hybrid infrastructure in Semarang in Indonesia.

Box 3.6. Clustered investment pathways for hybrid water infrastructure in Semarang

The city of Semarang in Indonesia is facing multiple interconnected water-related challenges. Climate change and urbanisation are increasing the city's exposure and vulnerability to flooding. In order to address not only the impacts but also the causes of these water-related risks, the city has identified several reinforcing interrelations between population growth and urban expansion, infiltration rates, frequency and risks of flooding, tax income, deterioration of maintenance levels of water infrastructure and declining groundwater resources.

To tackle the challenge holistically, the city has created five clusters of projects, aiming at starting a new dynamic between water security and economic growth. The five clusters considered are: micro-interventions; spongy mountain; rechannelling the city; feeding the industry; and recharging the aquifer. The implementation of several hybrid projects will proceed in phases, starting in 2020 with approximately one measure per cluster at small scale in order to a) create the evidence base, b) generate participation of communities, public and private sectors and c) build capacity of authorities to procure projects successfully and the private sector to deliver projects.

The Implementation Strategy aims at improving the bankability of each concept by enabling multi-sectoral investments and by making use of blended finance strategies. Different sources of finance will be mobilised such as Official Development Aid (ODA) targeting relevant SDGs, climate finance, municipality local revenue sources and efficiency gains driven by private sector participation. If investors are aware of the synergies embodied by the clusters, access to finance could become conditional upon successful implementation of previous projects within the clusters. Hence, strategic investment pathways comprised of phased hybrid infrastructure clusters could contribute to closing the implementation gap of water security strategies.

Source: (Altamirano, 2019[69])

References

ADB (2013), *Water utility asset management: A guide for development practitioners*, Asian Development Bank, https://www.adb.org/documents/water-utility-asset-management-guide-development-practitioners. [24]

Altamirano, M. (2019), *Hybrid (green-gray) water security strategies: a blended finance approach for implementation at scale*, Background Paper for the Roundtabe on Financing Water, 26-27 November, Manila, https://www.oecd.org/water/Session3b.Hybrid_(green-gray)_water_security_strategies.pdf. [69]

Andres, L. et al. (2019), *Doing More with Less Smarter Subsidies for Water Supply and Sanitation*, The World Bank Group, http://www.worldbank.org/gwsp. [32]

Barde, J. and P. Lehmann (2014), "Distributional effects of water tariff reforms – An empirical study for Lima, Peru", *Water Resources and Economics*, Vol. 6, pp. 30-57, http://dx.doi.org/10.1016/j.wre.2014.05.003. [36]

Browder, G. et al. (2019), *Integrating Green and Gray*, https://openknowledge.worldbank.org/handle/10986/31430. [52]

Cardascia, S. (2019), *Financing Water Infrastructure and Landscape Approaches in Asia and the Pacific*, Background paper Session 4, 5th Roundtable Meeting on Financing Water, 26-27 November, https://www.oecd.org/water/Session4.Financing_Water_Infrastructure_and_Landscape_Approaches_in_Asia_and_the_Pacific%20.pdf. [48]

Cassin, J. (ed.) (2021), *Why Governments Embrace Nature-based Solutions: The Policy Rationale*, Elsevier. [61]

Cassin, J., E. Gunn and J. Matthews (2021), *Nature-Based Solutions and Water Security.* [64]

Cassins, J., E. Lopez Gunn and J. Matthews (eds.) (2021), *Chapter 15. Funding and Financing to Scale Nature-based Solutions for Water Security*, Elsevier. [63]

Cooper, R. and J. Matthews (2020), *Water finance and Nature-based solutions*, K4D. [54]

Dadson, S. et al. (2017), "A restatement of the natural science evidence concerning catchment-based 'natural' flood management in the UK", *Royal Society*, https://doi.org/10.1098/rspa.2016.0706. [62]

De Bièvre, B. and L. Coronel (2022), "Investing in catchment protection: The Water Fund model", in *Investing in Water and Growth*. [68]

Dodane, P. et al. (2012), "Capital and Operating Costs of Full-Scale Fecal Sludge Management and Wastewater Treatment Systems in Dakar, Senegal", *Environmental Science & Technology*, Vol. 46/7, pp. 3705-3711, http://dx.doi.org/10.1021/es2045234. [31]

EAP Task Force (2013), *Improving the Use of Economic Instruments for Water Resource Management in Kyrgyzstan: The Case of Lake Issyk-Kul Basin*, OECD Publishing, Paris, https://www.oecd.org/env/outreach/2013_Kyrgyz%20report%20on%20Eis%20for%20WRM%20Eng%20Web.pdf. [33]

EFESE (2018), *Les milieux humides et aquatiques continentaux*, Ministère de la transition écologiques et solidaire, https://www.ecologie.gouv.fr/sites/default/files/Th%C3%A9ma%20-%20Les%20milieux%20humides%20et%20aquatiques%20continentaux.pdf. [67]

ERM, Stephen Myers and Hydroconseil (2005), *Models of Aggregation for Water and Sanitation Provision*, https://ppp.worldbank.org/public-private-partnership/library/models-aggregation-water-and-sanitation-provision. [43]

Fuente, D. et al. (2016), "Water and sanitation service delivery, pricing, and the poor: An empirical estimate of subsidy incidence in Nairobi, Kenya", *Water Resources Research*, Vol. 52/6, pp. 4845-4862, http://dx.doi.org/10.1002/2015wr018375. [35]

Grafton, R. et al. (2018), "The paradox of irrigation efficiency", *Science*, Vol. 361/6404, pp. 748-750, http://dx.doi.org/10.1126/science.aat9314. [41]

Gruère, G. and H. Le Boëdec (2019), "Navigating pathways to reform water policies in agriculture", *OECD Food, Agriculture and Fisheries Papers*, No. 128, OECD Publishing, Paris, https://dx.doi.org/10.1787/906cea2b-en. [39]

Gruère, G., M. Shigemitsu and S. Crawford (2020), "Agriculture and water policy changes: Stocktaking and alignment with OECD and G20 recommendations", *OECD Food, Agriculture and Fisheries Papers*, No. 144, OECD Publishing, Paris, https://dx.doi.org/10.1787/f35e64af-en. [15]

Haasnoot, M. et al. (2013), "Dynamic adaptive policy pathways: A method for crafting robust decisions for a deeply uncertain world", *Global Environmental Change*, http://dx.doi.org/10.1016/j.gloenvcha.2012.12.006. [70]

Haasnoot, M. et al. (2019), "Investments under non-stationarity: economic evaluation of adaptation pathways", *Climatic Change*, pp. 1-13, http://dx.doi.org/10.1007/s10584-019-02409-6. [71]

IDB (2018), *AquaRating: an international standard for assessing water and wastewater*, https://publications.iadb.org/publications/english/document/Aquarating-An-International-Standard-for-Assessing-Water-and-Wastewater-Services.pdf. [45]

Kapos, V. et al. (2019), *The Role of the Natural Environment in Adaptation*, https://cdn.gca.org/assets/2019-12/RoleofNaturalEnvironmentinAdaptation_V2.pdf. [57]

Kingdom, B. et al. (2018), *Better Use of Capital to Deliver Sustainable Water Supply and Sanitation Services*, World Bank, Washington, DC, http://dx.doi.org/10.1596/30870. [23]

Leflaive, X. and M. Hjort (2020), "Addressing the social consequences of tariffs for water supply and sanitation", *OECD Environment Working Papers*, No. 166, OECD Publishing, Paris, https://dx.doi.org/10.1787/afede7d6-en. [34]

Leigland, J., S. Trémolet and J. Ikeda (2016), *Achieving Universal Access to Water and Sanitation by 2030: The Role of Blended Finance*, World Bank, Washington D.C., https://documents.worldbank.org/en/publication/documents-reports/documentdetail/978521472029369304/achieving-universal-access-to-water-and-sanitation-by-2030-the-role-of-blended-finance. [10]

Linkov, I. et al. (2019), *The business case for resilience in water infrastructure investments*, http://dx.doi.org/10.1080/02626667.2018.1426858. [46]

Mehmood, H. et al. (2020), *Strategic Foresight to Applications of Artificial Intelligence to Achieve Water-related Sustainable Development Goals*, United Nations University Institute for Water, Environment and Health, Hamilton, Canada, https://inweh.unu.edu/wp-content/uploads/2020/04/Strategic-Foresight-to-Applications-of-Artificial-Intelligence-to-Achieve-Water-related-Sustainable-Development-Goals.pdf. [17]

Money, A. (2017), *Scaling-up financing through an attractive risk-return profile*, https://www.oecd.org/environment/resources/RT-Financing-Water-background-paper-session-A-Money-Oxford.pdf (accessed on 2 June 2020). [2]

Mumssen, Y., G. Saltiel and B. Kingdom (2018), *Aligning Institutions and Incentives for Sustainable Water Supply and Sanitation Services: Report of the Water Supply and Sanitation Global Solutions Group*, World Bank, https://openknowledge.worldbank.org/bitstream/handle/10986/29795/126016-WP-P159124-PUBLIC-7-5-2018-12-14-46-W.pdf?sequence=1&isAllowed=y. [20]

Narayan, S. et al. (2016), "The Effectiveness, Costs and Coastal Protection Benefits of Natural and Nature-Based Defences", *PLOS ONE*, http://dx.doi.org/10.1371/journal.pone.0154735. [59]

OECD (2021), *Scaling up Nature-based Solutions to Tackle Water-related Climate Risks: Insights from Mexico and the United Kingdom*, OECD Publishing, Paris, https://dx.doi.org/10.1787/736638c8-en. [50]

OECD (2021), *Sixth Roundtable on Financing Water: Discussion Highlights, Regional meeting: Europe, 7-8 December 2020*, https://www.oecd.org/water/6th-Roundtable-on-Financing-Water-in-Europe-Summary-and-Highlights.pdf. [66]

OECD (2021), *Toolkit for Water Policies and Governance: Converging Towards the OECD Council Recommendation on Water*, OECD Publishing, Paris, https://dx.doi.org/10.1787/ed1a7936-en. [14]

OECD (2020), *Financing Water Supply, Sanitation and Flood Protection: Challenges in EU Member States and Policy Options*, OECD Studies on Water, OECD Publishing, Paris, https://dx.doi.org/10.1787/6893cdac-en. [13]

OECD (2020), "Nature-based solutions for adapting to water-related climate risks", *OECD Environment Policy Papers*, No. 21, OECD Publishing, Paris, https://dx.doi.org/10.1787/2257873d-en. [49]

OECD (2020), *Strategic Investment Pathways: The Zambezi Basin case study*, https://www.oecd.org/water/OECD-(2020)-Strategic-investment-pathways-Zambezi-case-study.pdf. [5]

OECD (2019), *A Typology of Water-related Investments*. [4]

OECD (2019), *Biodiversity: Finance and the Economic and Business Case for Action*, OECD Publishing, Paris, https://dx.doi.org/10.1787/a3147942-en. [60]

OECD (2019), *Fourth meeting of the Roundtable on Financing Water, Regional Meeting Americas, 26-27 June, Washington DC, Discussion Highlights*, http://www.oecd.org/water/Summary-RTmeeting-26and27June.pdf (accessed on 2 June 2020). [65]

OECD (2019), *Innovation, Agricultural Productivity and Sustainability in Japan*, OECD Food and Agricultural Reviews, OECD Publishing, Paris, https://dx.doi.org/10.1787/92b8dff7-en. [28]

OECD (2019), *Making Blended Finance Work for Water and Sanitation: Unlocking Commercial Finance for SDG 6*, OECD Studies on Water, OECD Publishing, Paris, https://dx.doi.org/10.1787/5efc8950-en. [1]

OECD (2018), *Blended finance for water-related investments*, Background paper Session 1. 3rd Roundtable Meeting on Financing Water, 12 November, https://www.oecd.org/water/Background-Paper-3rd-Roundtable-Financing-Water-Blended-Finance-for-water-related-investments.pdf. [12]

OECD (2018), *Developing Robust Project Pipelines for Low-Carbon Infrastructure*, Green Finance and Investment, OECD Publishing, Paris, https://dx.doi.org/10.1787/9789264307827-en. [47]

OECD (2018), *Third meeting of the Roundtable on Financing Water, 12 November, Paris Summary and Discussion Highlights*, http://www.oecd.org/water/roundtable-financing-water-2018-summary-and-highlights.pdf (accessed on 2 June 2020). [30]

OECD (2016), *OECD Council Recommendation on Water*, https://www.oecd.org/environment/resources/Council-Recommendation-on-water.pdf. [8]

OECD (2016), *OECD Council Recommendation on Water.* [19]

OECD (2016), *Water, Growth and Finance*, https://www.oecd.org/environment/resources/Water-Growth-and-Finance-policy-perspectives.pdf. [22]

OECD (2015), *Water and Cities: Ensuring Sustainable Futures*, OECD Studies on Water, OECD Publishing, Paris, https://dx.doi.org/10.1787/9789264230149-en. [26]

OECD (2013), *Scaling-up Finance Mechanisms for Biodiversity*, OECD Publishing, Paris, https://dx.doi.org/10.1787/9789264193833-en. [74]

OECD (2013), *Water and Climate Change Adaptation: Policies to Navigate Uncharted Waters.* [55]

OECD (2012), *A Framework for Financing Water Resources Management*, OECD Studies on Water, OECD Publishing, Paris, https://dx.doi.org/10.1787/9789264179820-en. [72]

OECD (2011), *Economic Instruments for Water Management*, Working Party on Biodiversity, Water and Ecosystems. [38]

OECD (2010), *Innovative Financing Mechanisms for the Water Sector*, OECD Studies on Water, OECD Publishing, Paris, https://dx.doi.org/10.1787/9789264083660-en. [42]

OECD (2009), *Managing Water for All*, OECD Publishing, Paris, https://www.oecd-ilibrary.org/environment/managing-water-for-all_9789264059498-en. [25]

OECD (2009), *Private Sector Participation in Water Infrastructure: OECD Checklist for Public Action*, OECD Studies on Water, OECD Publishing, Paris, https://dx.doi.org/10.1787/9789264059221-en. [9]

OECD (2007), *Subsidy Reform and Sustainable Development: Political Economy Aspects*, OECD Sustainable Development Studies, OECD Publishing, Paris, https://dx.doi.org/10.1787/9789264019379-en. [40]

OECD (forthcoming), *Report on the implementation of the OECD Recommendation on Water*. [27]

OECD and ADB (2019), *Supporting the Mobilisation of Commercial Finance: Managing risk, improving performance and creditworthiness*, Background paper Session 5. 5th Roundtable meeting on financing Water, 26-27 November, Manila, https://www.oecd.org/water/Session5.Supporting_the_mobilisation_of_commercial_finance.pdf. [44]

OECD-WCC (2017), *Converting economic benefits of water security investments into financial returns*, Backround paper Session 3. OECD-WWC-Netherlands Roundtable on Financing Water, 12-13 April 2017, Paris, https://www.oecd.org/environment/resources/RT-Financing-Water-background-paper-session-3.pdf. [11]

Pories, L., C. Fonseca and V. Delmon (2019), *Mobilising Finance for WASH: getting the foundation right*, Water.org, IRC and The World Bank, http://documents1.worldbank.org/curated/en/725521553154723194/pdf/Mobilising-Finance-for-WASH-Getting-the-Foundation-Right.pdf. [3]

PPIAF (2020), *Non-revenue Water*, https://ppiaf.org/sectors/non-revenue-water. [73]

Reynaud, A. et al. (2016), *Review on International Best Practices on Charges for Water Management*, Toulouse School of Economics. [37]

Streeter, W. (2017), *Financing Water and Sewer Infrastructure in the Developing World*, Taylor & Francis. [7]

Sy, J. and S. Ahmed (2016), "In the market for good practices on performance-based contracts for non-revenue water management", *World Bank Blogs*, https://blogs.worldbank.org/ppps/market-good-practices-performance-based-contracts-non-revenue-water-management (accessed on 2 November 2020). [29]

Trémolet, S. et al. (2019), *Investing in Nature for Europe Water Security*, The Nature Conservancy, Ecologic Institute and ICLEI. London. [51]

UNEP (2019), *Peatlands store twice as much carbon as all the world's forests*, https://www.unep.org/news-and-stories/story/peatlands-store-twice-much-carbon-all-worlds-forests (accessed on 24 March 2021). [53]

United Nations (2018), *World Water Data Initiative - Summary*, Sustainable Development Goals Knowledge Platform, https://sustainabledevelopment.un.org/content/documents/hlpwater/12-WorldWaterData.pdf. [16]

Vermaat, J. et al. (2015), *Assessing the societal benefits of river restoration using the ecosystem services approach*, http://dx.doi.org/10.1007/s10750-015-2482-z. [58]

WMO (2018), *WMO steps up action on water*, https://public.wmo.int/en/media/press-release/wmo-steps-action-water (accessed on 16 November 2020). [18]

World Bank (2017), *Easing the transition to commercial finance for sustainable water and sanitation*, http://documents.worldbank.org/curated/en/182521503466225465/pdf/119048-WP-REPLACEMENT-PUBLIC.pdf. [6]

World Bank (2017), *Implementing nature-based flood protection: Principles and implementation guidance*, http://documents.worldbank.org/curated/en/739421509427698706/pdf/120735-REVISED-PUBLIC-Brochure-Implementing-nature-based-flood-protection-web.pdf. [56]

World Bank and UNICEF (2017), *Sanitation and Water for All: Priority Actions for Sector Financing*, https://www.oecd.org/environment/resources/Session%204%20Sanitation%20and%20water%20for%20all%20-%20priority%20actions%20for%20financing.pdf. [21]

Notes

[1] Relevant data include: the state of water resources (quantity and quality), now and in the future, quality of water supply and sanitation services, exposure and vulnerability to water-related risks.

[2] A recent re-examination of the issue of the affordability of WSS services finds that affordability measures are best delivered through targeted social measures, rather than through the water bill (Leflaive and Hjort, 2020[34]). The most appropriate responses vary according to national and local contexts, and usually combine: a capacity to target households most in need of support; low transaction costs, use of existing data and social programmes; and synergies with water conservation measures. Different tariff structures and levels have differentiated social impacts. See (Leflaive and Hjort, 2020[34]).

[3] For more detail, see e.g. (OECD, 2012[72]); (OECD, 2016[8]).

[4] Securing the revenue streams from these policy instruments for specific purposes requires earmarking. While the earmarking of revenues from environmentally related taxes (e.g. to fund spending on pesticide reduction policies) promote transparency and help garner public support and thereby the political acceptability of the tax, it also bypasses or pre-empts the annual budgets, where departments compete for funds on an equal footing, and creates a precedent for other government agencies to have their own earmarked funds (OECD, 2013[74]).

[5] Non-revenue water can result from physical losses (due to e.g. poor asset quality and/or O&M, lack of leakage control), commercial losses (due to e.g. illegal connections and water theft, under-use of customer water meters, data and monitoring errors) and losses for authorised purposes that are not billed (e.g. for firefighting or certain consumer groups) (PPIAF, 2020[73]). Non-revenue water can be addressed through a range of interventions targeted at the multiple drivers of losses.

[6] Note by Turkey: The information in this document with reference to "Cyprus" relates to the southern part of the Island. There is no single authority representing both Turkish and Greek Cypriot people on the Island. Turkey recognises the Turkish Republic of Northern Cyprus (TRNC). Until a lasting and equitable solution is found within the context of the United Nations, Turkey shall preserve its position concerning the "Cyprus issue". Note by all the European Union Member States of the OECD and the European Union The Republic of Cyprus is recognised by all members of the United Nations with the exception of Turkey. The information in this document relates to the area under the effective control of the Government of the Republic of Cyprus.

[7] More broadly, "water-harmful subsidies" may include the provision of water, power and other relevant services (piped water supply; irrigation water from the public network; drainage of land via collector drainage networks, etc.) at below their real cost (including exemptions and reductions for some users). They also include absolving economic agents from the full charge for their impacts on the water-environment, in terms of water quality or quantity (EAP Task Force, 2013[33]).

[8] See for example, the approach of dynamic adaptive policy pathways (Haasnoot et al., 2013[70]) and the application of this approach to investments under non-stationarity (Haasnoot et al., 2019[71]).

4 Mobilising additional sources of funding and finance

This chapter presents a range of options to mobilise additional sources of funding and financing for water-related investment, by generating revenue streams, reducing investment risks, effectively using intermediaries and making use of blended finance where appropriate. The chapter documents a wide range of financing approaches and specific practical examples to illustrate how they have been applied in distinct contexts. Finally, the chapter reflects on opportunities for adapting and scaling up to new contexts.

There are a range of options to mobilise additional funding and financing for water-related investments. Governments can employ a variety of economic and financial policy instruments to influence the behaviour of individuals, communities and organisations to help achieve water policy goals. These instruments can also help to generate revenues for water management and the delivery of water and sanitation services (discussed in Chapter 3 on the enabling environment). In addition, a broader range of sources of capital can be mobilised.

Public finance is likely to continue to play a central role in financing water-related investments, with concessional finance playing an important role particularly in developing countries. Yet, in light of the constraints on public finance and substantial investment needs, crowding in contributions from a wider range of financiers can help to scale up investment in contexts where there is an attractive risk-return profile.

Encouraging access to commercial finance can strengthen financial discipline of water service providers and promote the development of domestic capital and credit markets. Commercial finance includes public finance (such as sovereign wealth funds or public pension funds) as well as private finance, which seeks market rate returns (OECD, 2019[1]). In the water sector, it ranges from microfinance loans, to larger, long tenor loans to bonds, which can be offered to service providers, local governments, individual users or communities (World Bank, 2017[2]; OECD, 2015[3]). Commercial capital brings with it greater requirements for accountability, reporting and transparency to fulfil due diligence requirements of commercial actors. Private financiers are increasingly interested in investment opportunities with Environmental, Social and Governance (ESG) attributes. Further, mobilising commercial capital can free up public funding that can be reallocated to other uses (World Bank Group, 2016[4]).

In distinction to other sources of funding, commercial finance needs to be repaid. It requires compensation such as repayment at a future date plus remuneration in the form of interest or dividends. While other sources of revenue can close the financing gap, commercial finance can only bridge this gap. (OECD, 2010[5]) Figure 4.1 gives an overview of potential sources of revenue streams for water security, distinguishing between repayable finance and revenues for WSS and water security in broader terms. Repayable finance is broken down between concessional finance (provided by public actors and including a grant element) and commercial finance.

Figure 4.1. Potential sources of revenue streams for water security

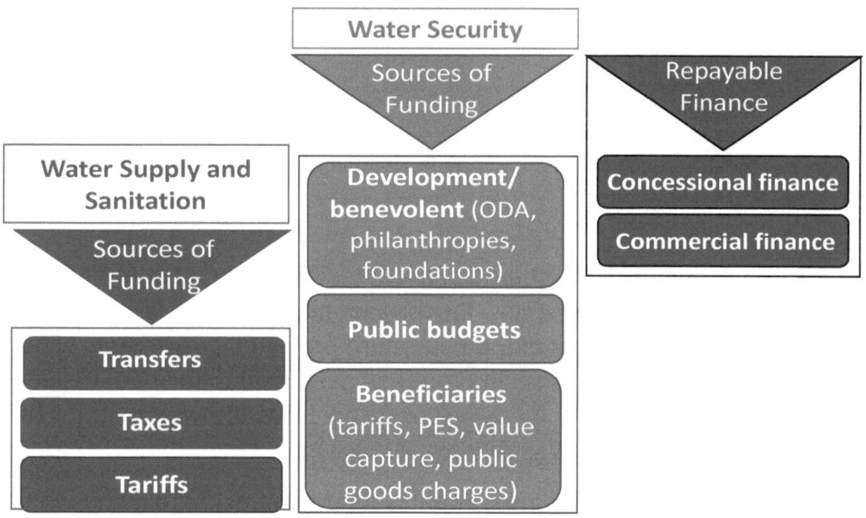

Source: Adapted from (OECD, 2010[5])

To date, commercial finance for the water sector has not reached the scale commensurate with the challenge of bridging the investment gap. In Europe, commercial finance covers only 6% of the total expenditure on WSS (OECD, 2020[6]) and a very minor share of all funding on watersheds investments (Bennett, Leonardi and Ruef, 2017[7]).

Recent OECD analysis (2020[8]) of institutional investment holdings in "green" infrastructure underscore the limited role commercial finance plays in the water sector. The analysis shows that institutional investment in water supply infrastructure accounts for a mere 1.6% of all investment holdings mapped in the analysis (excluding listed stocks). Only USD 17 billion is currently invested in water supply-related assets. As shown in Figure 4.2, the majority of investments are held by pension funds (USD 12 billion). The investment landscape of the sector is also much less diverse in terms of instruments and vehicles used to channel private capital to other infrastructure sectors.

Figure 4.2. Institutional investment in water supply infrastructure (excl. direct investment in stocks) – USD 16.73 million

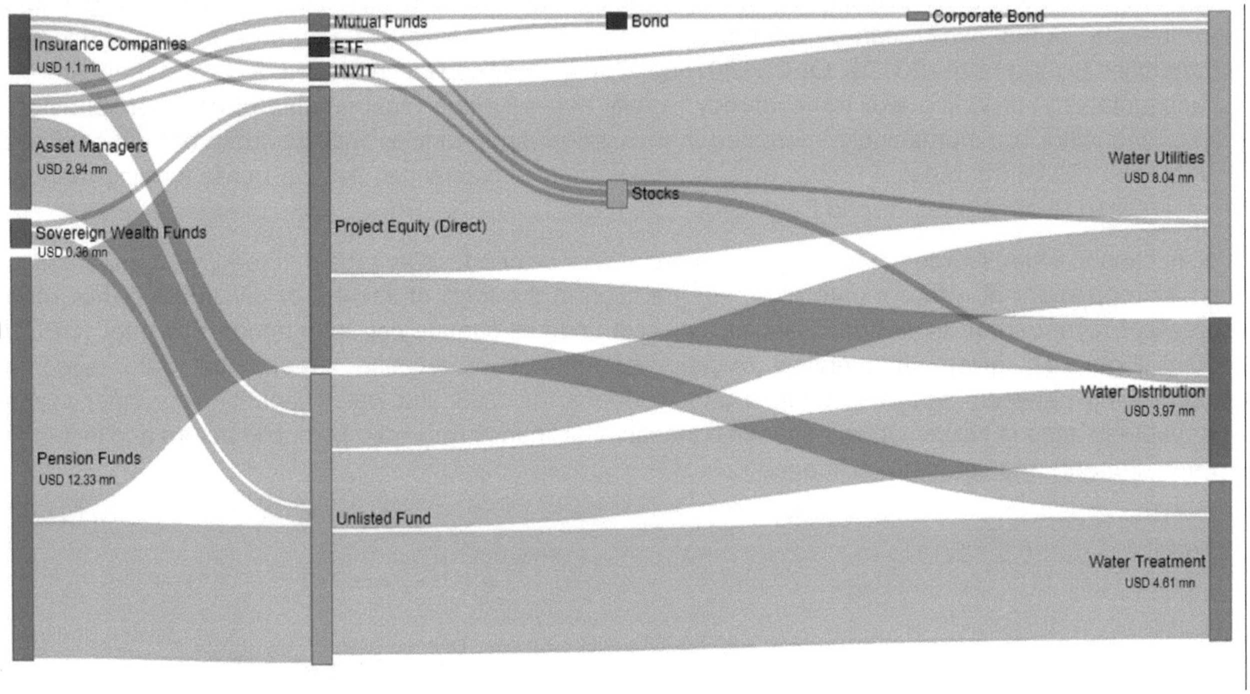

Notes: Holdings of institutional investors domiciled in OECD and G20 countries (as on February 2020). The figure excludes direct stock holdings. Further, while some nodes appear to have unequal left and right sides, this is just a visual effect and they are always balanced.
Source: (OECD, 2020[8])

As discussed in Chapter 2, the distinct characteristics of the water sector pose challenges for the mobilisation of commercial finance. Generally, the engagement of private investors and commercial lenders is determined by the attractiveness of the risk-return profile of investments which depends on two factors: i) a stable revenue stream; and ii) how the range of risks related to water security investments are shared between public and private actors. Investors often perceive the water sector as a 'high risk / low return' sector (OECD, 2018[9]; OECD, 2010[5]; Alaerts, 2019[10]).

Strengthening the enabling environment for investment is fundamental to providing the conditions that can attract commercial finance. In addition, a variety of instruments and approaches can help to address various barriers by securing stable revenue flows from water-related investments and attenuating the different types of risks and unfavourable attributes. Strategically deploying public and development funding along with risk mitigation instruments, such as via blended finance, can help to overcome the hurdles for commercial investment and play a critical role in mobilising additional commercial finance (OECD, 2019[1]).

4.1. Generating revenue streams

Revenue streams fulfil several functions: they (1) cover the costs of service provision, (2) can be a source of capital needed to maintain or enhance asset quality, and (3) provide a means to leverage repayable (commercial) finance. Stable revenues are the main driver of financial sustainability and essential to attain creditworthiness. From the investors' point of view, one main determinant is the creditworthiness of the borrower, which depends on the ability to recover costs and to service their debt obligations. It is therefore essential to create and clearly define predictable revenue flows from water-related investments and to invest in the enhancement of borrowers' creditworthiness. Public funds can be used for investment or technical assistance to improve functionality and performance of service providers, positively affecting their creditworthiness (OECD, 2019[1]). It can also be used to lower the average cost of capital, thereby creating the conditions for financially bankable projects.

The Beneficiary Pays Principle can be applied through raising revenue from actors (water utilities, corporates, property developers, etc.) who benefit from water security investments in their local area. For example, benefits from improved catchment management can be generated for actors operating in the area, through higher turnover, lower expenditures for water treatment or improved quality of their products. By strategically linking these returns to an investment, local actors may have the incentive to provide non-repayable capital in improvements in water resources management that spur such operational benefits. The brewery Heineken, for instance, invests in the Monterrey Metropolitan Water Fund in Mexico and the mineral water companies Vittel-Nestlé and Volvic support farmers with cash or in-kind payments to adopt eco-friendly farming practices (Trémolet, S. et al., 2019[11]; OECD, 2020[6]). Box 4.1 provides further insights into the Water Fund model and other selected country examples.

The Polluter Pays principle can be applied through property rights or marketable permits and thus providing the conditions to mobilise additional revenue flows. One example are environmental offset markets where actors with negative impacts on water resources or ecosystems can buy certificates that provide funding for restoration projects to compensate. The American private investment firm Ecosystem Investment Partners (EIP), for instance, manages investments in large-scale ecosystem restoration and conservation. With committed capital from institutional investors, such as pension funds, they launch projects for flood protection, improving water system operations, etc., which generate credits that can be sold on the environmental offset market. In 2019, EIP had USD 885 million in assets under management and has restored 180 square km of wetlands and over 280 km of streams (EIP, 2020[12]). In Europe, the European Commission is currently elaborating approaches to implement the Polluter Pays Principle, particularly in the context of an extended producer responsibility. As one example, this could translate into chemical companies having to pay for more stringent water treatment.

Whether it is appropriate to apply the Beneficiary Pays Principle vs. the Polluter Pays Principle depends on the particular contextual circumstances and what is considered as the "duty of care" by the relevant actors. The Beneficiary Pays Principle is typically employed when providing an incentive for actors to generate benefits on a voluntary basis additional to what is required by the current regulatory regime. The Polluter Pays Principle is typically applied via a dedicated policy instrument (e.g. an environmental tax) as part of the regulatory regime.

Box 4.1. Payments for freshwater ecosystem services

The Water Fund Model

Water Funds are collective investment vehicles, developed by The Nature Conservancy and the Inter-American Development Bank's (IADB) Latin Water Funds Partnership. They pool grant funding from donors, local communities and commercial actors within the spatial area and basin to finance investments in water security through nature-based solutions. Activities include payments for environmental services, including watershed management and biodiversity conservation, water resource management and adaptation measures to mitigate negative impacts on water resources due to climate change. Water funds offer no direct financial return on investment; instead, the profitability of the capital provision arises from the positive impacts on local actors reliant on water resources. The brewery Heineken, for instance, invests in the Monterrey Metropolitan Water Fund (FAMM) in Mexico, which, to date, has leveraged USD 9.1 million with an implementation area of 1 387 ha. Since the establishment of a first Water Fund in 2000, another 35 funds have been set up in South and North America, Kenya and South Africa. Water Funds are an effective tool to tackle governance failures in multi-stakeholder settings and can mobilise multiple types of funding sources. Yet, development finance remains essential to support the setup of these complex structures that bring together the needs of the various commercial actors as well as the different sources and expectations regarding returns.

Source : (Trémolet, S. et al., 2019[11]; OECD, 2019[1]; Latin American Water Funds Partnership, 2020[13])

Payments for Ecosystem services in France

France launched its Biodiversity Plan in 2018 with a dedicated objective to put in place payments for ecosystem services to protect biodiversity and water quality. With a budget of EUR 150 million over three years, the government undertook a public tender for payments for ecosystem services (PES) pilot projects, which are tested in over 120 regions. The most successful projects will be implemented with a 5-year contract between farmers and beneficiaries such as local communities, associations, national parks, etc. Giving a value to soil conservation practices, water quality and biodiversity restoration can be accompanied with further requirements to limit or stop the use of herbicides, such as glyphosate. These payments schemes are hence a mechanism to recognise farmers' contributions to the creation of direct environmental benefits, which exceed mandatory standards. In addition, French water agencies increased their financial support dedicated to the transition towards an ecological agriculture by EUR 50 million per year starting in 2020.

Source : (Ministère de la transition écologique et solidaire, 2019[14]) (Ministère de la transition écologique et solidaire, 2018[15])

Eco-Compensation Schemes in the People's Republic of China

In 2008, the government of the People's Republic of China (hereafter 'China') has launched an Eco-Compensation pilot for watersheds, in which upstream stakeholders compensate downstream stakeholders for ecological damage and water pollution. The payment for watershed services (PWS) programmes focus on the creation of development zones, emissions trading schemes, water use right trading programs, trans-boundary water pollution programs and water resources conservation zones. The first cross-province PWS pilot program was implemented in the Xin'anjiang River watershed between Anhui and Zhejiang provinces in 2011. Between 2008 and 2016, ecological transfer payments to Key Ecological Function Zones have risen from CNY 6 billion across 230 counties to CNY 80 billion across 700 counties, nationally. While inspired by market-based approaches, the Chinese Eco-Compensation scheme does not entirely match the definition associated with purely market-based PWS projects. Stakeholders are upstream and downstream local governments (rather than private actors) and the schemes are subject to governmental command-and control-measures.

Source: (Lu et al., 2018[16]; Zhang and Bennett, 2011[17]; Cardascia, 2019[18])

4.1.1. Reducing investment risks and sharing risks among stakeholders

Commercial investors are cautious about uncertainty regarding any of the risks related to an investment opportunity. As discussed in Chapter 2, investors are confronted with a range of risks, including business risks (e.g. credit risks), macroeconomic risks (e.g. currency risk), regulatory and political risks (e.g. changing regulations or political unrests), commercial and technical risks (e.g. performance risks for innovative approaches such as NbS). A lack of analytical tools aggravates the challenge to assess and address these risks, lowering the attractiveness of the risk-return profile of water-related investments. Concerns around small ticket sizes and high transaction costs further dampen financiers' appetite to invest in the water sector. Adequate contractual arrangements or blended instruments and mechanisms can mitigate a variety of these risks, share the remainder with the public sector or commercial co-investors, or take a certain level of risk off the financier's own book.

Credit enhancement, including guarantees

Credit enhancements improve the credit profile of structured financial products or transactions. For example, they can be employed to allow existing revenue streams to be used as collateral (OECD, 2019[1]). Traditional loan securitisation or political risk insurance are other instruments making use of public finance to improve the risk-return profile of water-related projects thus unlocking additional sources of finance. (OECD, 2020[6]; World Bank, 2017[2])

Public guarantees are an effective tool to reduce credit risk for commercial investors against non-payment. Public funds can be used strategically to mitigate for financial risks, resulting in lower cost of capital. Structured funds, for example, allow donor governments to use concessional finance in a first loss position to provide a risk cushion for commercial investors. Guarantees can also be applied for political, regulatory, contractual or currency risks. (World Bank Group, 2016[4]; OECD, 2019[1])

The use of guarantees should be carefully assessed in order to ensure that governments and donors do not take on excessive risk in terms of contingent liabilities. Guarantees should also be designed to avoid crowding out private finance. While designing guarantee schemes, donors should pay particular attention to ensuring their financial sustainability. Guarantees should ideally be time-bound, with credible expectations that they will be phased out over time. (Garbacz, Vilalta and Moller, 2021[19])

Pooled financing

Pooled approaches can help overcome the high credit risks and transaction costs of individual small projects by grouping them together. Pooling can bundle multiple water service providers and diversify borrower risk, allowing to tailor different risk and return profiles for individual investors (OECD, 2019[1]). Transaction costs can be shared among participants, enhancing the efficiency of the transaction. Pooling can help to attain scale of investment and thus facilitate access to capital markets or institutional investments (since most institutional investors require significant minimum investment sizes) (Streeter, 2017[20]; OECD, 2010[5]). The collective approach enables the pooled facility to issue bonds and on-lend to service providers, which is particularly relevant for small service providers and decentralised municipalities (World Bank Group, 2016[4]).

Increasing transparency by using performance benchmarking and credit ratings

Credit ratings can raise transparency by providing independent assessment of the financial health of service providers, allowing investors to better assess potential investment risks. Sovereign credit ratings can give investors insights into the level of risk associated with investing in the debt of a particular country, including political risk. Moreover, water-related risks are increasingly recognised as a material factor for credit ratings of corporates. Systematically adjusting future cash flow expectations and valuations of companies for ESG factors, of which water is one, is one way for investors to identify how these water risks may affect company valuations. The recommendations of the Financial Stability Board's Task Force on Climate-related Financial Disclosures (TCFD) are an important initial development in this regard (OECD, 2018[21]).

In light of growing demand, the finance industry is creating more products and services related to ESG ratings, indices, and funds. The number of firms providing ESG ratings have proliferated along with the number of ESG indexes and funds. While ESG methodologies are improving and becoming more transparent, scoring remains in a state of transition. ESG ratings can vary greatly from one ESG provider to another and the different methodologies used to translate raw data into a more sophisticated rating are subject to criticism because of the wide variance in the results. (Boffo and Patalano, 2020[22])

Benchmarking is another important tool to measure and report technical and financial health of operators. For instance, the International Benchmarking Network for Water and Sanitation Utilities (IBNet) provides access to comparative information on core cost and performance indicators of water and sanitation utilities worldwide (IBNet, 2020[23]). Practical examples of the implementation of these instruments are given in the section on the role of blended finance below.

4.1.2. Matching supply and demand for finance: The role of intermediaries

One critical limiting factor for commercial investments is a lack of well-prepared, bankable projects. On the demand side of finance, project developers often lack the skills necessary to support their funding applications with adequate documentation. On the supply side, financiers have limited knowledge of the water sector and there is a lack of financial instruments, which fit the needs of the sector. Public investment in capacity building and technical assistance could increase project developers' ability to design sound business cases, support project preparation and provide guidance on project implementation models or on documentation, including cost-benefit analyses and financial statements.

Intermediary institutions can be set up to better link the interests and capabilities of the water and financing industries (Trémolet, S. et al., 2019[11]; Alaerts, 2019[10]). Grant finance can be channelled through project preparation facilities to support project identification, appraisal and due diligence and piloting (OECD, 2010[5]). Upfront preparation costs traditionally represent 3% of total project costs, but can run as high as 10% (World Bank Group, 2016[4]) and could thus be covered via public funds. Intermediary institutions provide specialised knowledge and expertise and contribute to increasing the number of bankable projects (Cooper and Matthews, 2020[24]; Trémolet, S. et al., 2019[11]). The Dutch-seed funded Water Finance Facility, for instance, initiated the first country facility, the 'Kenya Pooled Water Fund', which was launched in 2018 (van Oppenraaij et al., 2022[25]). Other examples are dedicated, so called 'water banks', such as the Netherlands Water Boards Banks or Natural Capital Finance Facilities (see discussion below).

A recent analysis of the role of intermediaries to facilitate finance for water-related investments documented the wide range of organisations playing various roles at the interface between demand for finance (e.g. water agencies, utilities or other service providers) and supply of finance (e.g. financing institutions) (Lardoux de Pazzis and Muret, 2021[26]). These entities, referred to in the analysis as "intermediaries", include those working upstream on the enabling environment for finance facilitation; transaction advisory supporting partnership development (of which financing is one component), private sector lending windows of donors and international financial institutions, and dedicated financing facilities. These intermediaries play multiple roles along the investment value chain, in various geographies and at various scales (international, national, regional, local).

The analysis identifies and analyses a diverse sample of 52 intermediaries active in deploying one or more key functions across the investment value chain for three specific sub-sectors: utilities, small scale water and sanitation service providers and nature-based solutions. The analysis assesses the extent to which the activities of these intermediaries is aligned with the critical functions needed to mobilise finance across the sub-sectors. It identifies gaps, redundancies and misalignments and calls for a shift from the current opportunistic approach to a more strategic approach in the design and activities of intermediaries, supported by governments and financial institutions. Key findings are summarised below[1].

A constellation of intermediaries playing various roles along the water investment value chain constitutes a striking feature of the water sector

The water sector is characterised by an abundance of players and intermediaries performing a diversity of functions. Understanding the roles and responsibilities of actors within the sector is made difficult by this extraordinary diversity of entities. This has clearly been to the sector's disadvantage when it comes to attracting investors who need to be provided with clarity and perspective, as well as certainty about the alliances needed to set up and manage bankable projects.

The sole provision of financial mechanisms is not sufficient to attract and facilitate water-related investments

The analysis of intermediaries shows that there is an abundance of organisations focused on providing financial mechanisms (e.g. grants, loans, equity, guarantees, collective investment vehicles, etc.) for water-related investments, revealing a strong concentration of activity at the transaction level. At the same time, there is a lack of bankable projects in the sector that can benefit from these financial mechanisms. The strong focus on the transaction level paradoxically leaves both the demand side (e.g. water agencies and service providers) and the supply side (e.g. financiers) underserved.

From the service providers' perspective, this can appear to be a highly fragmented market, resulting in significant transaction costs to identify the relevant intermediaries worth approaching. Moreover, most of the available financing mechanisms do not create incentives towards operational efficiency and improvement for service provides. Such incentives would support efforts to improve the creditworthiness of service providers and their capacity to access finance. Rather, interventions focus on providing viability gap funding and employing de-risking instruments at the transaction level but do not encourage the service providers to achieve higher operational standards. The proliferation of actors focused on providing financing mechanisms at the transaction level also increases competition to facilitate financing, in a context where the number of viable bankable projects remains limited.

A better alignment between the challenges specific to each water sub-sector and the key functions performed by intermediaries is needed

The design and implementation of public policies, investment preparation, and the development of human capital rank amongst priority functions needed to mobilise finance across all water sub-sectors covered in the analysis (e.g. utilities, small scale service providers, and NbS). However, each sub-sector differs in terms of the critical functions needed to facilitate financing due to their distinctive risk-return profiles and the relative maturity in terms of a dedicated track record to access finance. Water utilities are the most mature sub-sector in terms of access to finance, but still face deeply-rooted misperceptions that deter investors, and require strong efforts of business promotion. In contrast, small-scale service providers, and nature-based solutions require a different kind of support from the intermediaries: notably, ensuring that conducive policies and regulation are in place and supporting the coordination amongst multiple local stakeholders and new types of innovative partnerships.

By mapping the functions of intermediaries against the priority activities for each sub-sector, one can clearly observe that many activities identified as critical for a given sub-sector are among those which are rather neglected by the intermediaries reviewed. This observation, combined with the considerable focus of intermediaries on the provision of financing mechanisms, further reinforces the finding that the focus on the transaction level is not well-aligned with the critical need to foster a more conducive business and policy environment to enable water-related investments.

Anchoring the role of intermediaries at the relevant geographic scale is a prerequisite to optimise their intervention

Several examples of intermediaries reviewed in this analysis illustrate how the articulation of functions performed and the geographical scale of intervention can reinforce the relevance of their intervention (for example, in the case of the Cities Development Initiative for Asia (CDIA) and WWF Bankable Water Solutions). A key consideration is the importance of proximity to the local level to provide credibility to the actions of intermediaries who can thus offer solutions better adapted to the needs of the local players and to the characteristics of the local markets. Knowledge of specific local conditions and access to key decision makers is highly valued by investors and financiers.

Intervention at the regional level has the potential to foster economies of scale, while maintaining proximity to activities on the ground. The analysis highlights that greater attention could be placed on interventions at the regional level, which only a small share of the intermediaries reviewed in this sample currently focus on.

Gaps and redundancies in the activities of intermediaries call for a shift to a more strategic approach

Intermediaries' activities are often driven by an opportunistic approach and political agendas, or are simply reflected by the dynamism of water entrepreneurs. There is a need to shift to a more strategic approach in order for intermediaries to address the full range of service providers' and financiers' needs along the investment value chain. The strikingly strong role played by the abundance of non-profit organisations raises the question of how to promote coordinated action in a sector with a highly diversified landscape of actors.

Consideration also needs to be given to ways to enhance the complementarity of intermediaries, the consistency of their interventions and their collective effectiveness to attract domestic and/or foreign finance. In some cases, integration with other intermediaries either horizontally or vertically may be considered. Identifying the missing links and overlaps of the value chain in the local and regional ecosystems is essential. Gaps may be more of a concern than redundancies and initiatives to fill those gaps should be encouraged.

Governments and financial institutions have a role to play

The results of this analysis imply a need to shift from the current opportunistic approach to a more strategic approach, under the direction of governments and in partnership with financial institutions, with primary efforts on transformative changes through strengthening the enabling environment for investment rather than transactional activities.

Key actions include:

- Strengthening the policy, regulatory and institutional frameworks of the sector
- Generating demand for quality services
- Supporting initiatives to fill gaps in the investment value chain currently underserved by intermediaries
- Showcasing the water sector as an opportunity for the private sector to grow business
- Supporting and facilitating transactions with a focus on improving business fundamentals and innovative partnerships.

4.1.3. *Growing interest to align finance with environmental objectives*

Sustainable finance is gaining increasing attention from investors, financial institutions and governments and there is an opportunity for water-related investments to attract financing seeking environmental and social impact. Water-related investments contribute to climate action, notably climate adaptation and resilience, by better managing increasing risks of floods, droughts, water stress and water quality degradation. Further, the water sector can contribute to mitigation efforts, with water-related activities potentially causing over 10% of anthropogenic greenhouse gas emissions (Kerres et al., 2020[27]). Water and wastewater utilities, for example, contribute to 30% to 40% of a municipality's energy use (WaCCliM, 2020[28]). In the United Kingdom, water companies produce almost one third of the country's industrial and waste process emissions (Water UK, 2020[29]). Investments in energy efficiency could therefore be a valuable contribution to CO_2 emission reduction efforts.

In order to tap into the growing demand from investors for sustainable projects, water investments should make visible the range of benefits they deliver, for climate action, biodiversity and the environment generally. At the same time, efforts to avoid "green-washing" or "blue-washing" are imperative.

As noted above, at present, there is no common understanding or harmonised definition of what is considered a green or sustainable investment. While standards or metrics exist, the multiplicity and heterogeneity of definitions is often cited as an important barrier to scaling up sustainable investment. Differences in policies and standards relating to sustainable investments can result in market fragmentation and increased uncertainty, constraining the financing of transition-compatible assets and projects. (OECD, 2020[30]; Och, 2020[31])

Taxonomies for Sustainable Activities

The development of sustainable finance taxonomies can serve to reduce these uncertainties and to define clear metrics and thresholds for what is considered a sustainable project. This could increase investors' confidence and establish market clarity, and thus facilitating the mobilisation and reallocating of financial capital towards sustainability objectives.

Within its Action Plan for Sustainable Finance, the European Union (EU) is currently developing the EU taxonomy, establishing a unified classification system for sustainable economic activities with clearly defined thresholds and legal obligations for financial market participants, large companies, the EU and its member states. The EU taxonomy is unique in its approach to interlink six environmental objectives[2] based on a 'Do No Significant Harm' Principle.

Technical screening criteria define the metrics and thresholds for about 80 economic activities[3]. The screening criteria for the two environmental objectives *Climate Change Mitigation* and *Adaptation* entered into force in January 2022. A delegated act with the detailed criteria for the four remaining objectives will be published in 2022 and enter into force in in January 2023. The Platform on Sustainable Finance has published recommendations for these technical screening criteria in 2021. (European Commission, 2020[32]; European Commission, 2021[33])

Water-related activities under the EU taxonomy

The EU taxonomy explicitly includes water resources as one of the six environmental objectives notably the *Sustainable use of water and marine resources*. Thus, economic activities, which substantially contribute to this objective (while not doing significant harm to any of the other objectives), will be classified as taxonomy-compliant. Eligible activities are, for example, actions that improve water management and efficiency, including by protecting and enhancing the status of aquatic ecosystems or by promoting sustainable water use. Other activities include the protection of human health and of the environment from water pollution.

Further, the sixth environmental objective *Protection and restoration of biodiversity and ecosystems* also encompasses water-related investments, especially linked to nature-based solutions. Eligible activities contribute to the protection, conservation or restoration of biodiversity and ecosystems, and thereby enhancing ecosystem services (European Commission, 2020[32]). Water plays a vital role for the functioning of all of these services and has therefore the potential to make substantial contributions to this target.

Box 4.2 gives an overview of the already elaborated criteria for the objectives *Climate change mitigation* and *Adaption* related to activities in the water sector. More detailed information on EU taxonomy developments in relation to water can be found in the background paper for the 6th Roundtable meeting on Financing Water (OECD, 2020[34]).

Box 4.2. Screening criteria for water-related activities for the environmental objectives *Climate change mitigation* and *Climate change adaptation*

Screening criteria for mitigation

The screening criteria for mitigation related to water include economic activities leading to improved energy efficiency. The renewal of water collection, treatment and supply systems counts as eligible sustainable activities if it (a) lowers the average energy consumption of the system by at least 20% compared to own baseline performance averaged for three years (or by at least 10% for waste water systems), or (b) if it reduces leakage and closes the gap by at least 20% between current leakage level and an Infrastructure Leakage Index (ILI) of 1.5. The construction, extension and operation of water collection, treatment and supply systems are eligible activities, if (a) the leakage level equals to or us lower than 1.5 (ILI), or if (b) the average energy consumption of the system equals to or is lower than 0.5 kWh per cubic meter billed/unbilled authorised water supply. Wastewater (collection and treatment) systems need to demonstrate net zero energy use on an annual basis, in order to be eligible.

Screening criteria for adaptation

Eligible economic activities contributing to climate change adaption implement solutions for a list of climate-related risks, which include floods, sea level rise, droughts, water stress, changing precipitation patterns, temperature variability and permafrost thawing. The adaptation solutions shall favour nature-based solutions or rely on blue or green infrastructure to the extent possible. Non-life insurance related to the underwriting of the listed climate-related perils are also included as sustainable activities.

Adaptation solutions are "monitored and measured against pre-defined indicators and remedial action is considered where those indicators are not met".

Source: (European Commission, 2020[35]; European Commission, 2020[36])

Implications for water-related investments

Investments in water-related projects are often hampered by a lack of experience of investors and financial institutions with the sector as well as both real and perceived risks. By defining water resource management as one of the key environmental objectives, the EU taxonomy raises the water sector's visibility for financial actors and could raise investors' awareness and interest. (OECD, 2020[30]; Schütze et al., 2020[37]) By increasing transparency, the EU taxonomy provides investors with more information on what they are investing in and can reduce reputational risks. This could help to attract more retail, as well as institutional savings into sustainable investment, including water-related investments. (OECD, 2020[30]) For example, a study has shown that currently, only about 5% of the total asset value held by European insurers may be taxonomy-compliant, indicating the possibility for insurers, as major long-term investors, to contribute more significantly to sustainable infrastructure projects (Scholer and Cuesta Barbera, 2020[38]).

One characteristic of water-related projects is the potential to meet several environmental objectives, such as nature-based solutions or integrated watershed management, improving water quality, biodiversity, pollution control at the same time. These projects could gain prominence due to the EU taxonomy or other taxonomies of sustainable finance in other regions that would integrate water-related investments. Such taxonomies may encourage crosscutting investments allowing for multiple environmental improvements. For issuers, the taxonomy provides clear guidance on how to capture environmental performance in specific contexts, and to deal with the challenge of trade-offs between the various environmental objectives. However, in practice, the fragmentation of distinct aspects of water resources management and water and sanitation service delivery across specific taxonomy categories could undermine efforts to take a holistic, systemic approach to financing water-related investments.

Certain water-related investments, such as those delivering new access to water and sanitation services to previously underserved communities, could be classified as contributing primarily to social objectives and falling under the environmental objective of 'sustainable use of water and marine resources' or others. If finance is increasingly channelled towards sustainable investments, it could become challenging to attract funds for these types of water-related investments, if not included in the taxonomy. The Platform on Sustainable Finance is currently working on a possible taxonomy extension on social objectives and specifically recommends the inclusion of services for basic human needs, such as water, including wastewater management (European Commission, 2021[39]; Platform on Sustainable Finance, 2021[40]; Platform on Sustainable Finance, 2021[41]).

Underpinning the **EU Green Bond Standard**, the taxonomy could also scale up water-related investments in the form of green bonds. Currently, the demand for green bonds outstrips the capacity of issuers to identify eligible 'green' projects and assets of financing. The EU taxonomy provides clear and standardised requirements for eligible projects and could thus reduce related cost, time and effort (OECD, 2020[30]). It could hence improve the market's ability to identify new projects and widens the range of eligible activities, including water-related activities (TEG, 2019[42]). When demonstrating taxonomy-alignment, water-related projects could raise funds on the green bond market, opening up opportunities for new investors and scaling up sources of finance. Yet, the impact of the EU Green Bond Standard on the water sector's representation on the green bond market could remain limited, without efforts to develop investment opportunities with an attractive risk-return profile and to pool smaller-scale investments.

A disadvantage of the taxonomy and its linked initiatives could be the required reporting procedures that could be complex, burdensome and costly for issuers and investors. It could be difficult for financial market participants and corporates to demonstrate multi-criteria compliance and can hence involve significant time and costs. Data gaps could create an additional burden and could hamper the use of the taxonomy. (OECD, 2020[30]; Och, 2020[31]) It would hence be crucial for the water sector, that project developers are able to provide relevant data and to demonstrate compliance with the taxonomy at reasonable cost. Public funds could be used to support water utilities and other project developers with technical assistance to develop bankable and taxonomy-aligned projects.

International outreach and other sustainable finance taxonomies

Other sustainable finance taxonomies have been developed in various regional and national contexts. China, for example, has developed frameworks for a 'green industry', 'green lending' and 'green credit and green bonds', usually referred to as the Chinese taxonomy. The latter contains detailed criteria and thresholds for its six objectives, which contain the water-related categories 'Water saving and unconventional water use' under the broader objective *Resource conservation and recycling*, and 'Natural ecological protection', 'Ecological agriculture' and 'Disaster control' under the objective *Ecological protection and climate change adaptation* (OECD, 2020[30]). Other examples stem from Japan, which published an updated Green Bond Guideline in 2020, Colombia, which started the development of a green taxonomy, or the ASEAN region with its ASEAN Green, Social and Sustainable Bond Standards. (IPSF, 2020[43])

Overall, patchy global standards could be a hurdle to joint financing efforts of large-scale projects, such as water-related investments, and could deter investors from taking on multilateral or cross-border projects (Anthony, Yuan and Xia, 2021[44]). Further, as financial markets are global in nature, investors seeking to build portfolios of sustainable investments need to have confidence that standards across jurisdictions are sufficiently comparable. The International Platform on Sustainable Finance, composed of experts from both the public and private sector, strives to compare, harmonise and develop and update the different initiatives and frameworks. Stakeholder engagement, including from the water sector, is encouraged and vital in order to help shaping the taxonomy frameworks in an effective way.

4.1.4. The role of blended finance: Illustrations from developing countries

Concessional finance is playing an important role in developing countries to help finance investments in water security in developing countries. However, development finance flows, and particularly concessional finance flows, are not sufficient to address total financing needs and achieve the 2030 Agenda for Sustainable Development. (OECD, 2019[1])

Development finance can be used strategically to blend in additional commercial finance. Blended approaches aim at mobilising additional capital for investments for sustainable development in developing countries and can act as risk-reducing mechanism to increase lenders' confidence. By deploying development finance in a way that addresses investment barriers preventing commercial actors from providing capital in SDG-relevant sectors, such as water and sanitation, blended finance operates as a market building instrument. It can thus provide a bridge from reliance on grant and other donor finance towards commercial finance. Similar approaches to use public funding strategically to mobilise commercial finance for water investments are also relevant in OECD countries, as are the use of blended finance instruments and mechanisms to de-risk investments. This section focuses on the developing country context.

Blended finance can help shift funds that are currently not directed to sustainable development to countries and sectors that have significant investment needs in order to deliver on the SDGs. Beyond addressing a financing gap, blended finance should aim to have a transitory nature, designed to enable stand-alone commercial investment in the long-run, by providing confidence, capacities and track record in markets where commercial investors are not yet present. To date, the use of blended finance models for water-related investments remains limited. Only USD 2.1 billion out of USD 157.2 billion mobilised through official development finance from 2012-2017 globally went to the WSS sector. This 1.36% share of private finance mobilised compared to the overall sample reveals the limited attractiveness of the sector to commercial investors. The banking and financial services, energy, industry, mining and construction sectors mobilised over 18 times the amount mobilised in the water and sanitation sector from 2012-17; mobilisation in agriculture was over twice as much (OECD, 2019[1]). Recent data from 2016-18 confirm this trend, with the WSS sector accounting for only 1% of commercial finance mobilised by development finance (Figure 4.3.).

In terms of instruments, between 2012 and 2017, blended finance instruments differed depending on the sector. Guarantees, for example, mobilised 58% of the private finance in the WSS sector, while only 40% in all other sectors; syndicated loans mobilised 29% for WSS and 17% for the other sectors. Direct investment represented 17% of the private investment mobilised in all other sectors, comparative to 7% mobilised in the WSS sector (OECD, 2019[1]). Direct investment in companies or special purpose vehicles (SPVs) accounted for the majority of commercial finance mobilised for WSS (69%) over the 2016-18 period (Figure 4.3).

Figure 4.3. Blended Finance by Selected Sector 2016-18

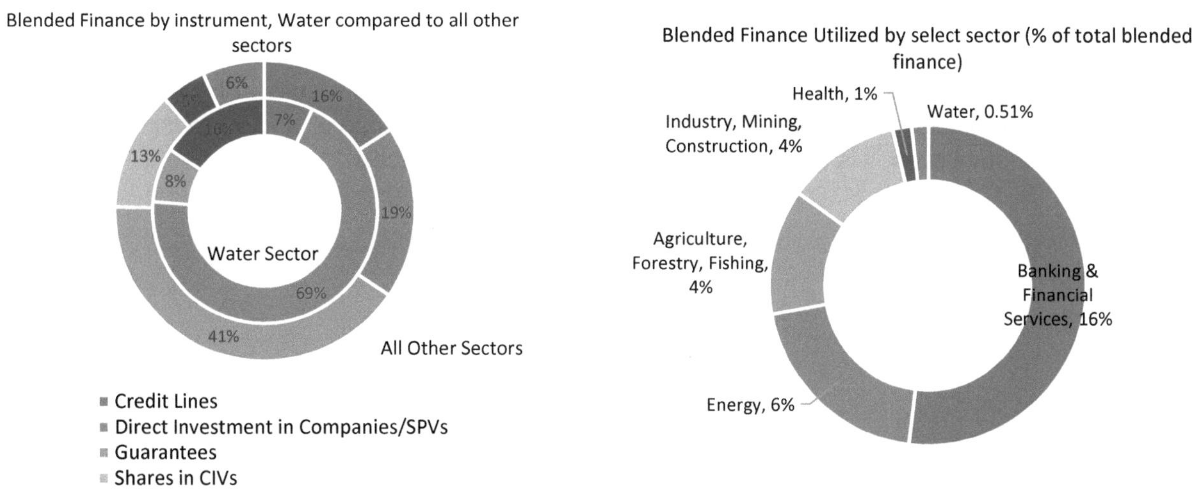

Note: In the left figure, the percentages are of all blended finance from 2016 to 2018; we excluded the largest sector "unallocated/unspecified 66%" to better show the selected sectors in context. In the right figure, "All Other Sectors" includes unallocated/unspecified and all remaining sectors

Source: Authors, based on OECD DAC data on amounts mobilised from the private sector by official development finance interventions: https://www.oecd.org/dac/financing-sustainable-development/development-finance-standards/mobilisation.htm

The fact that water and sanitation services are locally sourced and provided, and flood risks and irrigation best managed at a basin scale, makes it vital to closely cooperate with local actors and to align with local development needs. This also helps avoid excessive reliance on concessional finance and to avoid crowding out commercial finance by creating market distortions and undermining financial sustainability of the sector. Further, blended finance should be designed in conjunction with efforts to improve the enabling environment for commercial investments. Due to the public good dimension of water services and the common pool feature of water resources, the water sector requires strong regulatory and policy frameworks and robust allocation regimes (see Chapter 3 on the enabling environment). Yet, in developing countries, the water sector often faces a weak enabling environment with absent regulations or insufficient enforcement. Blended finance cannot compensate for an unfavourable enabling environment, but rather needs to be accompanied by efforts to promote a stable and conducive policy environment.

A diagnostic tool to assess the readiness for blended finance at country level

Blended finance is a relevant structuring instrument for projects that are either bankable or near-bankable. In the case of near-bankable projects, blended finance can play an enabling role – for example in underwriting credit risks for projects that lack collateral. However, many projects that are deemed bankable (i.e. that could be financed on market-based terms) are unable to attract financing because of the lack of domestic liquidity or capital availability. As a consequence, blended finance is necessary despite a project's viability for market-based finance. To the extent that this lack of domestic liquidity is due to risks related to the specific country context or weakness in the enabling environment (as distinct from the specific project), then reducing those risks and perceptions of risk should pave the way for greater uptake of commercial finance (Money, forthcoming[45]).

Blended finance can be applied as a structuring instrument to achieve one of two objectives: to reduce the perceived risk of a project, relative to its expected return; or to enhance the expected return of a project, relative to its perceived risk (Figure 4.4). In practice, most blended finance transactions are oriented towards the reduction of risk. These risks are heterogeneous in nature and vary in salience from one country to another. As set out in (Money, forthcoming[45]), the *perception* of these risks is also heterogeneous, depending on the actor and their motivations and incentives to act. Understanding these perceptions, and how they vary within and across countries and among relevant actors provides valuable insight in assessing the "readiness" for blended finance at country level and tailoring the blended finance approach to address specific local conditions. Reducing risk perceptions results in lowering the average cost of capital for projects. In the case of water, where revenues are scarce, and increasing returns may harm affordability objectives, it is an avenue to unlock access to finance.

Figure 4.4. Application of blended finance to reduce risk or enhance return

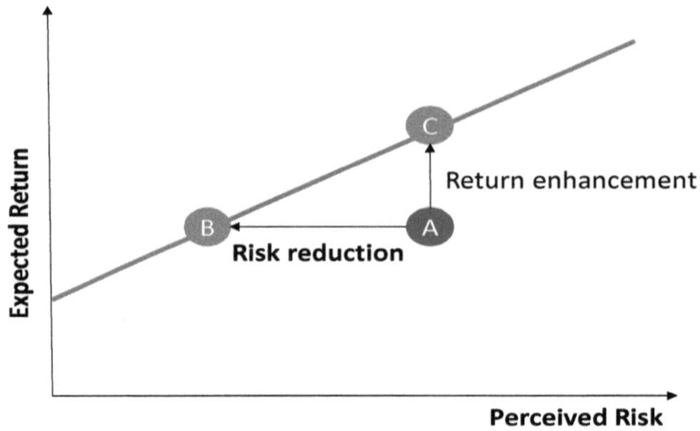

Note: Shifting from point A towards point B reduces risk to achieve bankability; shifting from point A towards point C enhances returns to achieve bankability.
Source: (Money, forthcoming[45])

To gather empirical data on perceived risks an indicator scorecard has been designed to collect data from a range of financial actors (see Money (forthcoming[45]) for further details on the rationale and approach). The indicators are grouped in three categories: liquidity, bankability and capacity. Liquidity refers to the availability of capital in the amount, denomination, duration and cost that is necessary for the viability of blended finance. Bankability refers to the availability of projects that could be financed on market terms, and considers inter alia creditworthiness, performance, resilience, sustainability and growth prospects. Capacity refers to the institutional, regulatory, policy, market and human capacity requirements that need to be met for blended finance projects to be implemented. The indicators are presented as a series of statements against which respondents provide a score based on a Linkert scale.[4]

To apply the scorecard in a practical way, data would be collected and consolidated by relevant respondent categories. In the context of a national policy dialogue on financing water, the results could inform discussions between policy makers, development partners and financial market actors to target elements where strengthening the enabling environment is required. It could also inform the tailoring of blended finance instruments to the local context. Updated on a periodic basis, the scorecard could provide a longitudinal marker of changing risk perceptions regarding readiness for blended finance across a range of countries. (Money, forthcoming[45])

Blended finance instruments and practical examples

The following section will discuss different blended finance instruments in various contexts, such as large investments in water supply and sanitation, multi-purpose water infrastructure and micro-finance for off-grid sanitation or small-scale irrigation investments.

Guarantees

Guarantees are the most commonly used credit enhancing tool in the blended financing of water and sanitation utilities. The Philippine Water Revolving Fund, for example, had a primary and secondary guarantee in place, the former granted by the private Local Government Unit Guarantee Cooperation (LGUGC), covering a maximum of 85% of the bank's exposure, backed by the second guarantee from the USAID Development Credit Authority (up to 50% of the LGUGC's exposure). (OECD, 2019[1])

Another example is the AGRI3 Fund, a blended finance structure aiming to catalyse private finance for sustainable agriculture, reforestation, CO_2 reduction and improvement of rural livelihoods. Launched in 2020 as partnership between Rabobank and UNEP, The Sustainable Trade Initiative IDH and the Dutch Entrepreneurial Development Bank FMO, the AGRI3 Fund aims at de-risking commercial loans by providing guarantees and thus unlocking at least USD 1 billion. The fund is composed of a USD 250 million guarantee 'Finance Fund', to which Rabobank and the Dutch Government have each committed USD 40 million, and a USD 50 million 'Technical Assistance Facility', managed by IDH. The fund targets guarantees of between USD 2 and 15 million to enable projects between USD 5 and 25 million, with tenors up to 12 years. Lower amounts are possible for initial project stages, if they are scalable that full implementation leads to commitment in the target range (IDH, 2020[46]). Figure 4.5 visualises the different components and financing structure of the AGRI3 Fund.

Figure 4.5. The AGRI3 Fund structure

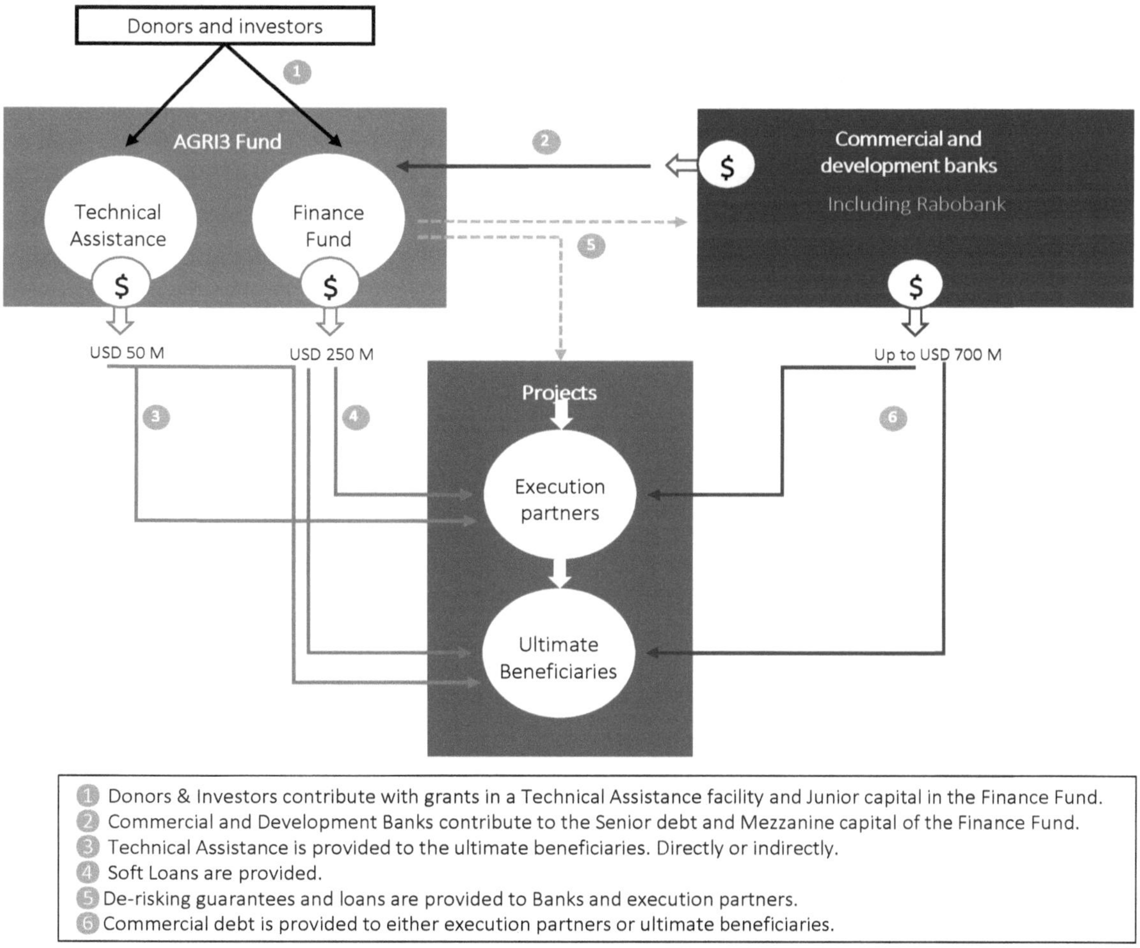

Source: Authors, adapted from IDH (2021), *AGRI3 Fund Technical Assistance Facility, Financing Structure of the Fund.*, https://www.idhsustainabletrade.com/landscapes/agri3-fund/.

Credit enhancements

In Jamaica, the Jamaica Credit Enhancement Facility placed an USD 3 million grant from the Global Environment Facility-funded Caribbean Regional Fund of Wastewater Management project (CReW) in a reserve account as a guaranteed fund, and, with a 4:1 leverage of financial resources, allowed the fund to provide a secondary collateral against the USD 12 million loans from the National Bank to the national water and sanitation utility of Jamaica. (OECD, 2019[1])

In Chile, the National Irrigation Commission manages a cost-share grant programme to support small-scale initiatives for irrigation development and management. Small and medium sized owners can complement their investments in irrigation and drainage projects for community or individual works with public grants. Small producers who benefit from the Agricultural Development Institute can receive financing of up to 90%, and small farmer organisations up to 70% of total costs (Panez, Roose and Faúndez, 2020[47]). Since the according law entered into force in 1986, about 23 000 farmers have benefitted from the program, which contributed to develop irrigation on 200 000 ha, including a growing number of small farmers over time. The programme also enabled 500 000 beneficiaries to shift to pressurised irrigation, representing a total area of 325 000 ha. (Gruère, Ashley and Cadilhon, 2018[48]).

Investment funds or collective investment vehicles

Pooling mechanisms can use different types of instruments, including equity, debt or guarantees to invest in specific sectors or regions. Figure 4.6 illustrates the example of the USD 230 million Philippine Water Revolving fund (PWRF), which aims at sharing risk-return profiles, lowering borrower costs and marketing water and sanitation projects to private finance institutions. With a concessional loan from JICA, the Development Bank of the Philippines (DBP) blends public funds with commercial financing from finance institutions at a 75%-25% ratio from each source respectively. The PWRF revolves principal repayments on the loans, while interest payments are used to service the blended finance from DBP and local banks. A credit line is set up by DBP to mitigate the liquidity risks of the banks involved, which they can use to disburse their share of the blended loans.

Figure 4.6. The Philippine Water Revolving Fund financing structure

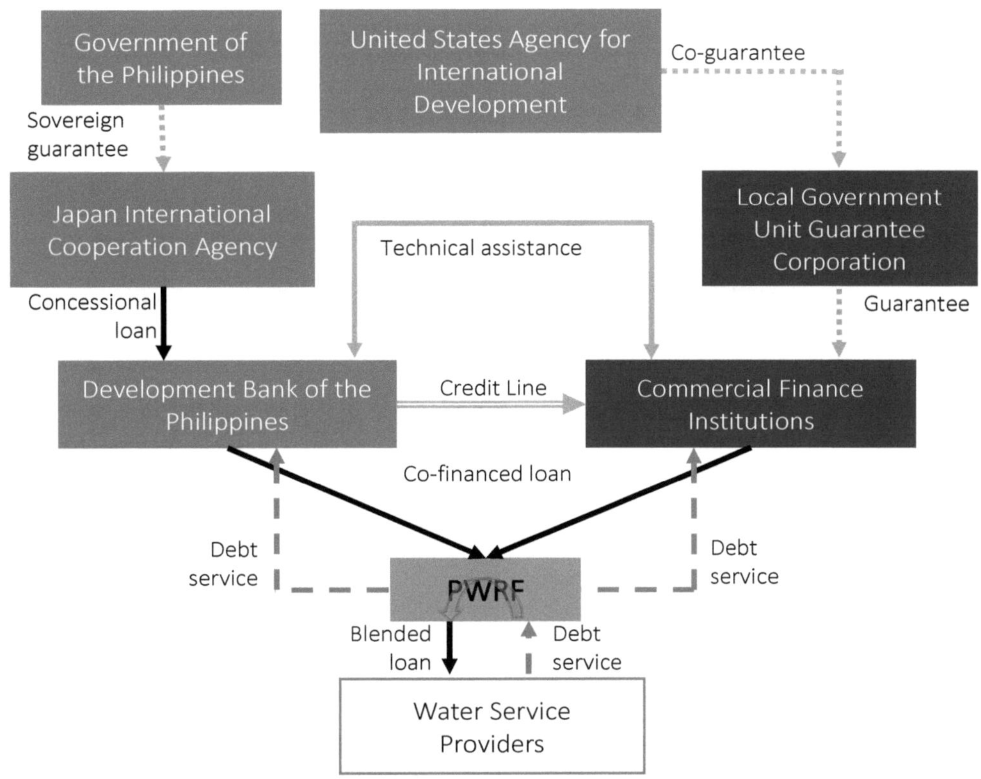

Source: (OECD, 2019[1])

The Dutch Fund for Climate and Development (DFCD) is another blended finance fund which aims at mobilising private sector investment in projects related to climate adaption and mitigation in developing countries. It seeks high impact investments to protect and enhance the health of critical ecosystems and increase communities' resilience to climate change and extreme weather events. The fund is managed by a pioneering consortium of Climate Fund Managers (CFM), the World Wildlife Fund (WWF), SNV Netherlands Development Organisation and is led by the Dutch Entrepreneurial Development Bank, FMO. It is funded by Netherlands Ministry for Foreign Affairs with a total value of EUR 160 and will run until 2037. Its structure consists of three separate but operationally linked facilities with specific sub-sector focusses and roles across the project lifecycles: (i) The Origination Facility, (ii) the Land-use Facility and (iii) the Water Facility, which is led by Climate Fund Managers. The latter aims at financing investments in WSS, restoration and sustainable and climate-resilient management of wetlands, headwaters and floodplains and ocean infrastructure. The Water Facility Structure, called "Climate Investor 2", consists of three financing elements, a EUR 50 million Development Fund, a EUR 500 million Construction Equity Fund and a EUR 500 million Refinancing Fund. Tailored investment instruments allow investors to participate in specific project stages to meet their preferred risk-return requirements. Project developers benefit from continuous access to capital at different stages of the project. Figure 4.7 gives an overview of this financing structure. A total of EUR 75 million of DFCD's EUR 160 million will be allocated to the Water Facility to be deployed in about 30 projects, currently operating in 12 different countries. (DFCD, 2021[49]; SNV, 2021[50]; CFM, 2021[51])

Figure 4.7. The Dutch Fund for Climate and Development financing structure

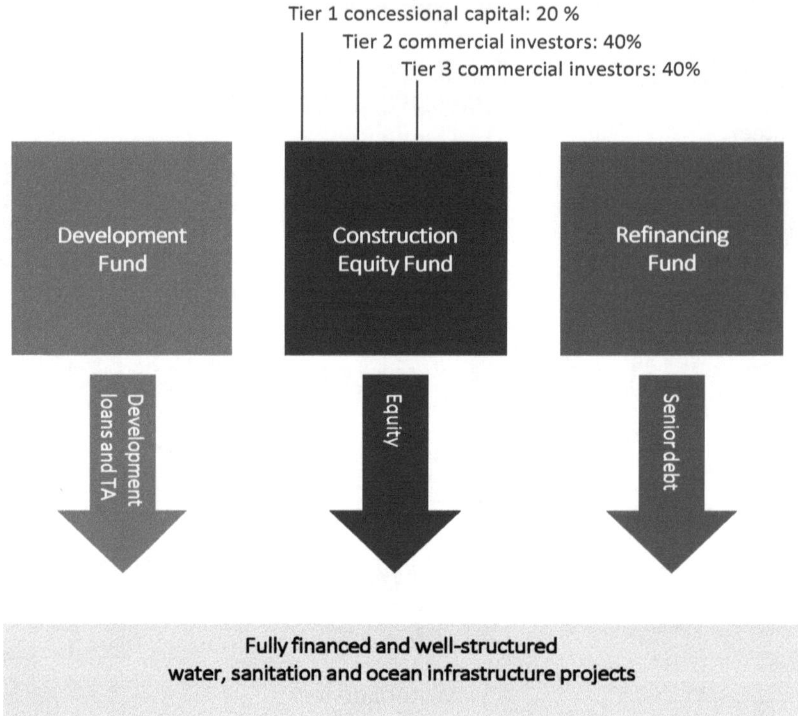

Note: Refinancing Fund to be launched.
Source: Authors, adapted from *Presentation, Seventh Roundtable on Financing Water, Aart Mulder*. https://www.slideshare.net/OECD_ENV/presentation-seventh-roundtable-on-financing-agricultural-water-aart-mulder.

Micro-finance

Small-scale off-grid sanitation, wastewater treatment on the household level and irrigation on the small-scale farm-level are less appealing from a commercial investment perspective due to limited capital absorption capacity and higher risk due to partially unproven technology. Micro-finance can help overcome this barrier and can enable households and individual farmers to access loans and to self-finance water-related investments.

With an USD 240 000 grant by Water.org, Gramalaya in India established the microfinance institution Gramalaya Urban and Rural Development Initiatives and Network (GUARDIAN), which focuses solely on water and sanitation engaging in micro lending to households to support the purchase of water and sanitation assets at a household level such as toilet construction, rainwater harvesting equipment and household purifiers. With the grant funding from water.org, GURARIDAN mobilised commercial financing from a local pubic-sector bank, and Indian Overseas Bank and social investors Acumen and Milaap (Share, 2012[52]).

The Philippine example of technical advisory services and loans helped small-scale farmers to access finance for irrigation and water management investments. The thrift CARD SME Bank partnered with the International Finance Corporation (IFC) and designed an agro-finance strategy, trained loan officers on credit assessment in the sector and developed a credit scoring tool to assess viability of each crop and to understand production cycles. Linking the repayment schedule to the production cycle minimized repayment risks, and overall loan disbursement and the number of client farmers grew substantially. After a successful pilot phase, IFC provided a seven-year concessional loan package at competitive market rates to CARD SME Bank in 2016. The proceeds of the loan were blended with CARD SME Bank funds and disbursed to client farmers, tailored to their needs. Loans would range from between three months to three years with volumes between about 500 and 85 000 EUR and are accompanied by advisory services enhancing farmers' awareness of new technology, innovations and production and marketing strategies. With this approach, CARD SME Bank's loan disbursement rose by 241% between 2016 and 2017 to reach underserved small-scale farmers and agribusinesses. With this new access to finance, farmers were able to expand production, input supply, and transportation and to improve their income. (SAFIN IDB, n.d.[53]).

Special Purpose Vehicles

Special Purpose Vehicles (SPVs) can be used to finance multipurpose water infrastructure (MPWI) and landscape-based approaches, which refer to investments that deliver multiple water-related benefits and which can include cross-sectoral benefits such as energy production, agriculture and biodiversity conservation. Traditionally, MPWI are large-size projects with a great heterogeneity of project characteristics.

SPVs are typically owned by a consortium of project sponsors that can raise further debt funding if needed. Projects with a power element, such as hydropower production, can help generating clearly defined revenue streams and are thus especially valued by commercial investors. For example, the Nam Theun 2 power station in Laos is funded via power purchase agreement between the Electricity Generating Authority of Thailand and Électricité du Laos, a state owned utility. In this case, off-taker or counterparty risk is driven by the public sector's ability to honour contractual obligations.

Blended finance instruments for multi-purpose water infrastructure

Blended finance instruments for multi-purpose water infrastructure include equity and debt, guarantees to mitigate risk for commercial financiers and grant funding to bridge investment gaps with the ambition to mobilise commercial financing from local and international financial institutions. In the case of the Nam Theun 2 project in Thailand, direct investment in project finance vehicles via loans and equity were used strategically, leading to a share of 85% of commercial finance in the USD 1 300 million project costs. Figure 4.8 shows a simplified structure of the Nam Theun 2 financing scheme in which a total of 27 institutions including MDBs, DFIs, Export Credit Agencies and Thai Banks were involved. The state-run business Lao Holding State Enterprise owns the SPC Nam Theun 2 Power Company and has raised a combination of debt (e.g. AFD, EIB and ADB) and grant funding (AFD, World Bank's IDA) in both LCY and USD, which overall reduces the currency volatility risk for the project company.

In Jordan, for example, the viability gap grant funding of USD 93 million from the Millennium Challenge Corporation (MCC) and a USD 20 million grant from the national government allowed to leverage an additional USD 110 million from the private financiers for the expansion of the As-Samara wastewater treatment plant.

Figure 4.8. A simplified Nam Theun 2 financing scheme

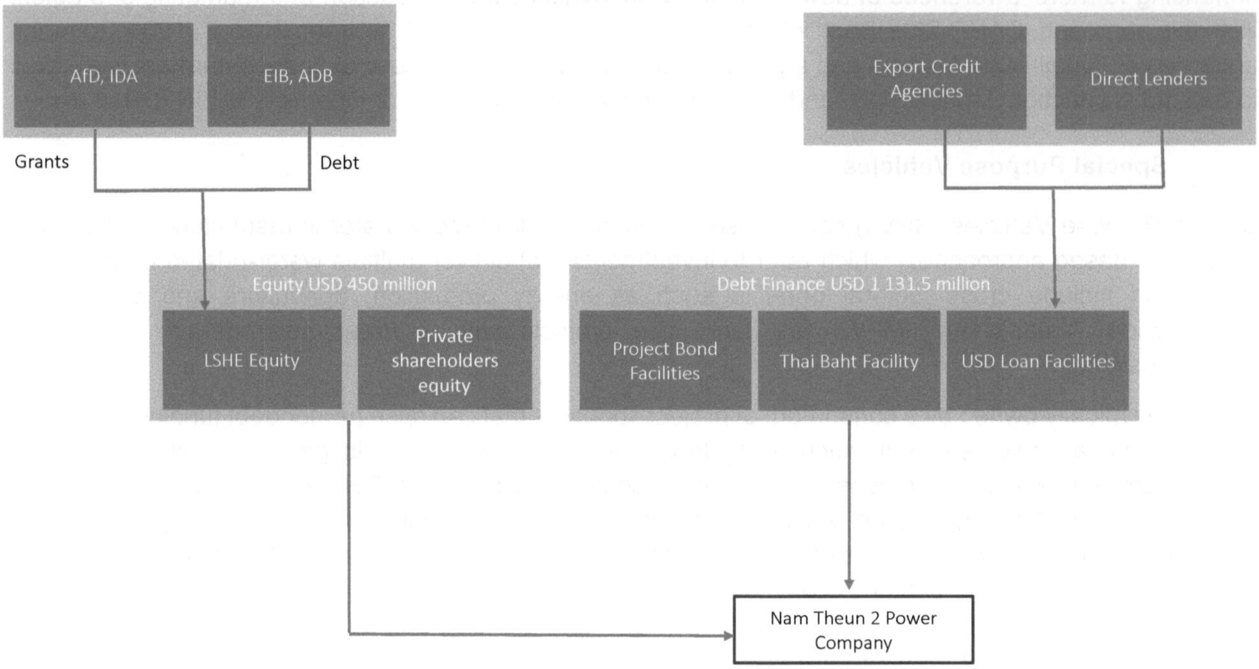

Source: (OECD, 2019[1])

Technical assistance

Technical assistance plays a key role for successful project development and implementation and can boost investors' confidence at multiple levels. Technical assistance is an integral part of blended finance arrangement and can be provided in kind or through grants. In the project preparation phase, technical assistance can come in the shape of policy advice to local government institutions, such as in Rwanda for the structuring of the newly established national water and sanitation utility WASAC, ensuring a successful off-take of the wastewater treatment plant from the Kigali Water Limited company when the Build-Operate Transfer agreement expires (OECD, 2019[1]).

Technical assistance for project development is especially relevant for MPWI projects, given their long preparation and financing tenors, making them vulnerable to changing circumstances. For landscape-based approaches, mechanisms which mobilise and bring together local actors with a stake in improved resources management across the value chain can help materialise explicit and implicit revenue streams. One example are Water Funds, described in more detail in Box 4.1.

4.2. Tailored financing vehicles and approaches to create opportunities for scaling up investment

Private investors and particularly institutional investors are increasingly looking for opportunities to grow their sustainable finance portfolios but often lack adequate financial products to channel their investments (Trémolet, S. et al., 2019[11]; OECD, 2020[30]). They require appropriate investment vehicles that satisfy fiduciary requirements and provide investment opportunities at scale. Appropriate vehicles for water-related investments would account for and help overcome the specificities of the water sector, such as the need for long tenors, small ticket sizes, limited creditworthiness and the lack of clearly defined revenue streams. The following section presents different financing vehicles in various contexts and different types of water-related investments.

4.2.1. Use-of-proceeds bonds

Bonds are a fixed income financial instrument to raise capital from investors through the debt capital market. The bond issuer raises a fixed amount of capital from investors, which is payed back after a specific time period with an agreed amount of interest. Bond finance can facilitate the flow of capital for water-related investments with clearly defined revenue streams. Bonds with long tenors, typical of the water sector, can attract institutional investors such as pension funds. Traditionally, bonds have been the asset class favoured by OECD pension funds and insurance companies, which in 2018 invested on average 45% and more than 50% of their portfolio respectively in bonds and bills (OECD, 2019[54]; OECD, 2020[55]). Investors increasingly show interest in use-of-proceed bonds, whose proceeds are earmarked for particular projects and purposes and which need to meet specified standards, concerning for instance social responsibility or sustainable development.

Green Bonds

One example for use-of-proceeds bonds are green bonds which are designated as "green" by the issuer or another entity, whereby a commitment is made to use the proceeds in a transparent manner, and exclusively to finance or refinance green projects, assets or business activities with an environmental benefit. Since the first green bond has been launched in 2007, issuance has been growing steadily up to cumulative USD 1.4 trillion by 2021. More than USD 350 billion have been issued globally in the first three quarters of 2021, the biggest shares coming from Germany and the United States (CBI, 2021[56]). Looking at sectors, the majority of proceeds were used for investments for energy and buildings and only 9% fell to the water sector in 2019 (CBI, 2020[57]). Reasons for this relatively small share are some clear limitations for certain water-related investments. Generally, bonds are largely used as refinancing instruments while project bonds only represent 1% of total bond market (and less than 50% of the green bond market) (TEG, 2020[58]). Further, green bonds are mostly accessible to large-scale, creditworthy issuers, who can provide clear revenue streams associated with their repayment, which can be challenging especially for landscape-based approaches or investments on water resource management. The international bond market prefers large minimum sizes (EUR 300 to 500 million), rendering it difficult for small- and medium-sized companies or municipalities (often the case for water utilities) to get access to bond finance (TEG, 2020[58]). In this context, an important role falls to intermediaries, working to pool small and medium sized demands for financing, facilitating access to bond finance.

One example of green bond issuance for the water sector is **Anglian Water**, the first utility company in the United Kingdom to issue a green bond in 2017, having raised GBP 830 million in green bonds since then. The company finances projects for water abstraction, water resource management and drought and flood resilience schemes and has segmented its investment plan into 12 categories according to their green and social characteristics. This allows the bank to tap into diverse pools of investors with different priorities for financial, social and environmental returns. The debt raised by the bank through UK-registered companies, is listed on the London stock exchange, their first year bond will mature in 2025 with a return to investors of 1.625 per cent (Anglian Water, 2020[59]; Trémolet, S. et al., 2019[11]).

Sustainability Awareness Bonds

Similar to green bonds, the European Investment Bank (EIB) has launched Sustainability Awareness Bonds (SABs) to raise debt financing focused in particular on water-related projects. Water supply, sanitation and flood protection projects, which contribute to four defined sustainability objectives[5], can raise funds through this bond. While SABs attract sustainably responsible investors, they offer beneficial loan conditions, such as long maturity and low interest rates, for project developers. In 2018, the EIB issued its first EUR 500 million SAB, followed by another USD 1 billion global SAB in May 2020 (EIB, 2020[60]).

One example is the Emscher rehabilitation project in Germany, one of Europe's largest environmental projects. EUR 450 million of the EUR 1 250 million total costs are provided through SAB. In addition to its large volume, the loan has a long maturity of up to 45 years and interest rates can be fixed, allowing to benefit from current low interest rates. The project concerns the restructuring of a regional wastewater system and the restoration of the Emscher river bed, resulting in both social and environmental benefits and the creation of natural and recreational space (EIB, 2017[61]).

Another project financed via SAB bonds is the Dhaka Environmentally Sustainable Water Supply project in Bangladesh. It aims at developing a new sustainable surface water resource to help covering the increasing water demand. Additionally, it will enable to reduce extraction from over-exploited groundwater resources and thus improve the city's resilience to adverse impacts form climate change. EUR 100 million of the EUR 493 million project costs will be covered via SAB bonds, directed to the Bangladesh Ministry of finance, which will on-lend to the Dhaka Water Supply and Sewerage Authority. The procurement for the different project components will be carried out according to ADB guidelines, and the operation will be covered by the EU Guarantee for EIB loans outside the EU. (EIB, 2013[62])

Environmental Impact Bonds

Environmental impact bonds are pay-for-success financing structures, where private actors' pre-finance investments in environmental improvements and public funders commit to reimbursing them, when specific environmental outcomes have been met. They allow to transfer performance risk to investors, which lightens the burden on public funds and can increase efficiency. Environmental Impact Bonds can be the financial vehicle for green infrastructure, smart sewer and storm water infrastructure and coastal wetlands restoration (Trémolet, S. et al., 2019[11]). The first Environmental Impact Bond was launched in October 2016 by DC Water in Washington to reduce storm wastewater runoff by replacing one water runoff tunnel with large-scale green infrastructure, an approach which by then had not been deployed at scale. The USD 25 million bond was sold to the impact investors Goldman Sachs Urban Investment Group and Calvert Impact Capital, with a three tired structure, based on three possible outcomes: for 'as-expected performance', no extra payments will be paid, in case of 'over-performance', DC Water will make an outcome payment to the investors of USD 3.3 million and in case of 'under-performance', the investors will make a risk share payment of that same amount to DC Water. (Goldman Sachs, n.d.[63])

Environmental impact bonds help to attract investors who wish to align their financial returns with positive environmental impact and, by having a strong focus on outcomes, can help building a broader evidence base and inform future planning.

4.2.2. Special purpose vehicles to overcome the small-scale nature of water authorities

As mentioned earlier, different types of green bonds are mostly accessible for large-scale projects with stable revenue streams, while small-scale projects might face difficulties to raise debt financing. The Italian example of "hydrobonds" is a tool to mitigate the fragmented and small-scale nature of Italian water authorities. In 2014, eight water utilities in the Veneto Region (owned by the Viveracqua Consortium) side-stepped the bank loan market and accessed the capital markets by creating mini-bonds which were then pooled to form the so-called "hydrobonds". A special purpose vehicle[6] was created and fully subscribed to these bonds (see Figure 4.9). This tool enabled the aggregation of small scale needs of a number of players to then be put on the market concertedly. The bonds were structured and bought by the EIB and other financial institutions, allowing the small-scale water suppliers in the Veneto region to raise EUR 500 million for capital expenditure (Rees, 2018[64]; Gatti, 2018[65]). SPVs need to be adjusted to local conditions and project specificities, in many cities or regions, a public development bank can assist in tailoring the approach to local needs. SPVs could also be promoted by special investment funds to be set up by a legitimate and trusted organisation. When accepted by all stakeholders, SPVs can build trust in project implementation both in the short and the long term.

SPVs are not only an efficient tool for small-size projects, but are also typically used for large scale multi-purpose water infrastructure (MPWI) projects and are owned by a consortium of project sponsors, as mentioned above. These companies have limited recourse to their owners' assets and hence depend on the quality and cash flow of the asset, which can be generated through tariffs and power purchase agreements. An example are the pre-agreed tariffs for transport, electricity and water services between the Ugandan government and the Kalangala Infrastructure Services SPV, a MPWI project providing transport, water piping, wastewater plant construction services. (OECD, 2019[1])

Figure 4.9. Financial structure based on the issuance of mini-bonds

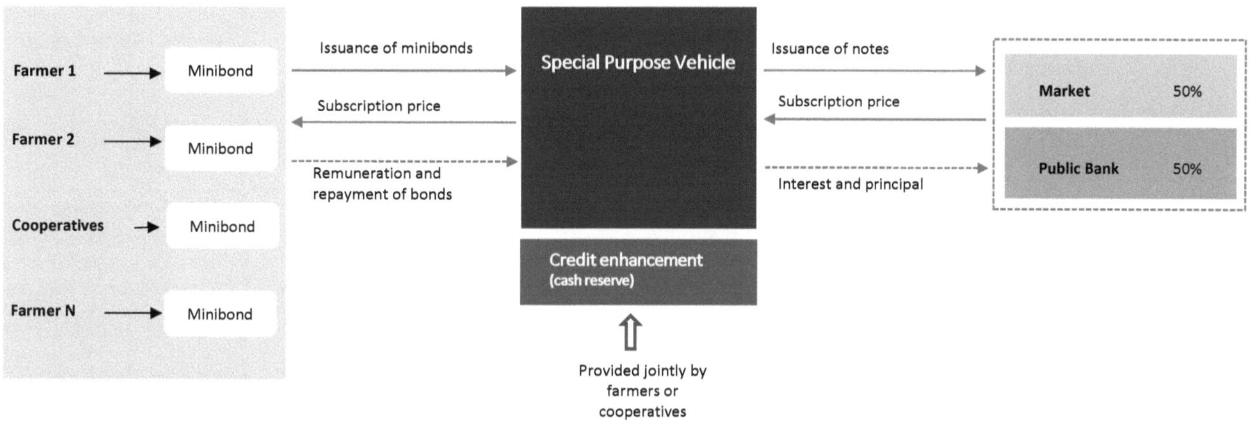

Source: Authors, adapted from (EIB, 2019[66])

4.2.3. Revolving funds

Revolving funds can be an effective model to attract commercial finance and to ensure available funding for water-related projects in the future. The **Clean Water and the Drinking Water State Revolving Funds (SRF)** in the United States are examples how priority water infrastructure projects can be financed through public loans, which leverage non-public sources of finance. The U.S. Environmental Protection Agency has partnered with the states and capitalises the SRFs with annual grants, states provide a 20% match. The states are responsible for the operation of their SRF programs, which function like environmental infrastructure banks: They provide assistance through loans with below market interest rates with periods of up to 30 years, through refinancing, guarantees or purchase of local debt and bond insurance. As money is payed back, the state makes new loans to other eligible high priority water projects; repayments and interest earnings are recycled back into the programme, financing future projects (see Figure 4.10) (EPA, 2020[67]; Gebhardt, 2019[68]).

A key element of the U.S. SRF model is its integration with the U.S. capital market, where SRFs raise additional capital to supplement their lending capacity. The SRF bond sector has received AAA median rating, which allows SRFs to borrow at the best financing terms from the private capital market. Building on federal investments of USD 66.2 billion, the state Clean Water and Drinking Water SRFs have provided USD 179.1 billion to water systems and communities through 2019 (EPA, 2020[67]; Gebhardt, 2019[68]).

The programs are designed to be a sustainable source of funds. Sustainable fund operations are assured by the stipulation in the Federal Acts that federal and state equity contributions, and program earnings, be held in the SRFs in-perpetuity and used solely for the purposes prescribed by the Acts. The longer that federal appropriations and state match dollars are made available, the more financially resilient and less dependent the SRFs are on future appropriations to sustain robust support to eligible financial assistance recipients. The result has been an ever-rising level of funding certainty that benefits all SRF stakeholders, including contract project developers and equipment vendors. Consistent funding has become a program bellwether that has produced tangible long-term benefits by enabling SRF administrators to largely match financial and technical assistance needs year in and year out. The beneficial result has been a persistently strong signal to the water infrastructure investment sector that planning and project development efforts will be rewarded with funding at better than market terms (Gebhardt, Zeigler and Mourant, 2022[69]).

This model could find replication where national or subnational governments can concentrate sufficient financial resources to produce stable high credit mechanisms that can offer favourable market terms, independent of a country's own credit strength. One example of the successful use of a revolving fund mechanisms in a developing-country context is the previously mentioned Philippine Water Revolving Fund. Gebhardt, Zeigler and Mourant (2022[69]) provide a checklist of enabling conditions that should be considered in efforts to adapt U.S. water financing experience in other countries.

Figure 4.10. Illustration of U.S. State Revolving Funds

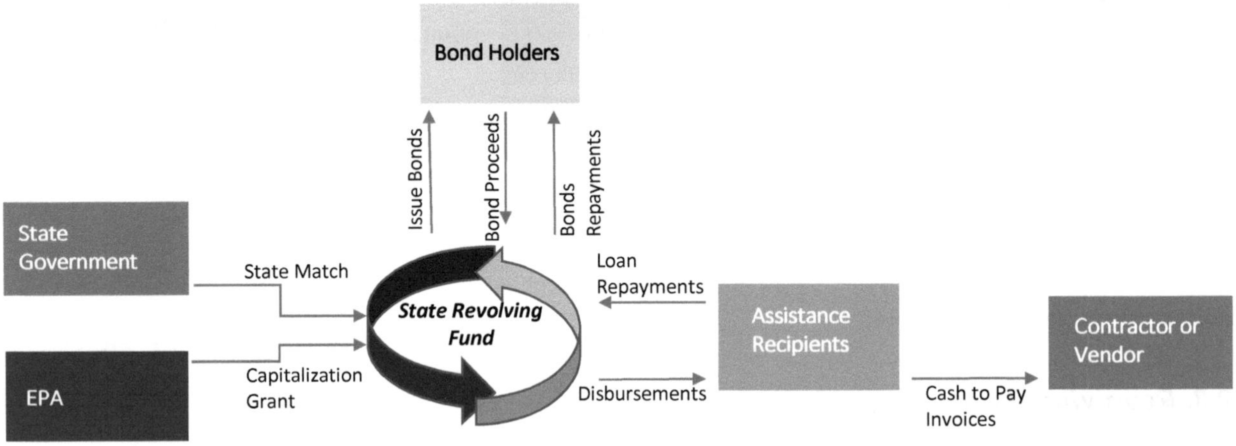

Source: Authors, adapted from CWSRF Branch - PD-US Gov-EPA, Public Domain, https://en.wikipedia.org/w/index.php?curid=19972913

4.2.4. Dedicated financing institutions and funds to mobilise investment for water

NWB Bank is a dedicated financial institution helping to raise and distribute funding for water-related projects and other sectors. As national bank, a majority is owned by the Dutch water authorities, with minority shares owned by the Dutch state and provinces. The bank lends to local and regional authorities responsible for water management as well as for the health care, education and public housing sectors. It raises funds on the international capital market and has issued so-called water bonds. Funds raised via these use-of-proceeds bonds are earmarked for projects to mitigate and to adapt to climate change through waterway management and flood protection and to promote biodiversity projects such as water treatment projects. Thanks to a zero-default history, the bank has received its first AAA credit rating in 1996, giving access to finance at affordable conditions, and has received the highest rating for sustainability of their use-of-proceeds issuance from Cicero rating agency in 2019. In 2020, the bank has lent EUR 976 million to water authorities and for several years and it has been involved in financing Public-Private-Partnerships (NWB Bank, 2020[70]; NWB, 2020[71]). NWB is a fairly unique institution in the European context that other countries could use for inspiration. It was the inspiration behind the establishment of the Kenya Pooled Water Fund, a local capital market financing mechanism to mobilise water and sanitation infrastructure investments in Kenya (van Oppenraaij et al., 2022[25]).[7]

In Europe, the **European Fund for Strategic Investment** (EFSI) is an example of a dedicated fund to mobilise commercial finance for strategically important projects through EU funding. The European Commission (EC) provides guarantees to EIB for projects supported by the EFSI and manages directly the assets covered by these guarantees. The projects are subject to the normal EIB project cycle governance, in addition to an EFSI specific governance structure, ensuring compliance with EFSI objectives. Thanks to a credit enhancement by the EC, the residual risk of the lending products are reduced significantly, unlocking additional and affordable private finance. By the end of 2019, additional investment totalled EUR 458 billion. (EIB, 2020[72]; EIB, 2019[73])

In South-East Asia, ADB has launched the **ASEAN Catalytic Green Finance Facility** in April 2019 to strategically unlock private investment for infrastructure projects in the region, which contribute to environmental sustainability goals, including resilient water infrastructure and multi-sectorial projects. The facility will mobilise a total of USD 1 billion from the ASEAN Infrastructure Fund, ADB and other development partners such as KfW, EIB and Afd. The funds will be used to cover a portion of capital or operational costs to achieve bankability and for credit enhancement support. Minimum revenue guarantees (of at maximum 7 years) will help to improve the projects' rate of return and first loss structures can improve the projects' risk profile. The facility thus facilitates the development of new financial products and models which meet the needs of the different types of projects. Technical assistance helps to develop new targets and performance measures and builds awareness and capacity to identify and structure relevant projects. The facility is in its pilot phase and aimed at identifying six to eight potential projects by the end of 2021. (ADB, 2020[74])

The **Sustainable Water Impact Fund**, established in partnership between Renewable Resources Group (RRG) and the Nature Vest, The Nature Conservancy (TNC), seeks to provide competitive, risk-adjusted returns to investors by acquiring land and water assets to improve the management of surface water, groundwater and farming practices. The fund attracts capital from institutional investors with a traditional 10-year fund structure and closed with over USD 900 million in April 2020 (of which USD 300 million were provided by Goldman Sachs through client commitments (Goldman Sachs, 2020[75])). TNC is technical advisor to the Fund, assessing the conservation opportunities of portfolio investments and to helping ensure investments continue to deliver the targeted benefits and intended impacts. One of the first projects is the investment in partly transforming a large dairy and feed-crop farm in California into groundwater recharge storage basins, which can provide wetland habitat for migratory birds. Other projects include an avocado and walnut farm in Chile and other land and asset investments in California, Chile and Australia. (TNC, 2020[76]) Box 4.3 gives the example of dedicated development funds for climate action relevant for water.

Box 4.3. Development funds for climate action relevant for water

The Green Climate Fund

The Green Climate Fund (GCF) has been established within the framework of the UNFCCC to assist developing countries in adaptation and mitigation practices to counter climate change. As of July 2020, a total of USD 10.3 billion has been pledged, of which USD 8.31 billion confirmed by 45 countries and regions and one city. Approved projects comprise a total value of USD 30.3 billion, including GCF financing and co-financing. In terms of regions, projects are mostly located in Asia-Pacific (38%) and Africa (36%), followed by Latin America and the Caribbean (21%) and Eastern Europe (5%). The GCF structures its support through a combination of grant, concessional debt, guarantees or equity instruments to leverage blended finance and crowd-in private investment for climate action.

Water-related investments that contribute to climate action have benefitted from the fund. In Jordan, for example, the fund finances a USD 33.3 million project aiming to improve water use efficiency in agriculture, and thus ensuring water and food security and protecting livelihoods in light of climate change. The financial support consists of a USD 25 million GCF grant, topped up with a total of USD 3.8 million of grants through co-financing arrangements and USD 4.5 million co-financed in-kind payments. The project was approved in March 2021 and is projected to benefit over 210 000 people.

The Adaptation Fund

Another example of dedicated climate funds is the Adaptation Fund, also established under the UNFCCC, which has committed USD 783 million to climate adaptation and resilience activities since 2010. Its financing mainly stems from sales of certified emission reductions under the Clean Development Mechanism. Additionally, the Fund receives contributions from governments, the private sector and individuals. The Fund finances projects in nine sectors, including agriculture (16%), water management (14%), disaster risk reduction (14%) and coastal zone management (9%).

A project addressing disaster risk reduction is located in Uruguay and Argentina, aiming at building resilience in vulnerable coastal cities and ecosystems of the Uruguay River. The 6-year project includes the implementation of sustainable infrastructure adapted to the adverse effects of climate change, community- and ecosystem-based adaptation measures, as well as the implementation of integrated climate risk management and early warning systems. From the total grant of approximately USD 14 million, USD 2.8 million have already been transferred since project approval in July 2019.

Another project is located in Zanzibar: a USD 1 million grant is allocated to a coastal management project, financing the construction of water harvesting infrastructures and the promotion of soil and water conversation techniques for improved water protection and crop productivity.

Source: (Green Climate Fund, 2021[77]; Green Climat Fund, 2021[78]; Adaptation Fund, 2019[79]; Adaptation Fund, 2019[80]; Adaptation Fund, 2020[81])

4.2.5. Public-Private Partnerships (PPP)

PPP for flood protection under the EFSI

One example for a water-related project funded by the EFSI has the shape of a public-private partnership for flood protection in the Netherlands. The project concerned an upgrade of the Afsluitdijk dyke, ensuring compliance with flood directives in the future, and was awarded through a tender process to the private consortium Level, which is responsible for the design, construction, financing and maintenance over 25 years. The EFSI has supported the EUR 550 million project with a EUR 330 million loan. Besides increased flood protection and adaptation to climate change, the project also includes components to re-establish fish migration, the improvement and maintenance of a National Motorway and can boost the local economy through projects on recreation, tourism, nature and innovative sustainable energy sources. Payments to the consortium are based on the availability of the infrastructure, allowing for potential performance deductions (The Afsluitdijk, 2020[82]; World Construction Network, 2019[83]; EIB, 2018[84]). This example shows how flood protection can be addressed effectively through cooperation between public and private entities as well as through cross-sectoral approaches (flood protection, transport, tourism, environmental protection), allowing for different types of revenue streams.

PPP in Chile for dam construction and irrigation

In Chile, the government has set up a PPP arrangement for dam construction, which would secure irrigation for agriculture. Since 2005, the Chilean government launched the construction of two large dams, Convento Viejo Etapa II, awarded in 2005 and currently operating, and Las Palmas, awarded in 2018, currently under construction. Together, these two dams allow increased irrigation security for 67 000 ha land with capacities to supply irrigation needs of over 290 million cubic metres. The former project also generates electric energy with a capacity of 16.4 MW, and is connected to the Central Interconnected grid System. The Convento Viejo dam was developed as a pilot project with a cost-share mechanism: the state financed a part of the total cost, private investors built, exploit and maintain the dam, and the end users pay the license holder for water stored. Initially, the approach had faced opposition from farmers fearing higher costs of water. Eventually, the project led farmers to shift their production to high-value agriculture (e.g. fruit trees) or to sell their land to other farmers (Gruère, Ashley and Cadilhon, 2018[48]). For the 2021 – 2025 period, three additional dams are in a planning stage.

PPPs in the People's Republic of China

ADB's Private Sector Operations Department (PSOD) is promoting PPP to finance WSS investments and arrangements including the prevention and rehabilitation of pollution in water bodies. One significant arrangement is the Integrated Water Management Project in China, for lake and river pollution prevention and rehabilitation initiatives that involve multiple environmental interlocking facilities (wastewater and sludge treatment plants, sewage collection systems) and services (riverbank reinforcement, wetland development). The innovation of this programme is that it is the first ADB non-sovereign financing programme to support an emerging PPP model for integrated wastewater management. An USD 150 million loan from ADB mobilised USD 300 million of commercial co-finance, accompanied with a smaller loan (USD 215 000) for technical assistance. The programme has revealed the scope for mobilising private sector participation in well-prepared, bankable projects. Similarly, by involving multiple environmental interlocking facilities and services, different private actors can be mobilised across a range of projects. (Money, 2018[85])

Generally, PPPs are a form of outscoring of operational and financial responsibility to the private sector (and have been used at scale in China). While, typically, PPP projects in the WSS sector are narrowly characterised by the Build-Operate-Transfer model, in China, PPP models are taking a broader concept, encompassing the long-term alliances between local governments, private developers and third-party financers to fund water remediation, flood control and pollution prevention projects. For example, in order to reduce the credit risk faced by private financiers, users' payments for water, wastewater and waste treatment are ring-fenced from the local government's budgets. This allowed smaller cities, with less creditworthy municipal governments to have access to commercial finance (Money, 2018[85]). Overall, private investment in the Chinese water and wastewater sector more than doubled in 2019 to USD 3.3 billion (GWI, 2020[86]).

4.2.6. Risk-financing instruments

Risk-financing instruments are a mechanism to promote the sharing and transfer of risks and losses and reduce (at least part of) the burden on public funds in case of disasters (e.g. floods and droughts). Insurance can serve as a risk-communication tool which can help individuals to rationalise their land use choices in at-risk areas and can incentivise behaviour to reduce exposure. Flood insurance schemes, for example, if properly designed, could provide a strong incentive for risk-reduction behaviour – thus also reducing the need for public investment on the long run. In agriculture, adjusted crop insurance premiums which reflect water-holding capacity, can incentivise farmers to adopt more sustainable soil management practices and thus increase their resilience to drought. Risk sharing arrangements can operate at multiple levels, from individual households and business, to local communities and national or regional levels.

As an example of a risk sharing arrangement on the national level, France has established the natural disaster insurance system CatNat, a public-private compensation system that covers losses that cannot be insured in private markets, such as flooding. Under CatNat, it is mandatory for insurers to extend property and vehicle insurance contracts to cover damages caused by natural disasters. The premiums are not based on local natural disaster risks but are fixed by the Government following a principle of national solidarity. (Poussin, Botzen and Aerts, 2013[87]) Similarly, the British government has negotiated voluntary agreements with British insurance companies to help households in flood risk areas to find affordable home insurance holders and taxpayers. It aims to provide available and affordable insurance without placing unsustainable costs on wider policy (Surminskia and Hudsonb, 2017[88]). Flood Re, a joint initiative by the government and insurers, allows for risk sharing between the government and private insurers, with an aim to keep household premiums affordable. In Romania, homeowners are legally required to purchase a home insurance covering damages from floods, landslides and earthquakes. Nonetheless, legal clauses exempt some households from this obligation on the basis of socio-economic criteria, leading to a share of on 38% of dwellings covered by insurance (Surminskia and Hudsonb, 2017[88]).

In the agricultural sector, insurances are generally relatively expensive and premiums are heavily subsidised. Out of 65 developed and developing countries, almost two-thirds subsidized premium costs with an average subsidy rate of 47% (Mahul and Stutley, 2010[89]; FAO, 2018[90]). For developing countries, it remains difficult to provide subsidised coverage for numerous small-scale family farmers. Approaches such as weather-index-based insurances aim to address this challenge: The insurance holds, when rainfall or temperature exceed or fall under a specific threshold, and measurements are taken by weather stations or satellite technology. This reduces assessment and operational costs for insurers, reducing the premium costs. In India, for example, the Weather-based Crop Insurance Scheme had a coverage of about 1.7 million hectares in 2016 (Gulati, Terway and Hussain, 2018[91]). In sub-Saharan Africa, the Agriculture and Climate Risk Enterprise (ACRE) is the largest index insurance programme among developing countries in which farmers pay a market premium, and the first agricultural insurance programme globally to reach smallholders using mobile technologies. Their insurances range from weather indexed coverage, soil moisture indexed to vegetation indexed coverage (ACRE, 2021[92]). However, these programmes still require public support through subsidies. (Greatrex et al., 2015[93])

4.3. Concluding remarks

The inventory of financing approaches summarised above underscores the range of new opportunities to harness domestic commercial finance for water investments. Governments have a decisive role to play to ensure the enabling environment is in place to take advantage of these opportunities. Success will depend on the enabling environment, which goes beyond water and encompasses the finance sector, capital markets and broader factors related to countries' governance and political stability.

Governments can also foster the development of commercial finance and capital markets able to lend at an affordable cost and appropriate long term maturity to water related projects. Appropriate vehicles for water-related investments need to overcome the specificities of the water sector, such as the need for long tenors, small ticket sizes, limited creditworthiness and the lack of clearly defined revenue streams. Transparency is needed for financiers to properly asses and price risk. Governments can also signal their intention and financial capacity to tender water projects over a multi-year time span. Project-level analyses need to be supplemented by the design, review and assessment of investment pathways.

References

ACRE (2021), *AcreAfrica*, https://acreafrica.com/ (accessed on 17 March 2021). [92]

Adaptation Fund (2020), *Enhancing Climate Change Resilience of Coastal Communities of Zanzibar*, https://www.adaptation-fund.org/project/enhancing-climate-change-resilience-of-coastal-communities-of-zanzibar-2/ (accessed on 20 April 2021). [81]

Adaptation Fund (2019), *Adaptation Fund, Infosheet*, https://www.adaptation-fund.org/wp-content/uploads/2018/04/AF-infographic-Eng-May2019-WEB.pdf (accessed on 20 April 2021). [79]

Adaptation Fund (2019), *Climate Change adaptation in vulnerable coastal cities and ecosystems of the Uruguay River (Argentina, Uruguay)*, https://www.adaptation-fund.org/project/climate-change-adaptation-vulnerable-coastal-cities-ecosystems-uruguay-river-argentina-uruguay-2/ (accessed on 20 April 2021). [80]

ADB (2020), *ASEAN Catalytic Green Finance FAcility An ASEAN Infrastrucutre Fund Initiative, Operations Plan 2019-2021*, https://www.adb.org/sites/default/files/institutional-document/575911/acgf-operations-plan-2019-2021.pdf (accessed on 5 October 2020). [74]

Alaerts, G. (2019), "Financing for Water—Water for Financing: A Global Review of Policy and Practice", *Sustainability*, Vol. 11/821, http://dx.doi.org/10.3390/su11030821. [10]

Anglian Water (2020), *Annual Integrated Report 2019*, Anglian Water Services Limited, Cambridgeshire. [59]

Anthony, I., J. Yuan and S. Xia (2021), *Promoting China-European Union Cooperation on Green and Sustainable Finance, Policy Brief*, Stockhold International Peace Research Institute, https://www.jstor.org/stable/pdf/resrep29591.pdf. [44]

Bank, E. (ed.) (2018), *Netherlands: EUR 330m EIB support under Juncker Plan for Afsluitdijk flood defence works*, https://www.eib.org/en/press/all/2018-131-eur-330m-eib-support-under-juncker-plan-for-afsluitdijk-flood-defence-works-in-the-netherlands (accessed on 7 July 2020). [84]

Bennett, G., A. Leonardi and F. Ruef (2017), *State of European Markets 2017 Watershed Investments*, Forest Trends' Ecosystem Marketplace, https://www.ecostarhub.com/wp-content/uploads/2017/06/State-of-European-Markets-2017-Watershed-Investments.pdf (accessed on 21 July 2020). [7]

Boffo, R. and R. Patalano (2020), *ESG Investing: Practices, Progress and Challenges*, OECD Publishing, Paris, https://www.oecd.org/finance/ESG-Investing-Practices-Progress-Challenges.pdf (accessed on 8 September 2021). [22]

Cardascia, S. (2019), *Session 4. Financing Water Infrastructure and Landscape Approaches in Asia and the Pacific*, OECD, https://www.oecd.org/water/Session4.Financing_Water_Infrastructure_and_Landscape_Approaches_in_Asia_and_the_Pacific%20.pdf. [18]

CBI (2021), *Sustainable Debt Market Summary Q3 2021*, https://www.climatebonds.net/files/reports/cbi_susdebtsum_q32021_03b.pdf. [56]

CBI (2020), *2019 Green Bond Market Summary*, https://www.climatebonds.net/files/reports/2019_annual_highlights-final.pdf. [57]

CFM (2021), *Climate Fund Managers. Funds*, https://climatefundmanagers.com/funds/#CIO (accessed on 12 March 2021). [51]

Cooper, R. and J. Matthews (2020), *Water finance and Nature-based solutions*, K4D. [24]

DFCD (2021), *Dutch Fund for Climate and Development. Our approach*, https://thedfcd.com/our-approach/ (accessed on 12 March 2021). [49]

EIB (2020), *EIB issued its first USD Global Sustainability Awareness Bond*, https://www.eib.org/en/investor_relations/press/2020/fi-2020-22-first-usd-global-sab.htm (accessed on 22 June 2020). [60]

EIB (2020), *Facts & Figures*, European Investment Bank. [72]

EIB (2019), *European Investment Bank Financial Report 2018*, European Investment Bank. [73]

EIB (2019), *Feeding future generations, How finance can boost innovation in agri-food, Executive summary*, European Investment Bank, https://www.eib.org/attachments/thematic/feeding_future_generation_summary_en.pdf. [66]

EIB (2017), *Germany: The EU bank provides a new EUR 450m loan for the Emscher rehabilitation project*, https://www.eib.org/en/press/all/2017-199-450-millionen-euro-eu-bank-stellt-weiteren-kredit-fur-emscher-umbau-bereit (accessed on 7 July 2020). [61]

EIB (2013), *Dhaka Environmentally Sustainable Water Supply*, https://www.eib.org/fr/projects/pipelines/all/20130229 (accessed on 3 November 2020). [62]

EIP (2020), *Delivering the Value of Nature Resotred*, https://ecosystempartners.com/ (accessed on 22 July 2020). [12]

EPA (2020), *United States Environmental Protection Agency: Learn about the Clean Water State Revolving Fund (CWSRF)*, https://www.epa.gov/cwsrf/learn-about-clean-water-state-revolving-fund-cwsrf (accessed on 3 July 2020). [67]

European Commission (2021), *Implementing and delegated acts*, https://ec.europa.eu/info/law/sustainable-finance-taxonomy-regulation-eu-2020-852/amending-and-supplementary-acts/implementing-and-delegated-acts_en (accessed on 23 March 2021). [33]

European Commission (2021), *Platform on sustainable finance*, https://ec.europa.eu/info/business-economy-euro/banking-and-finance/sustainable-finance/overview-sustainable-finance/platform-sustainable-finance_en (accessed on 23 March 2021). [39]

European Commission (2020), *Draft Annex 1, Annex to the Commission Delegated Regulation*. [35]

European Commission (2020), *Draft Annex 2, Annex to the Commission Delegated Regulation*. [36]

European Commission (2020), *Regulation (EU) 2020/852 of the European Parliament and of the Council of 18 June 2020 on the establishment of a framework to facilitate sustainable investment, and amending Regulation (EU) 2019/2088*. [32]

FAO (2018), *The State of Agricultural Commodity Markets 2018. Agricultural trade, climate change and food security*. [90]

Garbacz, W., D. Vilalta and L. Moller (2021), "THE ROLE OF GUARANTEES IN BLENDED FINANCE", *OECD Development Co-operation Working Papers, No 97 OECD Publishing, Paris.* [19]

Gatti, S. (2018), *Project Finance in Theory and Practice: Designing, Structuring and Financing Private and Public Projects*, Academic Press, Elsevier. [65]

Gebhardt, J. (2019), *U.S. EPA Water Infrastructure Finance Models*, Background Paper Session 2. 4th Roundtable on Financing Water, 26-27 June, Washington, D.C., https://www.oecd.org/water/Session2.US-water-infrastructure-finance-models.pdf. [68]

Gebhardt, J., R. Zeigler and A. Mourant (2022), "Water Infrastructure Financing: The Experience of the U.S.", in *Investing in Water and Growth*. [69]

Goldman Sachs (2020), *Goldman Sachs 2019 Sustainability Report, Sustainable Finance The Imperative and the Opportunity*, https://www.goldmansachs.com/our-commitments/sustainability/sustainable-finance/documents/reports/2019-sustainability-report.pdf. [75]

Goldman Sachs (n.d.), *Fact Sheet: DC Water Environmental Impact Bond*, https://www.goldmansachs.com/media-relations/press-releases/current/dc-water-environmental-impact-bond-fact-sheet.pdf (accessed on 10 October 2020). [63]

Greatrex, H. et al. (2015), "Scaling up index insurance for smallholder farmers: Recent evidence and insights", *CCAFS Report No. 14, CGIAR Research Program on Climate Change, Agriculture and Food Security (CCAFS). University of Copenhagen, Denmark.* [93]

Green Climat Fund (2021), *Projects & Programmes, FP155 Building resilience to cope with climate change in Jordan through improving water use efficiency in the agriculture sector (BRCCJ)*, https://www.greenclimate.fund/project/fp155 (accessed on 20 April 2021). [78]

Green Climate Fund (2021), *GCF at a glace*, https://www.greenclimate.fund/ (accessed on 20 April 2021). [77]

Gruère, G., C. Ashley and J. Cadilhon (2018), "Reforming water policies in agriculture: Lessons from past reforms", *OECD Food, Agriculture and Fisheries Papers*, No. 113, OECD Publishing, Paris, https://dx.doi.org/10.1787/1826beee-en. [48]

Gulati, A., P. Terway and S. Hussain (2018), *Crop Insurance in India: Key Issues and Way Forward*, https://www.think-asia.org/bitstream/handle/11540/8052/Working_Paper_352.pdf?sequence=1. [91]

GWI (2020), *Global Water Intelligence, China buoys rising water PPP investment statistics*, https://www.globalwaterintel.com/news/2020/31/china-buoys-rising-water-ppp-investment-statistics (accessed on 5 October 2020). [86]

IBNet (2020), *The International Benchmarking Network*, https://www.ib-net.org/about-us/ (accessed on 23 July 2020). [23]

IDH (2020), *IDG The sustainable trade initiative: AGRI3 Fund Technical Assistance Facility*, https://www.idhsustainabletrade.com/landscapes/agri3-fund/ (accessed on 11 March 2021). [46]

IPSF (2020), *International Platform on Sustainable Finance, Annual Report*, https://ec.europa.eu/info/sites/info/files/business_economy_euro/banking_and_finance/documents/international-platform-sustainable-finance-annual-report-2020_en.pdf. [43]

Kerres, M. et al. (2020), *Stop Floating, Start Swimming, Water and climate change - interlinkages and prospects for future action*, Deutsche Gesellschaft für Internationale Zusammenarbeit (GIZ), https://www.everydrop-counts.org/imglib/pdf/Water%20Climate%20Report%202020.pdf. [27]

Lardoux de Pazzis, A. and A. Muret (2021), "The role of intermediaries to facilitate financing for water-related investment". [26]

Latin American Water Funds Partnership (2020), *Metropolitan Water Fund of Monterrey (FAMM)*, https://www.fondosdeagua.org/en/the-water-funds/water-fund-maps/metropolitan-water-fund-of-monterrey-famm/ (accessed on 4 November 2020). [13]

Lu, Y. et al. (2018), "Payments for Watershed Services and Practices in China: Achievements and Challenges", *Chinese Geographical Science*, Vol. 28/5, pp. 873-893, http://dx.doi.org/10.1007/s11769-018-0981-3. [16]

Mahul, O. and C. Stutley (2010), *Government Support to Agricultural Insurance Challenges and Options for Developing Countries*, World Bank. [89]

Ministère de la transition écologique et solidaire (2019), *Les actions du plan biodiversité, dossier de presse*, https://www.ecologie.gouv.fr/sites/default/files/2019.07.04_dp_final_plan_biodiversit%C3%A9.pdf. [14]

Ministère de la transition écologique et solidaire (2018), *Plan Biodiversité*, https://www.ecologie.gouv.fr/sites/default/files/18xxx_Plan-biodiversite-04072018_28pages_FromPdf_date_web_PaP.pdf. [15]

Money, A. (2018), *Financing the water value chain without a sovereign guarantee: Case studies of private sector participation in water distribution and wastewater treatment in China*, https://www.oecd.org/water/Session2.Financing_the%20water_value_chain_without_a_sovereign_guarantee.pdf (accessed on 5 October 2020). [85]

Money, A. (forthcoming), "Country-level indicators to support blended finance for water related investments", *OECD Environment Working Paper*. [45]

NWB (2020), *NWB Bank*, https://nwbbank.com/en (accessed on 7 July 2020). [71]

NWB Bank (2020), *Annual Report 2019*, Nederlandse Waterschapsbank N.V. [70]

Och, M. (2020), *Sustainable Finance and the EU Taxonomy Regulation - Hype or Hope?, Working Paper No. 2020/05*, Jan Ronse Institute for Company and Financial Law, KU Leuven, https://poseidon01.ssrn.com/delivery.php?ID=0680960011260250990640921141121271171220110050350100281040910990241220160740070670910310070000420330070270681141011150031160660490070880220071060851031161200921071050240200000220740221130010640950821180940720000. [31]

OECD (2020), *Developing Sustainable Finance Definitions and Taxonomies*, https://doi.org/10.1787/134a2dbe-en. [30]

OECD (2020), *Financing Water Supply, Sanitation and Flood Protection: Challenges in EU Member States and Policy Options*, OECD Studies on Water, OECD Publishing, Paris, https://dx.doi.org/10.1787/6893cdac-en. [6]

OECD (2020), *Global Insurance Market Trends 2019*, https://www.oecd.org/daf/fin/insurance/Global-Insurance-Market-Trends-2019.pdf (accessed on 7 August 2020). [55]

OECD (2020), *Green Infrastructure in the Decade for Delivery: Assessing Institutional Investment*, Green Finance and Investment, OECD Publishing, Paris, https://dx.doi.org/10.1787/f51f9256-en. [8]

OECD (2020), *Recent developments on the EU sustainable finance agenda and the implications for water*, Background paper. 6th Roundtable Meeting on Financing Water, 7-8 December, https://www.oecd.org/water/Session4-Recent-developments-on-the-EU-sustainable-finance-agenda-and-the-implications-for-water.pdf. [34]

OECD (2019), *Making Blended Finance Work for Water and Sanitation: Unlocking Commercial Finance for SDG 6*, OECD Studies on Water, OECD Publishing, Paris, https://dx.doi.org/10.1787/5efc8950-en. [1]

OECD (2019), *Pension Markets in Focus*, http://www.oecd.org/daf/fin/private-pensions/pensionmarketsinfocus.htm (accessed on 7 August 2020). [54]

OECD (2018), “Financing Water, Investing in sustainable growth, Policy Perspectives”, *OECD Environmental Policy Paper No. 11*, https://www.oecd.org/water/Policy-Paper-Financing-Water-Investing-in-Sustainable-Growth.pdf. [9]

OECD (2018), *Third meeting of the Roundtable on Financing Water, 12 November, Paris Summary and Discussion Highlights*, http://www.oecd.org/water/roundtable-financing-water-2018-summary-and-highlights.pdf (accessed on 2 June 2020). [21]

OECD (2015), *Water Resources Allocation: Sharing Risks and Opportunities*, OECD Publishing, https://dx.doi.org/10.1787/9789264229631-en. [3]

OECD (2010), *Innovative Financing Mechanisms for the Water Sector*, OECD Studies on Water, OECD Publishing, Paris, https://dx.doi.org/10.1787/9789264083660-en. [5]

Panez, A., I. Roose and R. Faúndez (2020), “Agribusiness Facing Its Limits: the Re-design of Neoliberalization Strategies in the Exporting Agriculture Sector in Chile”, *Land*, Vol. 9/66, http://dx.doi.org/doi:10.3390/land9030066. [47]

Platform on Sustainable Finance (2021), *EU Taxonomy & Platform Social Taxonomy Outreach, Presentation in Webinar on social Taxonomy*, https://ec.europa.eu/info/sites/default/files/business_economy_euro/banking_and_finance/documents/finance-events-210226-presentation-social-taxonomy_en.pdf. [40]

Platform on Sustainable Finance (2021), *Report on Taxonomy extension options linked to environmental objectives, Public Consultation*, https://ec.europa.eu/info/sites/default/files/business_economy_euro/banking_and_finance/documents/sustainable-finance-platform-report-taxonomy-extension-july2021_en.pdf. [41]

Poussin, J., W. Botzen and J. Aerts (2013), "Stimulating flood damage mitigation through insurance: an assessment of the French CatNat system", *Environmental Hazards*, Vol. 12/3-4, pp. 258-277, http://dx.doi.org/10.1080/17477891.2013.832650. [87]

Rees, M. (2018), *A sexy name to pay for the pipes (part of the series "a Dictionary of Finance"*, https://www.eib.org/en/podcasts/italian-hydrobond# (accessed on 6 July 2020). [64]

SAFIN IDB (n.d.), *Providing Fertile Ground for lending in the Philippines Case Study*, https://5724c05e-8e16-4a51-a320-65710d75ed23.filesusr.com/ugd/f6ddfc_2686745531644eb3a2ea245f656e0c95.pdf (accessed on 17 March 2021). [53]

Scholer, M. and L. Cuesta Barbera (2020), "The EU Sustainable Finance Taxonomy from the perspective of the insruance and reinsurance sector", *Financial Stability Report*. [38]

Schütze, F. et al. (2020), "EU taxonomy increasing transparency of sustainable investments, DIW Weekly Report", *Deutsches Institut für Wirtschaftsforschung (DIW), Berlin*, Vol. 10/51, pp. 485-492, http://dx.doi.org/10.18723/diw_dwr:2020-51-1. [37]

Share (2012), *Small-scale finance for water and sanitation*, https://assets.publishing.service.gov.uk/media/57a08aa3e5274a27b20006cb/EUWI_and_SH. [52]

SNV (2021), *Dutch Fund for Climate Resilience and Development (DFCD).*, https://snv.org/project/dutch-fund-climate-and-development-dfcd (accessed on 12 March 2021). [50]

Streeter, W. (2017), *Financing Water and Sewer Infrastructure in the Developing World*, Taylor & Francis. [20]

Surminskia, S. and P. Hudsonb (2017), "Investigating the Risk Reduction Potential of Disaster Insurance Across Europe", *The Geneva Papers*, Vol. 42, pp. 247-274. [88]

TEG (2020), *EU Technical Expert Group on Sustainable Finance (TEG) Usability Guide, TEG proposal for an EU Green Bond Standard.* [58]

TEG (2020), *Technical Report, Taxonomy: Final report of the EU Technical Expert Group on Sustainable Finance.* [94]

TEG (2019), *EU Technical Expert Group (TEG) Report, Proposal for an EU Green Bond Standard.* [42]

The Afsluitdijk (2020), *The Afsluitdijk. Futureproof again*, https://theafsluitdijk.com/ (accessed on 7 July 2020). [82]

TNC (2020), *2020 Impact Report, Investing in Nature*, The Nature Conservancy, Nature Vest, https://www.nature.org/content/dam/tnc/nature/en/documents/NatureVest-2020-Impact-Report.pdf. [76]

Trémolet, S. et al. (2019), *Investing in Nature for Europe Water Security*, The Nature Conservancy, Ecologic Institute and ICLEI. London. [11]

van Oppenraaij, J. et al. (2022), "Tapping Local Capital Markets for Water and Sanitation: The Case of the Kenya Pooled Water Fund", in *Investing in Water and Growth.* [25]

WaCCliM (2020), *Water and Wastewater Companies for Climate Mitigation, How are we driving the transition towards a climate-smart and sustainable urban water sector?*, https://wacclim.org/our-approach/ (accessed on 23 March 2021). [28]

Water UK (2020), *Water industry launches world's first sector-wide plan to deliver net zero carbon emissions by 2030*, https://www.water.org.uk/news-item/water-industry-launches-worlds-first-sector-wide-plan-to-deliver-net-zero-carbon-emissions-by-2030 (accessed on 23 March 2021). [29]

World Bank (2017), *Easing the transition to commercial finance for sustainable water and sanitation*, http://documents.worldbank.org/curated/en/182521503466225465/pdf/119048-WP-REPLACEMENT-PUBLIC.pdf. [2]

World Bank Group (2016), *Sanitation and Water for All: Priority Actions for Sector Financing*. [4]

World Construction Network (2019), *Work begins on €550m project to strengthen Afsluitdijk in Netherlands*, https://www.worldconstructionnetwork.com/news/work-begins-on-550m-project-to-strengthen-afsluitdijk-in-netherlands/ (accessed on 7 July 2020). [83]

Zhang, Q. and M. Bennett (2011), *Eco-Compensation for Watershed Services in the People's Republic of China*, ADB. [17]

Notes

[1] For the full analysis and details related to the methodology, see (Lardoux de Pazzis and Muret, 2021[26]).

[2] The six EU environmental objectives are: Climate change mitigation, Climate change adaptation, Sustainable use and protection of water and marine resources, Transition to a circular economy, Pollution prevention and control, Protection and restoration of biodiversity and ecosystems.

[3] The economic activities are structured around the EU's NACE industry classification system, guaranteeing compatibility with EU Member States and international statistical frameworks and broad coverage of the economy (TEG, 2020[94]).

[4] The full analysis and indicator scorecard can be found in Money (forthcoming[45])

[5] Eligible projects need to contribute to the following four objectives: 1. Conservation of natural resources, 2. Pollution prevention and control, 3. Access to water and sanitation, 4. Natural disaster risk management.

[6]An SPV is created as a separate enterprise with its own balance sheet as a holding company for the securitization of debt, assuring repayment for investors. It is a well-known structure to commercial investors (OECD, 2019[1]).

[7] A detailed account of the rationale and process of setting up the Kenya Pooled Water Fund as well as the challenges of setting up such a local capital market financing facility can be found in (van Oppenraaij et al., 2022[25]).

5 Accelerating action on financing water: An agenda for the future

This chapter summarises the key themes explored to date in OECD work on financing water and the Roundtable on Financing Water. It charts a course for future work on financing water and new initiatives taking shape that can support countries' ambitions on the Sustainable Development Goal on water and sanitation.

Since its establishment in 2017, the Roundtable on Financing Water has provided a unique forum for action-oriented engagement between the water and the finance communities to promote the acceleration of investment that contributes to water security and sustainable growth. The past several years provide a strong basis upon which to continue to develop the Roundtable and its influence, as well as to deepen the substantive work supporting it.

OECD analytical work has helped to characterise the scale of the financing challenges across a diverse range of water-related investments (e.g. water supply and sanitation, flood protection, irrigation, water resources management, etc.) and explore options to address it through improved enabling environments and tailored financing approaches. Substantive work has focused on several key themes:

- Methods and analysis to estimate investment needs and financing capacities with work to date focused on Europe and the Asia-Pacific
- Options for leveraging public and development finance, notably with blended finance
- A focus on the project development process and strategic investment pathways, to inform the sequencing and design of investments
- The role of intermediaries in expediting water-related investments

5.1. An agenda for the future

Looking forward, the OECD's programme of work on financing water aims to raise the level of ambition, broaden engagement and contribute to key international processes and initiatives, including the United Nations Global Acceleration Framework for SDG6. Key activities include the ones listed below.

5.1.1. Launching the OECD Global Observatory on Financing Water Supply, Sanitation and Water Security

This work will provide a unique repository to:

- Document and share good practice on financing water-related investments
- Encourage peer-to-peer learning about the policies, institutional arrangements and financing approaches required to scale up investment
- Enhance thought leadership and horizon scanning for new developments.

5.1.2. Developing Diagnostic Tools and a Framework to guide country-level action

This work will:

- Develop a diagnostic tool to assess the enabling environment for water-related investment at country level. This includes quantitative and qualitative indicators assessing the strengths and weaknesses of the enabling environment.
- Develop an OECD Framework for Financing Water to distil policy recommendations on financing water, providing high-level guidance to strengthen the policies and institutional arrangements. The framework would cover:
  - the development of robust financing strategies in line with the ambition of water-related investments and domestic capabilities
  - making the best use of available assets (enhancing operational efficiency) and of financing resources (enhancing the efficiency of expenditure programmes)
  - scaling up investments that contributes to water-resilient sustainable growth.

- Together, these instruments would provide a robust analytical basis to inform Policy Dialogues on Financing Water at country level.

5.1.3. Pursuing analytical work to support aligning financing with a water secure future

This work will:

- Develop a conceptual framework and review of tools and methods to inform strategic investment planning and the assessment of options for distinct pathways and investment scenarios. Methods to inform planning and prioritisation under deep uncertainty deserve particular attention.
- Deepen the understanding of the materiality of water-related risks for the financial sector and how they can be addressed through prudential regulation, disclosure frameworks and risk management approaches.

5.2. Working in partnership

The activities listed above contribute to advancing, promoting and facilitating pragmatic financing options for investments that contribute to water security and sustainable growth. They will be implemented by the OECD in partnership with institutions active on these issues at global, regional or country levels. They can support dedicated discussions on the way to the UN Conference on Water scheduled in 2023.

Financing a water secure future requires going beyond what water policies and the water community can achieve. This requires engaging with others. Working in partnership is a key feature of the Roundtable, in recognition that a focus on water security alone will not be sufficient to generate the action required to finance a water secure future. This requires going beyond policymakers responsible for water to engage with policymakers responsible for sectors impacting water security (agriculture, energy, urban planning, among others), and the range of financiers, corporates, NGOs and experts who can help to drive action.

The Roundtable will support progress towards tailored, targeted analyses, recommendations and options of action. It will build on and collaborate with key international initiatives and engage in international fora, notably:

- Water in the context of adaptation to climate change and linkages to biodiversity (UNFCCC COP 26 the UN CBD COP 15). A dedicated meeting of the Roundtable focused on Climate Action was convened on 23-24 September, 2021.
- The G20. In 2020, the G20 Presidency put water on the G20 agenda. The OECD is ready to facilitate and substantiate further discussions on water at the G20, in the coming years.
- The 9th World Water Forum, Dakar, Senegal, March 2022
- The UN Conference on Water scheduled in 2023, and preparatory events
- The High-level Experts and Leaders Panel on Water-related Disaster Risks
- Water and health, in the context of SDG or other fora, as this topic gains traction in the aftermath of the COVID-19 pandemic.

Printed by Libri Plureos GmbH in Hamburg,
Germany